THE HORSE TRADE OF TUDOR AND STUART ENGLAND

——— OOO ———

Horses played a vital role in the economy of pre-Industrial England. They acted as draught animals, pulled ploughs, waggons and coaches, worked machines, and transported goods around the country. As saddle animals they enabled their riders to carry out a wide variety of tasks, and at all levels of society they were regarded as status symbols in a unique relationship with man shared by no other animal.

The Tudor and Stuart period was an important stage in the evolution of this relationship. Horses were needed in ever-growing numbers, and for a greater variety of tasks. As demand grew, improvements became necessary in the means of supply and distribution. This book is largely concerned with the latter aspect, namely the development of marketing institutions. The agents of change, the specialist dealers, were nominally condemned as rogues and cheats, whose actions raised prices and caused shortages. Dr Edwards argues that, far from being generally unscrupulous, the dealers were no better or worse than those amongst whom they lived and worked.

THE HORSE TRADE OF
TUDOR AND STUART ENGLAND

Peter Edwards

Senior Lecturer in History
Roehampton Institute of Higher Education

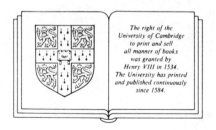

CAMBRIDGE UNIVERSITY PRESS

Cambridge

New York   New Rochelle   Melbourne   Sydney

Published by the Press Syndicate of the University of Cambridge
The Pitt Building, Trumpington Street, Cambridge CB2 1RP
32 East 57th Street, New York, NY 10022, USA
10 Stamford Road, Oakleigh, Melbourne 3166, Australia

First published 1988

Printed in Great Britain at the University Press, Cambridge

British Library cataloguing in publication data

Edwards, Peter
The horse trade of Tudor and Stuart
England.
1. Horse trading – England – History
2. Horses – England – Marketing –
History
I. Title
381′.4161′00942   HD9434.G7

Library of Congress cataloguing in publication data

Edwards, Peter (Peter Roger)
The horse trade of Tudor and Stuart England.
Bibliography.
Includes index.
1.Horse industry – England – History. I. Title.
HD9434.G73E654 1988 338.1′761′00942 87–24243

ISBN 0 521 35058 1

WV

For my mother and in memory of my father,
Alcwyn Edwards

CONTENTS

TABLES

———— OOO ————

GRAPH

———— OOO ————

MAPS

———— OOO ————

ACKNOWLEDGEMENTS

Many people helped me in the preparation of this book but my chief debt is to Dr Joan Thirsk who was unstinting in her support and encouragement. She read drafts of most of the chapters (in their various forms) and her constructive criticism saved me from many mistakes. Dr Thirsk also allowed me free access to transcripts of documents collected for volumes IV and V of *The Agrarian History of England and Wales*. Others too gave generously of their time, using their particular expertise to comment on sections of the work: Miss Daphne Machin Goodall on horse breeding, Dr John Chartres on marketing and trade, Dr John Styles on crime, and Dr Stephen Porter on the functions of horses. I had a fruitful correspondence with Dr Margaret Spufford on the subject of chapmen and she gave me a typescript of her book, *The Great Reclothing of England*, before publication. Dr John Chartres sent me two unpublished papers of his, one of which later appeared as an article in the *Economic History Review*. Dr Stephen Porter and Dr Wendy Thwaites provided me with photocopies of relevant parts of their theses, and Mr E. A. Veasey gave me a copy of his article on the Frizwell family of Bedworth. Miss Shabina Awan, and Drs Goodacre, Hull, Kerridge, Large, Spufford, Williams and Winchester allowed me to quote from their unpublished dissertations. In spite of my best endeavours, I have been unable to contact Dr Fleming and Messrs Chell, Cornwall and Tennant. I hope they will not object to my quoting from their theses. Mr Frank Emery extracted references to hill ponies from his transcripts of Welsh probate inventories, and Mr David Vaisey and Drs Joseph Bettey, Jack Fisher, David Hey and George Ramsay sent me other pieces of evidence. Sir Richard Graham of Norton Conyers Hall (North Yorks.) and Mr E. R. M. Pratt of Ryston Hall (Norfolk), kindly allowed me access to their family documents, whilst Viscount Daventry graciously gave me permission to publish the material printed as Appendix 4. Many other people unwittingly contributed to the book, when commenting on aspects of the work presented as papers at various conferences, seminars and meetings. If in spite of their good intentions, I persist in error, the fault is entirely mine.

During the course of my research I visited most of the County Record Offices in England and Wales and many of the more local ones too. Archivists and their staffs were unfailingly helpful, providing me with a mass of information and moving mountains of documents on my behalf. Documents printed as appendixes 3, 5, 6 and 8 have been reproduced by kind permission of the county record offices of Herefordshire and Worcestershire, Warwickshire, Lincolnshire and Northumberland respectively. I am also grateful to Staffordshire Record Office for allowing me to print appendixes 1 and 4. Appendix 9 is Crown copyright material in the Public Record Office and is reproduced by permission of the Controller of Her Majesty's Stationery Office. I am also grateful to the British Academy and to the Social Science Research Council for supporting my work with generous grants. Finally, and by no means least, I must thank my wife and family for their patience and forbearance. They have lived with the book for a long time and for my young daughters it has been an ever-present reality.

INTRODUCTION

I

Surprisingly little research has been done into the horse trade of pre-industrial England, an oversight which Professor J. H. Plumb commented upon in the Stenton Lecture of 1972, and which was also noted by Dr Joan Thirsk, speaking at the same event five years later.[1] Horses played such a vital role in the social and economic life of the country that answering questions about the sources of supply and the means by which they were marketed and sold should have been among the priority tasks which historians set themselves. As Dr Thirsk observed,

When we consider the age-long dependence of man on the horse coupled with the dramatic expansion of economic activity in the early modern period, it is remarkable how little interest historians have shown in the way that horses were made available to meet more insistent and fastidious demands.[2]

This lack of concern cannot be excused by the absence of information since the horse trade is very well documented. Apart from general sources such as manorial, parochial and borough records, estate papers, legal documents of various sorts and probate wills and inventories, there exists a special category of material, the toll book.[3] As a result of legislation passed in the reigns of Mary and Elizabeth, which aimed at reducing the incidence of horse stealing by tightening up controls of the trade, all transactions had to be entered into books set aside for that purpose. Historians have known of their existence for some time and have occasionally used them, but have never done so in a systematic way. This is all the more surprising when one considers the richness of the material, providing as it does, a range of information unrivalled among the sources for inland trade. Among the

1 J. H. Plumb, *The Commercialisation of Leisure in Eighteenth Century England* (Reading, 1973), p. 16, *n.* 58; J. Thirsk, *Horses in Early Modern England: for Service, for Pleasure, for Power* (Reading, 1978), p. 5.
2 Thirsk, *Horses*, p. 5.
3 *Infra*, pp. 55–60 for a fuller discussion of the uses of toll books.

items that can be looked at are details of prices and types of horses sold, their functions and such characteristics as sex, colour, age, size, pace and distinguishing marks. Information can also be obtained about the people involved in the trade – to whom they were selling horses and from whom they were buying, contacts between dealers and the scale of their operations. Comparisons can also be made between individual fairs, especially on those occasions when they overlap in time. Other details include catchment areas, periodicity, annual fluctuations and types of horses sold at particular fairs.[4]

II

Improvements had to be made in the production of horses and in the methods of distribution because, as in the marketing of other commodities, the population rise of the sixteenth and early seventeenth centuries created an extra demand. Developments in the use of horses for draught and carriage purposes were particularly important, for the expansion of trade that accompanied demographic growth necessitated more horses to pull waggons and carts or to carry packs on their backs. It has been calculated in a recent survey that the effective capacity of the road carrying industry may have gone up three or fourfold during the course of the two hundred years.[5] The adoption and spread of the heavy four-wheeled waggon, which after its introduction from the Low Countries at the beginning of Elizabeth's reign, complemented and to a certain extent replaced the traditional two-wheeled carts and wains, made the industry more efficient but at the same time increased the demand for horses.[6] The number of pack-horses also rose. In certain circumstances they possessed decided advantages and were especially effective over long hauls: they were faster, could travel over rougher ground, were more flexible in their number and required fewer men to attend to them.[7] Many thousands of horses were needed to service the varied enterprises of the nation. The important malt trade between Enfield and London, for instance, created such a heavy demand for pack-horses in the period before the Lea was made navigable, that on one morning early in Elizabeth's reign 2,200 animals were counted on the road between Shoreditch and Enfield.[8]

4 P. R. Edwards, 'The Horse Trade in Tudor and Stuart England', in F. M. L. Thompson, ed., *Horses in European Economic History: A Preliminary Canter* (Reading, 1983), pp. 113–14.
5 J. A. Chartres, *Internal Trade in England 1500–1700* (1977), pp. 40–1.
6 J. Crofts, *Packhorse, Waggon and Post* (1967), p. 7.
7 Edwards, 'Horse Trade', p. 117; J. A. Chartres, 'Road Carrying in England in the Seventeenth Century: Myths and Reality', *Ec.H.R.*, 2nd ser., 30 (1977), pp. 83–4.
8 D. O. Pam, 'Tudor Enfield, The Maltmen and the Lea Navigation', *Edmonton Hundred History Society, Occasional Paper*, N.S., no. 18, n.d.

The growth in the volume of traffic, especially the use of heavy waggons and their large teams of horses, affected the condition of the roads and it is debatable how much improvement was brought about by the employment of statute parish labour and later by the establishment of the first turnpike trusts. What is certain is that trade did increase and that expansion was not limited by the state of the highways.[9] Even in such inhospitable areas as south Yorkshire and north Derbyshire, a considerable number of wheeled vehicles, mainly wains, had been regularly in use on the roads since the Middle Ages.[10] Links were established between London and the provinces and by the end of the sixteenth century regular carrier services were operating between the capital and a number of towns. The provision of services further increased during the following century, according to Dr Chartres, growing appreciably between 1637 and 1681 and then accelerating between 1681 and 1715.[11] Clearly, in spite of the cost advantages enjoyed by river and coastal transport, especially in the movement of bulky items of low unit value, a good deal of internal trade was road based.[12] In the first place goods had to get to the wharves and later to be moved from them. In times of war, moreover, coastal traffic was more likely to be impeded than road transport and this influenced the judgement of many merchants.[13] In the textile industry road carriage was the normal mode of transport. The light weight and relatively high unit value of the commodity enabled it to withstand the greater cost of overland transport and this method was often quicker and more convenient too. Even where water communication was accessible, roads were often preferred because of the damage done to the wool by the damp.[14]

The population rise, by inflating the price of basic commodities, may have had an adverse effect on many people by lowering their real income and thereby their standard of living, but the commercial expansion that accompanied it offered opportunities for the enterprising individual who could acquire a horse. Dr Spufford has shown how important in the career of the pedlar-chapman was the purchase of a horse, since it enabled him to stay out longer and carry a more imposing stock of goods. If he throve, he could hitch his horse to a waggon and further improve his position. Significantly, whilst the median value of the stock of dealers on foot in the late seventeenth century was £12. 7s. 10d., that of horse owners was

9 Chartres, *Internal Trade*, pp. 40–1
10 D. G. Hey, *Packmen, Carriers and Packhorse Roads* (Leicester, 1980), pp. 91–102.
11 T. S. Willan, *The Inland Trade* (Manchester, 1976), pp. 12–13; Chartres, 'Road Carrying', *passim*, esp. p. 78
12 Chartres, *Internal Trade*, p. 30.
13 W. Albert, *The Turnpike Road System in England 1663–1840* (Cambridge, 1972), p. 7.
14 Chartres, *Internal Trade*, pp. 27–8; P. J. Bowden, *The Wool Trade in Tudor and Stuart England* (1971), pp. 75–6.

£22. 5s. 4d.[15] In the carrying trade, participants ranged from men with a single horse to individuals such as Joseph Naylor of Rothwell (W.R.Y.) who in 1718 possessed 101 head, but in between these two extremes scattered references indicate that people often owned about a half-dozen animals.[16] Opportunities for small operators were probably best in developing industrial areas, and among the people involved were local farmers who augmented their income by acting as part-time carriers in the slack periods on the farm. In the Neath area of Glamorgan many husbandmen from the late seventeenth century onwards used their horses to carry iron ore and coal, and coal horses became an important capital asset of those of their class who lived near a pit or an iron works.[17] The small man, however, was vulnerable not only to changes in the general pattern of trade but also, on a personal level, to the loss of his capital equipment, his horse. In the Shropshire parish of Myddle in 1700, Richard Gough recorded the case of Richard Maddock who had become a carrier but who had been broken by the death of an old horse.[18]

On the farm, horses gradually took over from oxen as draught animals, continuing a process that had been going on for centuries. In the Middle Ages the greatest advances had been made in the use of horses for harrowing and haulage, for oxen still predominated as plough animals. All-horse teams had made an appearance in East Anglia, the Chilterns and in the Home Counties and were more prominent on small peasant holdings than on demesne farms. Elsewhere, horses were used but combined with oxen in mixed teams, a device which speeded up the task of ploughing. By the end of the Middle Ages a certain rationalisation in the use of horses and oxen seems to have taken place, with farmers in particular areas intensifying their use of one animal or the other (though substantial farmers were still more likely than smaller scale cultivators to employ both horses and oxen). Various factors determined the choice. Horses, stronger, quicker and more agile animals, were particularly suited to light or stony soils, whilst oxen did comparatively better on stiff, heavy clays. Horses cost more to keep, however, and were almost valueless when their working life was over. Oxen, on the other hand, could be fattened and sold for a considerable sum.[19]

15 M. Spufford, *The Great Reclothing of Rural England* (1984), pp. 45, 49.
16 Somerset R. O., CQ 3/1/34 fo. 42; Richard Gough, *The Antiquityes and Memoyres of the Parish of Myddle* (Shrewsbury, 1875), p. 93; Hey, *Packmen*, p. 99.
17 M. I. Williams, 'Agriculture and Society in Glamorgan 1660–1760', unpubd Leicester University PhD Thesis (1967), p. 312.
18 Gough, *Parish of Myddle*, p. 93.
19 This paragraph is based on J. Langdon, *Horses, Oxen and Technological Innovation* (Cambridge, 1986), esp. pp. 112–14, 164, 220, 246 (harrowing); pp. 95–7, 114–15, 164, 175, 221–5 (haulage); pp. 100–12 (composition of teams); pp. 172–212 (peasants and

Farmers in early modern England had to make similar calculations, and if by the end of the period horses were being used in all parts of the country, they increased most rapidly in areas where they could be easily integrated into the local farming economy. The growing commercialisation of agriculture, by stimulating regional specialisation, had an important effect. Thus common field farmers with good access to markets for their corn readily turned to horses since they were also used for carting and could be fed on home-grown corn, pulses and vetches. In Leicestershire the substitution of horses for oxen is discernible from the 1530s and seems to have been initially associated with the growth in the acreage of oats. At first these horses were largely bred on the farm but as the area of common land shrank, farmers in the late sixteenth and early seventeenth centuries found it necessary to buy in young stock in order to make the best use of their grazing rights.[20] The decision to extend the use of horses was easiest to make in common field communities located in areas of light soil, where favourable conditions had led to the early use of the animal. Fodder was plentiful and as the soils were easy to plough, their speed, strength and agility gave them an advantage.[21] In contrast, oxen survived as draught animals in areas of heavy ground with ample pasture and where the steadier pull that the beasts could exert was more effective. This distinction can be seen in the mode of traction on the farms of south-eastern England in the seventeenth century, for horses had taken over at an early date on the downs but had failed to make the same progress in the weald.[22]

Another major consideration was the level of demand for carting, a factor which became more prominent as commercial agriculture developed. In this activity the functional superiority of the horse was crucial, a point that had already been recognised by farmers in the Middle Ages. Larger farmers, as in east Worcestershire, might keep their oxen to pull the

horses); pp. 97–9, 210–12 (late medieval rationalisation in practice); pp. 158–71 (debate over use of horses and oxen).

20 W. G. Hoskins, 'The Leicestershire Farmer in the Sixteenth Century', in *Essays in Leicestershire History* (Leicester, 1950), p. 177; J. Goodacre, 'Lutterworth in the Sixteenth and Seventeenth Centuries: A Market Town and its Area', unpubd Leicester University PhD Thesis (1977), p. 110; D. Fleming, 'A Local Market System: Melton Mowbray and the Wreake Valley 1549–1720', unpubd Leicester University PhD Thesis (1980), p. 38.

21 J. C. K. Cornwall, 'The Agrarian History of Sussex 1560–1640', unpubd London University MA Thesis (1953), pp. 94–5; C. W. Chalklin, *Seventeenth Century Kent* (1965), p. 104; Lambeth Palace Library, Probate Inventories of Cheam, East Horsley and Merstham (Surrey); R. W. Chell, 'Agriculture and Rural Society in Hampshire *circa* 1600', unpubd Leicester University M. Phil. Thesis (1975), p. 65; E. Kerridge, 'The Agrarian Development of Wiltshire, 1540–1640', unpubd London University PhD Thesis (1951), p. 127

22 Cornwall, 'Agrarian History of Sussex', pp. 94–5; Lambeth Palace Library, Probate Inventories of Burstow and Charlwood (Surrey); Chalklin, *Kent*, pp. 98, 104.

plough but increased the number of horses to do other jobs around the farm or to transport their produce to market. Poorer farmers could not afford the luxury of specialisation, however, and had long concentrated upon horses because of their greater flexibility. They could, of course, supplement their income by acting as part-time carriers.[23]

In the post-Restoration period horses were more widely dispersed around the country than ever before and were even making inroads into the strongholds of ox-draught. The acceleration in the pace of change at this time can, to a large extent, be seen as one of the responses made by substantial farmers to the problem of depressed corn prices. The introduction of large draught horses and heavy four-wheeled waggons onto the holdings of prosperous mixed farmers in lowland England were measures designed to promote greater efficiency and, by cutting costs, to maintain the profitability of the enterprises. Similar motives prompted enclosure and the development of more intensive rotations, the opening up of the downlands as corn-producing areas, the consolidation of holdings and the search for new markets both at home and abroad.[24] In this critical time for mixed farmers, the prosperous yeomen had a considerable advantage over their smaller neighbours. They could not only absorb greater levels of capital investment necessary to promote efficiency but also benefited from economies of scale. Regional studies, such as those undertaken on Lincolnshire and Oxfordshire, show that the larger farmers were conspicuously more successful than the smaller men in the late seventeenth and early eighteenth centuries and this consideration has an obvious bearing on the debate over the decline of the small land holder.[25]

Facilities for personal transport also improved during the course of the Tudor and Stuart period and further increased the demand for horses. By Continental standards horse ownership was widespread in England and the number of people who rode on horseback was one of the features noticed by foreign observers. In 1558 the Venetian ambassador, in a despatch to his master, remarked that peasants were accustomed to do so and therefore, he said, the country could be called the land of comforts.[26]

---

23 J. A. Yelling, 'Probate Inventories and the Geography of Livestock Farming: A Study of East Worcestershire 1540–1750', in J. A. Patton, ed., *Pre-Industrial England: Geographical Essays* (Folkestone, 1979), pp. 102–3.

24 C. Wilson, *England's Apprenticeship 1603–1763* (1984), p. 245; D. C. Coleman, *The Economy of England 1450–1750* (Oxford, 1977), pp. 122–4; Chartres, *Internal Trade*, p. 40.

25 Wilson, *England's Apprenticeship*, p. 250; Coleman, *Economy of England*, pp. 125, 128; B. A. Holderness, 'Aspects of Inter-Regional Land Use and Agriculture in Lincolnshire 1600–1850', *Lincs. History and Archaeology*, 9 (1974), p. 37; M. A. Havinden, ed., 'Household and Farm Inventories in Oxfordshire 1550–90', Oxford Record Society, 44 (1965) and H(istorical) M(anuscripts) C(ommission) Joint Publication, 10 (1965), pp. 275–8.

26 C(alendar of) S(tate) P(apers) V(enetian), VI, iii, 1557–8, p. 1672.

Inventories of the mid-sixteenth century do indicate a high proportion of horse owners but the information has to be treated with caution because only people of a relatively high social standing had their goods appraised. In particular, it was a more exclusive group than it was to become in the following hundred years when the inflationary spiral, by reducing the value of money, had the result of extending the circle of people for whom inventories were made.[27] With regard to the ambassador's observation, therefore, Dr Thirsk's suggestion that the word 'yeoman' should be substituted for the term 'peasant' is a reasonable one.[28] In the more difficult conditions of the late sixteenth and early seventeenth centuries a smaller proportion of people possessed a horse. As the income of many workers deteriorated in real terms, they had to put aside a comparatively larger amount to purchase staple items like food and clothing and to pay their rent, and the marginal horse owners found themselves caught in an economic squeeze. After the mid-seventeenth century the number of horse owners increased once more, the result not only of improvements in the general standard of living but also of developments in the organisation of the market. The rise, largely derived from an analysis of sets of inventories from different parts of the country, can be corroborated by other information. At Horbling (Lincs.), for instance, a series of parish rates were made in the seventeenth and eighteenth centuries, based on the ownership of a single animal, and they indicate a growth in the proportion of horse owners in the village after a low point in the reign of Charles I (Tables 1a and 1b).[29]

Horses could also be hired and as more people travelled the roads of the country, hackney services proliferated, especially in large centres of population. The celebrated Hobson of Cambridge possessed a string of 40, but small men were also involved, taking advantage of economic opportunities. According to the town leet records of Southampton in 1582, 'ev[er]y man allmost in this towne that hath a horse do vse to hyer owt to

27 J. M. Bestall and D. V. Fowkes, eds., 'Chesterfield Wills and Inventories, 1521–1602', *Derbys. Rec. Soc.*, 1 (1977); F. G. Emmison, ed., 'Jacobean Inventories', *Beds. Hist. Rec. Soc.*, N.S., 20 (1938); Havinden, 'Oxfords. Inventories'; P. A. Kennedy, ed., 'Nottinghamshire Household Inventories', *Thoroton Society Record Series*, 22 (1963); J. S. Moore, ed., *Clifton and Westbury Probate Inventories, 1609–1761* (1981); J. A. Yelling, 'Livestock Numbers and Agricultural Development 1540–1750', in T. R. Slater and P. J. Jarvis, eds., *Field and Forest: An Historical Geography of Warwickshire and Worcestershire* (Norwich, 1982), pp. 281–99.
28 Thirsk, *Horses*, p. 5.
29 Yelling, 'Livestock Numbers'; P. R. Edwards, 'Shropshire Agriculture 1540–1750', in G. Baugh, *Victoria County History of Shropshire*, forthcoming; inventory abstracts collected for J. Thirsk, ed., *The Agrarian History of England and Wales*; IV, 1500–1640 (Cambridge, 1967) and V, 1640–1750 (Cambridge, 1984). I am grateful to Dr Thirsk for allowing me to look at this information. Lincs. A.O., Horbling Probate Inventories, Horbling parish rates are Lincs. A.O., Horbling Parish Records, 7/1, 7/3, 12/2.

Table 1a. *Horbling (Lincs.) parish rate assessments: number of horses per holding*

Number of horses	1636	1701	1724	(1724–42)
0	24	17	10	8
	40.0%	26.6%	18.9%	14.3%
1–5	20	24	22	28
	33.3%	37.5%	41.5%	50.0%
6–10	10	10	6	10
	16.7%	15.6%	11.3%	17.9%
11–20	6	13	14	8
	10.0%	20.3%	26.4%	14.3%
21–30	—	—	—	1
				1.8%
Over 30	—	—	1	1
			1.9%	1.8%
Total holdings	60	64	53	56
Median (all)	1	3–4	3	2
Median (those with horses)	3	4	5	5

such as they lyke & also the hostelers of Innes be horse hyrers'. As a result the keeping of horses for hire was restricted to eight men, although within a few years the inhabitants were complaining that this system was worse than the old one, suggesting that the townspeoples' action had met a real demand.[30] Private travellers could also utilize the facilities of the postal service with its relays of horses. After its establishment in 1511 the service grew rapidly and by the end of the sixteenth century postal roads radiating out from London linked the capital with Dover, Falmouth, Milford Haven, Holyhead, Carlisle and Berwick. Subsequent development filled out the system and by 1666 a number of branch lines had been created.[31] Other travellers bought a horse at the outset of a journey with the intention of selling it at the end of the trip. At ports, for instance, some of the horses on sale at local markets and fairs were disposed of by people about to embark on board ship – mariners are recorded in surviving toll books at

30 Crofts, *Packhorse, Waggon and Post*, p. 23; F. J. C. and D. M. Hearnshaw, eds., 'Court Leet Records, I, ii, 1578–1602', *Southampton Record Society* (1906), pp. 228, 243.
31 Crofts, *Packhorse, Waggon and Post*, pp. 62, 61; H. Robinson, *The British Post Office: A History* (Princeton, NJ, 1948), pp. 64–5.

Table 1b. *Horbling parish inventories: number of horses per holding*

Number of horses	16th century	1600–46	post-1660
0	24 26.1%	32 45.7%	4 13.8%
1–5	27 29.3%	19 27.1%	9 31.0%
6–10	28 30.4%	12 17.1%	7 24.1%
11–20	8 8.7%	5 7.1%	7 24.1%
21–30	4 4.3%	2 2.9%	1 3.4%
31–40	1 1.1%	— —	1 3.4%
Total	92	70	29
Median (all)	3–4	1	6
Median (those with horses)	6–7	5–6	9

Bristol, Chester, Plymouth and Portsmouth and Irish merchants at Chester.[32]

Such developments helped to stimulate activity in the market place. Postmasters could impress horses to supply the post whenever necessary, but in the ordinary course of business had to buy their stock, as did the hackneymen. As more and more people became involved, the demand for horses grew, especially as hired horses did not last very long. The quality and condition of post and hackney horses were matters of constant debate, travellers complaining of poor standards and the hirers accusing the riders of ill-treating the animals. In consequence, hackneymen and postmasters were among the regular customers at horse fairs and often engaged in a little buying and selling on the side. For people who bought a horse merely to complete a journey, the development of horse fairs and the ease with which horses could be bought and sold, made this a feasible course of action, although, of course, they had to weigh up market conditions. Their

---

32 Toll Books. In 1610 Sir George Radcliffe, then a student at Oxford, thought about buying a horse on which to ride home. After weighing up the economics of the business, however, he decided against it; T. D. Whitaker, ed., *The Life and Correspondence of Sir George Radcliffe knight, Ll.D.* (1810), p. 53.

actions must have had an invigorating effect on the market, not only increasing the rate of turnover of stock but also helping to stimulate the flow of traffic between different parts of the country.

Coaching services developed too. In the early sixteenth century all that was available for transport were a few cumbersome vehicles built like small waggons slung on chains and known as 'chariots'. By the reign of Elizabeth, however, the Pomeranian coach with its elegantly built and furnished body, suspended on leather braces, had made its appearance.[33] The most luxurious models belonged to the gentry and nobility and cost a lot of money but as a mode of conveyance coaches grew rapidly in popularity, especially in London. In 1601 the House of Lords proposed a sumptuary measure to limit their use effectively to the leisured classes, but the bill was lost and the number of coaches continued to increase, causing severe congestion in parts of the capital.[34] In Coach and Sedan (1636) Henry Peacham has one of his characters, the surveyor, say that there were over 6,000 of them in London and its environs. At Whitehall, the character continues, 'you would admire to see them, how close they stand together (like Mutton pies in a Cookes-oven) that hardly you can thrust a pole betweene'. The main problem was caused by the rapid increase in the number of hackney coaches, those put out to hire, and in the year that Coach and Sedan was published, the King issued a proclamation which aimed at restricting the use of these vehicles.[35]

The seventeenth century also witnessed the gradual spread of stage-coaches along the roads of England, linking a number of towns to the capital and to one another. In 1637 all the services, except one that John Taylor noted, were to places within 30 miles of London. By the time that the Traveller's and Chapman's Instructor was published in 1705 the capital was connected with 180 towns and there were regular services to all parts of the country.[36] The growth in posting and stage-coach networks had a more general effect on commercial affairs too, because as they improved mobility and the dissemination of information, they helped to integrate the regional economies.

The upper classes adopted coaches partly as a means of ostentatious display: apart from the cost of the vehicles, a considerable sum of money had to be laid out for a matching set of fine coach horses. Top prices were paid for horses from abroad, particularly those with Flemish blood, a

---

33 Crofts, Packhorse, Waggon and Post, p. 112; D. M. Meads, ed., Diary of Lady Margaret Hoby 1599–1605 (1930), p. 245, n. 196; Hey, Packmen, p. 99.
34 Crofts, Packhorse, Waggon and Post, pp. 115–16.
35 Henry Peacham, Coach and Sedan (1636), fo. F1, C2; J. Bruce, ed., 'The Letters and Papers of the Verney Family', Camden Society, O.S., 56 (1853), p. 185.
36 Crofts, Packhorse, Waggon and Post, p. 125

situation that reflected not only the quality of these horses but also the dictates of fashion. In their general choice of horses the gentry and nobility gave greater prominence to non-economic criteria than did the population at large, valuing such points as colour, action, form and breed. They kept the largest stables and possessed the most varied stock. Estate records indicate that they owned many horses of small value and these included old, injured and diseased animals as well as those acquired as heriots or strays. What distinguishes their stables from those of other horse keepers, however, was the range of uses to which their horses were put and the high prices they paid for them. In particular, as they developed an interest in leisure pursuits, notably the manège, horse racing, hunting and coach travel, they refined their tastes and were prepared to pay top prices for suitable stock.

Whilst some activities such as horse racing and the manège remained essentially aristocratic pastimes, there were areas, as in the provision of draught and saddle horses, in which the influence of the upper classes extended over a wider section of society. They also provided income, employment and enjoyment for the population at large. On many estates, expenditure on horses and associated items was a major element in the budget and involved the disbursement of a good deal of money every year, catalogued under such headings as purchases, travelling costs, wages and stabling and maintenance charges (see Appendix 1). In one sense the estate was a microcosm of society and just as in the outside world the care and maintenance of horses gave employment to thousands of people in a variety of jobs, so there was plenty of work to be done in the stables of the leisured orders. The largest esablishments employed a considerable staff to look after their stock, ranging in rank from the yeoman of the horse down to the humble stable lad and including grooms, and coach- and huntsmen. On some estates blacksmiths, farriers, horse breakers and gelders were put on the payroll but if not, their jobs were carried out by individuals living locally, or sometimes, as in the case of the latter two occupations, by itinerant specialists. The skill in dealing with horses which blacksmiths and farriers naturally acquired as part of their job made them particularly useful to their masters and they were often used in a variety of ways. In the 1570s and 1580s George Middleton, a blacksmith, was employed by the Pagets of Beaudesert (Staffs.) as a breaker, farrier and horse dealer as well as a blacksmith.[37] Supervising the work of such men was an agent who on large estates would have had special responsibility for the horses (the yeoman of the horse) but on smaller ones may have had to oversee the livestock in general or even the entire farming enterprise. At the turn of the

37 Staffs. R.O., Paget of Beaudesert Colln. D(W) 1734/3/3/276, 279.

seventeenth century, John Pruce was in charge of the horses of the Cartwrights of Aynho (Northants.) and on one occasion, in 1709, was given the task of buying a set of coach horses for his master. By May he had obtained a set of six bay mares off gentry families in Leicestershire, Northamptonshire, Oxfordshire and Warwickshire, at prices ranging from £12. 1s. 0d. to £16. 2s. 6d. John received £1. 4s. 10d. in expenses and a gratuity of £6. 9s. 0d. for the job.[38]

Many other people from a variety of trades gained from the largesse distributed by the landed classes. Coachmakers could earn the most per item, but saddlers, bridle and bit makers and spurriers would have drawn a steadier, if smaller, income. Stables were often rebuilt, extended or improved – the central porch of the one at Arbury Hall (Warwicks.) is said to have been designed by Sir Christopher Wren – and this gave work to the building trades.[39] Fodder was normally found on the demesne, but if more were needed, it would have to be bought off neighbours or local farmers or at markets or fairs. Moreover, riding charges, a regular item of expenditure, included stabling costs of the horses needed on the various journeys made by gentry families and their agents. As the servants, especially on the larger estates, were often dressed in a special livery – Sir Henry Sidney's grooms in the 1570s wore black jerkins with blue buttons and yellow stockings – even tailors received something.[40] Tradesmen also profited from the passion of the gentry and nobility for horse racing. Meetings grew in number throughout the sixteenth and seventeenth centuries and often attracted large crowds. They were thus important economic events and it is therefore not surprising to note that many of the earlier ones had been organised by corporations as a means of attracting people to the town and encouraging trade.

The interest of the upper classes in good quality horses had a significant impact on the conduct of warfare too. During the Tudor and Stuart period a new type of cavalry mount replaced the old medieval destrier as the emphasis shifted from weight and size to speed and mobility.[41] Cavalry horses were major items of capital expenditure in equipping an army and the changing nature of warfare involved the officer class in substantial costs in upgrading their stock. The impetus was given early in the period by the toll on horses caused by Henry VIII's campaigns. When a thorough survey was made for the musters in 1539 it was revealed that practically no

38 Northants, R.O., Cartwright of Aynho Colln. C(A) 3489.
39 G. Nares, *Arbury Hall Guidebook* (1969), p. 5.
40 Thirsk, *Horses*, p. 7, quoting Kent A.O., U 1475/a56(3).
41 J. M. Brereton, *The Horse in War* (Newton Abbot, 1976), p. 38; M. Howard, *War in European History* (Oxford, 1976), p. 34; P. Young and R. Holmes, *The English Civil War* (1974), pp. 35–6, 45–6.

serviceable horses (animals of a certain size, strength and gait) could be obtained in southern England and by the end of the reign the North had been denuded too.[42] This discovery prompted the government to frame a number of measures designed to increase the number and improve the quality of native horses, and which were particularly aimed at enlisting the support of the privileged orders. In this sense the general interest which the gentry and nobility displayed in saddle horses was also geared to the needs of war. Good hunters, for instance, made ideal war horses, and for the riders excellent preparation for service in the cavalry.[43]

If over much of England the duty of providing cavalry horses rested with the landed classes, the situation was somewhat different on the northern border. Because of the lawlessness that prevailed in the area before the union of the crowns in 1603, the need for military preparedness was ever-present and thus responsibility was assumed by a larger section of society. Many tenants held their lands in return for doing border service for which, according to a document among the papers of Lord Howarth of Naworth, they had to keep, 'a goode and a sufficiente horse suche . . . as shalbe hable to do Service where any horsemanne ys to be charged'. These horses had to be able to carry a man for 20 to 24 hours without resting or at least be capable of taking a man 20 miles into Scotland and back again. The tenants also had to equip themselves with a steel cap, jacket, sword and dagger and either a bow, spear or a gun, as directed by the bailiff or land sergeant.[44]

III

The ways in which the growing and increasingly diversified demand for horses was met is the theme of this book. For some time, however, production lagged behind demand and prices rose. In this respect the horse trade mirrored the situation to be found in other industries. Agricultural prices had already begun to move upwards when Henry VIII came to the throne but the rise only became apparent in the 1520s. After a lull in the following decade, currency manipulations in the 1540s and 1550s accelerated the inflationary trend and affected industrial prices and wages too. The 1560s was a decade of relative stability, but thereafter a quickening in the pace of population growth increased the pressure upon supplies and the upward movement began again. The rise continued

42 Thirsk, *Horses*, pp. 10–11.
43 Young and Holmes, *English Civil War*, pp. 44–5.
44 Durham University, Dept. of Palaeography and Diplomatic, Howard of Naworth Colln. 201/9.

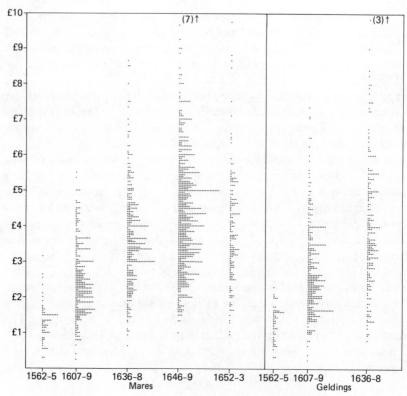

Prices of horses sold at Shrewsbury Fair, 1562–1653 (to nearest 1s.)

virtually unchecked until the mid-seventeenth century, and was greatly aided by such crises as the famine of the 1590s and the Civil War of the 1640s. The late sixteenth century was a crucial period; Dr Palliser has calculated that between 1547 and 1603 the price of grain almost quadrupled, whilst that of livestock and industrial goods doubled.[45] Dr Bowden's index, published in the *Agrarian History of England and Wales IV*, indicates a similar increase in the price of horses but in practice it may have been more considerable.[46] A detailed analysis of inventories from the North Shropshire Plain reveals that the mean valuation of horses went up from 7s. 2¼d. in the 1540s to £1. 7s. 1½d. in the 1600s, that is by 376.7 per cent (also see Graph 1).

45 D. M. Palliser, *The Age of Elizabeth: England under the later Tudors 1547–1603* (1983), pp. 140–1.
46 *Agrarian History*, IV, pp. 836–7.

During the Civil War horse prices reached a level that they were not to regain until the opening years of the eighteenth century. If the need of the army for horses had been limited to serviceable cavalry mounts, the economic effects of the demand would have been much more easily contained. However, horses were also required to move the armies' ordnance and baggage and this effectively spread the burden of provisioning the forces among the population at large. Both sides sought to protect stocks and preserve the local economy but the sheer scale of the operation, compounded by the use of inexperienced officials and the exigencies of war, often proved too much and inevitably shortages occurred.[47] The tendency for both sides to hire or impress draught- and pack-horses as and when the need arose, apart from those seized without ceremony, led to the sudden withdrawal of numerous horses from agriculture and carriage and created local difficulties.[48] Toll books were only scrappily kept during the war years, if they were at all, but on their reappearance the imprint of the conflict can be seen in the high prices listed there. Thereafter valuations decreased as the losses incurred during the war were made good.

Improvements did take place in the organisation of the market and, according to the available evidence, the horse trade shared in the developments that occurred in the conduct of internal trade. First of all, production was rationalised. Even if small-scale horse breeding persisted in many parts of the country, some areas began to specialise in the activity and, by increasing their output, provided the surplus stock needed to meet the growing national demand. The breeding grounds were generally, though not inevitably, located in pastoral regions and after two to three years there many horses were moved to other areas where they underwent a period of training. Rearing and training were predominantly the preserve of farmers in mixed farming areas where local supplies of fodder could be fed to the horses. Moreover, breeding in particular areas began to concentrate on the production of certain types of horses. Although many people continued to make do with all-purpose stock, there was a greater awareness of functional differences between the various breeds as the period progressed and this is reflected in the growing sophistication of the market and the wider range of animals on offer there. This was a development which fitted in well with the general trend in the economy of the time. As Dr Thirsk has written, the growth of rural industry and the home production of many commodities previously manufactured abroad not only provided customers with a wider choice of goods but also made

47 D. H. Pennington, 'The War and the Peace', in J. Morrill, ed., *Reactions to the English Civil War 1642–1649* (1982), pp. 115–35, *passim.*
48 *Ibid.*, p. 119.

them available in a range of styles and at different levels of quality and price.[49] Thus, at the end of the seventeenth century a pack-horse could be bought for less than £3, whereas a racer would cost £1,000.

Improvements were also made in breeding standards, especially at the upper end of the market where the gentry became more thoroughly involved. They were particularly responsible for the importation of foreign horses, the blood of which further advanced the quality of the native stock and made them suitable to perform specific tasks. Of course, foreign horses, notably from Spain and Italy, had come into the country in the Middle Ages. Many then had been employed as war horses and because of their size and quality, were extremely valuable animals.[50] These overseas trading links seem to have been broken off in the mid-fourteenth century however, at a time when there was a noticeable decline in the interest displayed by English kings in their studs.[51] This inevitably had an adverse effect on the quality of the stock and it was not until the reign of Henry VIII that effective steps were taken to remedy the situation (though his military campaigns further depleted the supply of horses).

Information on horses was disseminated in a number of ways. Undoubtedly, ordinary farmers and breeders relied heavily upon practical experience and the advice which they received from friends and neighbours, whereas the upper classes had the added benefit of literary manuals on horsemanship which after their first appearance in English in *circa* 1560 steadily increased in numbers.[52] The audience for which the authors were writing is evident from their emphasis upon good quality horses and the ways of improving them, but this was precisely the area where contemporaries thought attention was needed.

To cope with the increased volume of business and the development of the long-distance traffic, rationalisation took place in the means of distribution too. Horses continued to be sold at many markets and fairs but some centres became more important than others. By developing a specialisation in the sale of horses, separate from their general marketing activity, the more prominent fairs attracted custom from a wide area. Often the buyers were drawn to them because of the particular type of horses that could be obtained. Thus Penkridge (Staffs.) dealt in high-quality saddle horses, whereas Northampton was noted for its strong coach and carriage animals. Other places, situated on the junction of pastoral and mixed-farming areas, acted as pivotal points in the trade, supplying the former with brood mares and fillies, and the latter with

---

49 J. Thirsk, *Economic Policy and Projects* (Oxford, 1978), chapter 5, pp. 106–32, *passim.*
50 R. H. C. Davis, 'The Medieval Warhorse', in F. M. L. Thompson, ed., *Horses in European Economic History*, pp. 17–18.
51 *Ibid.*, pp. 17, 20.
52 Thirsk, *Horses*, pp. 17–21.

horses, colts and geldings. All markets and fairs, however, were threatened by the growth of private dealing, a practice which offered greater flexibility in the manner in which business was conducted. Its impact, although not as severe in the livestock trade as in other branches of commerce, was certainly felt and is reflected in the declining numbers of horses entered into the toll books of the post-Restoration period.

In conformity with the general pattern, the changes that occurred in the horse trade were largely brought about by the activities of a class of specialist dealers who alone had the time and the expertise effectively to provision the market on more than a purely local scale. For those with ambition and initiative and who were willing to take risks, circumstances provided the opportunities to make a reasonable living. Naturally the situation varied from commodity to commodity, depending upon such factors as location, scale of capital investment, level of demand and access to supplies and markets. Whatever their position, such people were rarely popular for many of their contemporaries were suspicious of their way of life and the manner in which they carried on their trade. The new and more informal means of organisation that they evolved to deal with the growth in demand made them less easy to control and provided them, it was thought, with unlimited opportunities for profiteering. Their mobility too seemed to strike at the foundations of society, adding a rootless element which threatened its existence. Horse dealers had a particularly poor reputation and the trade certainly had its seamier side. The importance of horses in the economy inevitably attracted some unsavoury characters to it, who operated on the edge of legality, if not beyond it. Such people often belonged to the 'criminal' sub-group of vagrants and itinerants as horse dealing easily fitted into their wandering life and all too readily merged into outright theft. The mere presence of such men in a locality was thought to constitute a serious threat to law and order, and hostility to them undoubtedly influenced attitudes towards the legitimate dealers who conducted their business openly and honestly.

Horse dealers were not a new phenomenon in the early modern period. In the thirteenth and fourteenth centuries, for instance, English kings acquired many of their Spanish and Italian horses through the medium of merchants who either brought them in for sale or who were sent out to obtain them. In 1214, Thomas Briton was allowed 200 marks to buy Spanish horses for the King, and another merchant, Walter Vinetarius of Bristol, had a safe conduct to go to Spain for others. In 1276–7, moreover, some of the merchants from whom Edward I bought horses were Italians.[53] These merchants seem to have concentrated their attention on quality stock for a high class market and to them horses probably formed

---

53 R. H. C. Davis, 'The Medieval Warhorse', pp. 17–18.

only a small part of a large widespread trade in a range of items. Others must have been involved in the trade too. Undoubtedly, the growing number of horses to be found on the farms and roads of medieval England encouraged dealing, especially in the favoured areas of the South and East, and there was a craft of horse coursers in London in 1422. Most people used multi-purpose horses, however, and as they were largely bred and sold locally, there were fewer opportunities for small-scale entrepreneurs than those presented by the expansion and diversification of the market in Tudor and Stuart times.[54]

The development of credit facilities helped in this process, offering a means whereby men of comparatively slender means could obtain a horse. For such people easy terms could be arranged. In a list of debts which Richard Wells of Wem (Shrops.) drew up in December 1602, three were from his fellow-parishioners for horses sold to them, one of whom, George Higginson Junior, was allowed to pay in weekly instalments of 1s. 0d. Similar arrangements were adopted at Bedale in the North Riding. In the petty court book of the manor kept at the turn of the sixteenth century are 60 entries relating to horses, of which 27 (45 per cent) comprise debts for part of the purchase price.[55]

According to the records, it was normal in credit dealings to discharge the debt in one instalment at a future specified date, paying only a small 'earnest' at the time the bargain was struck. As Dr Bowden found in the wool trade, three to six months was the customary period, although it could be as little as a week or as much as a year or more. To aid memory, important dates on the calendar were regularly chosen as the occasion for the settling of accounts, Michaelmas being a particularly popular one. Dates of fairs were also used and this indicates that in spite of the growth of private marketing, they remained important events. Personal deals between friends and relatives may have allowed for greater flexibility. In a letter to Mr Miles Stapleton in 1669, Edward Arden wrote, 'I leave honest Sorrell to you to dispose of: his good qualities will make amends for his age: if Mr. Flower will buy him and be good master, I will give him time for the money'.[56]

An analysis of the evidence indicates that the use of credit was enjoyed by the whole horse-buying population and was not confined to transac-

54 J. Langdon, *Horses, Oxen* ..., pp. 95–7, 114–15, 164, 175, 221–5, and private communication.

55 Lichfield Joint R.O., Probate, Richard Wells of Wem, 18 May 1603; North Riding R.O., Beresford-Peirse Colln., ZBA 17/1/19.

56 J. A. Chartres, 'The Marketing of Agricultural Produce', in *Agrarian History*, V, ii. p. 442; R. Surtees, *The History and Antiquities of the County Palatine of Durham* (1816; repr. 1972), p. cxliii.

tions between dealers or between friends and neighbours, areas in which business opportunities on the one hand and acquaintanceship on the other played a part. Neither was it limited to wholesale dealings, for it was clearly employed in many casual sales made by non-specialists. Dealers gave and took credit as a matter of course and details of a case heard in Chancery in 1642 reveal how extensively such men used the system. The information comes to light because of a dispute over the settlement of account and concerns two partners, Harvey Connaway and John Styles, whose large scale business was based at the Smithfield in London. Connaway claimed that they had long worked together and 'by reason thereof haue had much trading and entercourse of dealings togeather by lending of moneyes each to others vpon their respectiue occasions, & by selling hay horses and other Comodities each to the other'. They had made an arrangement, moreover, that if one of them needed horses, he could obtain them on credit from the other. Thus Connaway stated that he had sealed several bills, bonds and specialties, security for large sums of money which he had subsequently discharged, whilst Styles had borrowed a good deal of money from him, amounting to fully £1,000. Styles' account of the partnership inevitably differed but it also stressed the use of credit facilities.[57]

In their use of credit, in spite of what contemporaries said about sharp practice, dealers acted in the same manner as did other people. All the transactions recorded were listed as book debts and nowhere in the material surveyed is there a hint of usurious business being conducted, that is, deferring payment as a means of adding the rate of interest to the price. Rather, dealers, in common with others selling horses, gave credit as a means of securing the sale of the animal and helping to overcome the lack of ready money.[58] Nor did the common practice of exchanging horses, particularly popular with dealers, provide a way of earning a usurious increment on the transaction. Money was often given by one party or the other, but although one can read into this a disguised interest payment, in practice it comprised a monetary adjustment designed to correct differences in the value of the two horses.[59]

IV

In short, considerable developments occurred in the conduct of the horse trade which, as in the marketing of other commodities, were made in

57 P.R.O., C2/Charles I/C12/28. I am grateful to Prof. Jack Fisher for this reference.
58 Palliser, *Age of Elizabeth*, p. 294.
59 *Infra*, pp. 53–5.

response to changes in the level and nature of the demands placed upon it. Oxen continued to be used on the farm and on the road but horses were taking over in all parts of the country by the end of the era. The greater sophistication of taste also meant that whereas many horses were still employed in a general capacity, others had more specialised jobs to do. As a result, greater attention was paid to the particular qualities of individual breeds and this concern was similarly reflected in the importation of foreign stock to improve such characteristics as strength, speed and stamina. The initial impetus was given by the government, anxious to increase the supply of suitable horses for the army, and the measures taken were specifically aimed at the upper classes. Gradually, however, the benefits were felt among the population at large and by the end of the Stuart age the country's stock of horses was among the best and most varied in Europe, thereby stimulating an important export trade. Tens of thousands of horses were employed in one activity or another and clearly a considerable amount of business was generated, involving a host of people in occupations which used the animals. The dealers increasingly came to dominate the trade, and if contemporary opinion was stridently opposed to them, their role was nonetheless indispensable. Without them the markets and fairs would have remained localised and the resources of the country under-utilised.

During the sixteenth and seventeenth centuries prices rose considerably, especially in the hundred years before the Civil War. The needs of a rapidly growing population, together with the associated development of agriculture and trade and industry, formed the basis of this demand as horses of all types were needed in ever increasing numbers. The peak in demand, as for other commodities, came during the Civil War and this is reflected in the prices recorded in toll books and other sources of information that have survived for the war years and the period immediately afterwards. Prices were also affected by the unique position which horses held among animals for their use in leisure pursuits (with the possible exception of dogs) and as status symbols. This meant that non-economic criteria could influence values and the highest prices were paid for pads (easy-going saddle horses), and horses for racing and for the manège.

───── ○○○ ─────

HORSE BREEDING AND REARING AREAS AND THE IMPROVEMENT OF THE NATIVE STOCK

Small-scale horse breeding and rearing for an essentially local market continued in many parts of the country throughout the Tudor and Stuart period and these animals were sold at nearby markets and fairs or privately to friends and neighbours. Rarely expensive, the horses were utilised for a number of tasks on the farms and roads and in the industrial concerns of the locality. At Brewood (Staffs.) in the late seventeenth century, surviving toll books reveal that over three-quarters of the sellers and more than two-thirds of the buyers lived within ten miles of the town. Even at Penkridge, some five miles away and one of the leading centres in the country, the local population had their own fair. The significant development of the period, however, was the gradual emergence of specialised breeding and rearing areas which came into existence to meet the growing demand for horses of all types. As differences in the functional capabilities of particular breeds became more widely recognised, breeding standards improved, especially at the upper end of the market where the upper classes were more thoroughly involved. They were particularly responsible for the importation of foreign horses, the blood of which further advanced the quality of the native stock.

Though one should not over-exaggerate the trend, there was a growth in the long distance traffic in horses as stock was moved from one part of the country to another, often in a series of stages.[1] Many horses left their breeding areas to be reared elsewhere and by the end of their lives had travelled considerable distances and had passed through a number of hands before reaching their ultimate destination. The pattern formed was a complex one, for whereas there was an undoubted drift to eastern and south-eastern England from the breeding areas of the North, the West and the South-west, numerous cross-currents existed. Indeed, in the fens, eastern England possessed some of the best breeding grounds in the country, although after being moved westwards, many of the horses

---

1 *Agrarian History*, V, ii. p. 441.

eventually were taken to the South-east. In the trade in general much depended upon function and quality – breeding stock moved one way, horses to be trained another and everywhere towns and centres of industry exerted a pull. The upper classes with their more sophisticated requirements further complicated the picture; they needed a wide range of horses and were more likely to send their agents to find the sort of horses they wanted, wherever they could be found. The Midlands was a key area in the trade, lying as it did astride the major agricultural division of the country. Much of the long distance traffic passed across its borders and at the fairs horses brought in from outside mingled with others bred and reared locally. Here dealers from the region met their counterparts from elsewhere and the transactions they made with one another extended the range and scope of their trading connexions. As a result, the greatest concentration of horse fairs was to be found in the Midlands and they included leading centres like Northampton and Penkridge which enjoyed a national reputation.

Initially, a considerable proportion of the horses used in the country were bred locally. However, in some areas by the late sixteenth or early seventeenth centuries the pressure of a growing and increasingly varied demand, combined with the shortage of grazing ground, led the inhabitants to import their stock from outside. The availability of grass appears to have been a crucial factor in the decision to continue to breed horses or not, since as the animals did not give a quick return on investment, they were best kept in areas where pasture land existed in sufficient quantity to enable them to be fed cheaply. Wood-pasture regions were well-endowed in this respect but mixed farming communities with adequate resources were also engaged in horse breeding. Where conditions were less favourable farmers often concentrated upon rearing, training the young stock that they had purchased in the use of the collar before re-selling them after two or three years as mature draught horses. They grew fodder crops necessary to sustain draught animals and the horses improved in value whilst they were working for them. Thus breeding continued throughout the period in the Severn Valley and the Vale of Trent, for instance, but gave way to rearing in the east Midlands.[2] In the Lutterworth district of Leicestershire breeding was being widely practised in the mid-sixteenth century; farmers in the 1550s kept on average six horses, one-quarter of which comprised young animals, and overall the ratio of horses and geldings to mares was five to four. By the 1590s,

2 Shropshire, Derbyshire, Nottinghamshire, Leicestershire and Northamptonshire inventories, *passim*. I am grateful to Dr Joan Thirsk for letting me look at abstracts of inventories for *Agrarian History*, IV and V (hereafter sample inventories); Kennedy, Notts., inventories, *passim*.

1 Horse breeding and rearing areas (with particular reference to those mentioned in the text)

however, opportunities for breeding had diminished as the acreage of common pasture shrank, and in order to make the best use of the grazing rights allocated to them, farmers tended to buy in their horses as working animals. Young stock was now down to one-fifth of the total and there were nine horses and geldings for every four mares. Significantly, in parishes where enclosure of the common fields was taking place the proportion of young horses and the ratio between horses and geldings and mares remained the same as it had been in the mid-sixteenth century. At Oadby near Leicester the change from breeding to rearing occurred in the 1630s.[3]

Inventories reflect these differences in horse husbandry in the various regions, listing mares, fillies and foals in pastoral regions, mares and colts in areas of mixed farming where breeding was practised, and horses, colts and geldings in those parts where it was not. John Worlidge in 1675 drew a distinction between breeding and rearing districts, although, as just indicated, the contrast was not as clear-cut as he suggests.

Where you have good store of pasture, either in several, or in common, or in woods and groves, it is no small advantage to keep a team of mares for the breed; but where there is most of arable, and little of pasture land, horses or geldings are more necessary; which difference we may observe between the great breeding places for horses in the pastures and woodlands, and the naked corn countries; the one full of gallant lusty mares, the other of horses and geldings.[4]

At the beginning of the period a large proportion of the English horse population consisted of ponies with a maximum height of fourteen hands. They were bred in many parts of the country, especially on moors, heaths and fells where they often roamed in a semi-wild state until broken in. Heavier horses were bred and/or reared in improved grasslands and in the vales, whilst the largest of all came from the fens.

NATIVE PONIES

In northern England ponies bred in the dales and fells[5] mingled with the galloways of south-west Scotland, whilst on the Welsh border horses of a

---

3 Goodacre, 'Lutterworth', pp. 110–11; S. Awan, 'An Analysis of Agriculture and Society in Seventeenth Century Oadby, Leicestershire', unpubd undergraduate dissertation, Roehampton Institute of Higher Education (1980), p. 23.
4 John Worlidge, *Systema Agriculturae* (1675), p. 160.
5 J. Raine, ed., 'Wills and Inventories . . . of the Northern Counties of England', *Surtees Society*, 2 (1835), *passim*; A. Winchester, 'Rural Economy in Sixteenth Century Copeland', unpubd Durham Univ. PhD Thesis (1978), I, p. 124; J. V. Harrison, 'Five Bewcastle Wills 1587–1617', *T(ransactions of the) C(umberland and) W(estmorland) A(ntiquarian and) A(rchaeological) (S)ociety*, N.S., 67 (1967), p. 95; R. T. Spence, 'The Graham Lands on the Eve of the Jacobean Pacification', *T.C.W.A.A.S.*, N.S., 80 (1980),

common breed grazed on the hills of both countries.[6] Elsewhere, in the Midlands, they could be found on the heaths of east Shropshire, the moorlands and forests of Staffordshire and in the Peak District of Derbyshire.[7] Other notable centres lay on Dartmoor and Exmoor in the South-west and in the New Forest in Hampshire.[8] They were also bred in the more waterlogged parts of the fens of East Anglia, in places where the larger horses of the region would have floundered. This situation was recognised in the preamble to an Act of 1566 which stated,

Forasmuch as the moores, marishes and fenne groundes of the shires ... [of Cambridge, Huntingdon, Northampton, Lincoln, Norfolk and Suffolk] ... by reason of their rottenness and waterishness are not able to breed beare and bring forth such great breeds of stoned horses . . . without peril of miring and perishing of them . . .[9]

In the Lincolnshire fens before enclosure a great many rough, hardy horses were bred and reared, especially in Wildmor Fen where they were known as Wildmor Tits. Inventories of farmers from the fen-edge parish of Horbling include horses of this type which, apart from the terminology used, can be distinguished from the larger horses by their lower value. In March 1591/2, for instance, Thomas Clipsome left seven outliers and a foal worth £5, less valuable animals than his two mares and fillies (£4. 10s. 0d.) and his five housed horses (£7).[10]

These sturdy little animals were well adapted to the rigorous life they

p. 82; H. Thwaite, ed., 'Abstracts of Abbotside Wills 1552–1688', *Y.A.S. Record Series*, 130 (1967), *passim*; M. F. Pickles, 'Agrarian Society and Wealth in Mid-Wharfedale 1664–1743', *Y.A.S.*, 53 (1981), p. 67.

6 John Spreull, *The Accompt Current between England and Scotland Balanced* (1706), p. 56; William Camden, *Britannia*, trans. Philemon Holland (1610), p. 18; Daniel Defoe, *A Tour through the Whole Island of Great Britain*, ed. P. Rogers (Harmondsworth, 1971), pp. 600, 383.

7 P. R. Edwards, 'The Farming Economy of North-East Shropshire in the Seventeenth Century', Oxford Univ. D.Phil. Thesis (1976); pp. 119–20 for Shropshire horses; R. A. Lewis, ed., Staffordshire County Council Education Dept., Local History Source Book L19 (n.d.), pp. 12–13, for Staffordshire horses; for Derbyshire an admittedly much later writer noted that in the northern part of the county the horses were smaller, lighter and more slender and this made them better adapted to working in the uplands: J. Pilkington, *A View of the Present State of Derbyshire* (1803), p. 312.

8 M. A. Havinden and F. Wilkinson, 'Farming', in C. Gill, ed., *Dartmoor: A New Study* (Newton Abbot 1970), p. 171; E. T. MacDermot, *The History of the Forest of Exmoor* (Newton Abbot, 1973), p. 256; D. Machin Goodall, *The Foals of Epona* (1962), pp. 246–61; *Agrarian History*, IV, p. 70; Chell, 'Agriculture and Rural Society', table 5 between pp. 67–8, 74; J. H. Bettey, *Rural Life in Wessex 1500–1900* (Bradford-upon-Avon, 1977), pp. 19, 22.

9 8 Elizabeth I, c. 8.

10 W. H. Wheeler, *A History of the Fens of South Lincolnshire* (Boston, 1868), p. 411; Lincs. A.O., Horbling inventories, *passim*; for Thomas Clipsome, Lincs. A.O., INV 82/200.

had to lead. Cornwall, which, according to Richard Carew (1602), was unsuitable for large horses, 'being wet moors in some parts, and for the most very dry heath grounds', had, as a result, stock which was 'hardly bred, coarsely fed, low of stature, quick in travell and (after their growth and strength) able enough for continuance, which sort prove most serviceable for a rough and hill country'.[11] Accustomed to living in inhospitable conditions and fending for themselves there, these ponies, together with sheep, were suitable animals to keep and this encouraged many small farmers to breed them. Moreover, since they were hardy, active and sure-footed, they made ideal pack and work horses and provided breeders with a saleable commodity, especially as demand increased with the expansion of trade and industry from the mid-sixteenth century. Thus the measures instigated by Henry VIII to eliminate them because of their size, were ill-conceived and bound to fail.

Henry's actions were intended to increase the supply of large horses, which he felt to be threatened 'by reason that little stoned horses and Nags be suffered to pasture in forests etc. and to cover mares feeding there'. This sentiment was expressed in the preamble of an Act of 1540 which debarred everyone living in 25 specified counties from keeping stallions over the age of two and below fifteen hands on any common or waste ground. Elsewhere, the minimum height was set at fourteen hands. Horses that had broken out of closes were allowed one escape per year but their owners had four days to get them back. Annual drifts were to be made and all mares, fillies, foals and geldings thought to be too small either to produce foals of a reasonable stature or to provide useful labour were to be destroyed. This Act complemented an earlier one of 1536 which ordered all persons owning parks in all counties except the four northernmost ones to keep two brood mares of at least thirteen hands high. From May 1537, moreover, only stallions of fourteen hands or above were permitted to cover them.[12] Elizabeth made further attempts to put her father's measures into effect and writers such as Thomas Blundeville sought to influence opinion by pointing out the lack of serviceable horses in the country.[13] Over the period under review the stock of large horses did increase, but it did not do so at the expense of the smaller breeds which continued to thrive. Indeed, little attention was paid to the Acts. Moreover, the problems that they created in certain parts of the country were dealt with in an Act of 1566, the preamble of which has been quoted

11 Richard Carew, The Survey of Cornwall, ed. F. E. Halliday (New York, 1969), p. 107.
12 32 Henry VIII c. 13; 27 Henry VIII c. 6.
13 Thirsk, Horses, p. 15; Thomas Blundeville, The Foure Chiefest Offices Belongyng to Horsemanship (1580 edn.) fo. A. iii v.

above, whereby fenland breeders were exempted from the provisions of the 1540 measure. Nevertheless, no one could put onto the fens any stallion over the age of two and under thirteen hands high.[14] The evidence of the toll books shows that even after the Restoration small horses of under fourteen hands were still common.

In pastoral districts, holdings tended to be smaller than those in mixed farming areas, but farmers normally were able to augment their resources by the exercise of their rights of common on the wastes. It is true that in the lowlands – on the North Shropshire Plain for instance – the wastes were coming under attack, but in general there was no critical shortage of rough grazing land. In the north Shropshire parish of Myddle (4,691 acres) at least 1,000 extra acres had been brought into cultivation in the 150 years between the late fifteenth and early seventeenth centuries, but at the time of the enclosure award of 1813, 236½ acres remained to be dealt with. In north Shropshire too, many of the new improved pastures were made available to farmers for agistment or for short term leasing.[15] In the uplands, on the other hand, there were vast tracts of uncultivated land. In 1617 a deponent in an Exchequer case spoke of Exmoor as 'a large ground, many thousand acres in extent and thirty miles round at the least, time out of mind used for the pasture of great numbers of sheep, cattle and horse beasts'. In 1651 the Parliamentary commissioners estimated the extent of the royal forest there as some 18,000 acres where, according to a recent authority, up to 800 horses (among thousands of sheep and cattle) were grazing.[16]

Some of the best horses came from the Celtic fringe. The galloways of south-west Scotland, for instance, found a ready market in England, for they were among the largest of the native ponies (up to fourteen hands), could be employed for a wider range of tasks and were efficient and indefatigable workers. Defoe described them as the best breed of 'strong low horses in Britain, if not in Europe . . . These horses are remarkable for being good pacers, strong, easy goers, hardy, gentle, well broke, and above all, that they never tire, and they are very much bought up in England on that account'.[17] Montgomeryshire horses were similarly praised. 'This county is noted for an excellent breed of Welch horses, which though not very large, are exceeding valuable, and much esteemed all over England.' Herds of semi-wild horses roamed the extensive common pastures of the

14 8 Elizabeth I c. 8.
15 D. G. Hey, *An English Rural Community: Myddle under the Tudors and Stuarts* (Leicester, 1974), pp. 9, 34; Edwards, 'The Farming Economy . . .', p. 255.
16 MacDermot, *Forest of Exmoor*, p. 256.
17 Defoe, *Tour*, p. 600.

county and after being rounded up at the age of three, were brought to market.[18] These horses were equally suitable for riding as for work, but the hobbies of Ireland were particularly noted as saddle mounts. According to Blundeville, they were

> tender mouthed, nimble, light, pleasant and apt to be taught, and for the most part they be amblers, and therefore verie meete for the saddle, and to trauell by the way: yea and the Irish men both with dart, and with light spears, do use to skirmish with them in the field. And manie of them do proue to that use verie well by meanes they be so light and swift, notwithstanding I took them to be verie nesh and tender to keepe.[19]

Like galloways, hobbies were often to be found in the stables of the upper classes who valued them as tractable, easy-paced riding animals. They were also admired by foreigners, and Henry VIII in particular regularly made gifts of hobbies to other rulers, often in return for horses he had received himself, and he probably drew upon the stock of his own studs in Ireland.[20] In the reign of his daughter, Mary, the Lord Deputy of Ireland, Lord Fitzwalter, was ordered to make a survey of all the royal studs in the country and to see that the horses were employed in the service of the Crown. The progeny produced annually moreover was to be listed and carefully accounted for.[21]

Inventories of Yorkshire farmers living in the Dales, in Craven and on the North Yorkshire Moors, and those of their counterparts in such breeding areas as Shropshire and the Derbyshire Peak, suggest that many small farmers were engaged in horse breeding and that it provided them with a valuable source of income.[22] In a study of regional farming in Hampshire in the period 1575–1625, inventories of the New Forest area contained the highest mean number of horses (4.0) and the typical farmer had four or five in stock.[23] Wherever there were large open commons it is possible to find examples of ordinary farmers who owned a considerable head of horses. John Prees Morgan of Llandefaelogfach (Brec.), for instance, had a personal estate valued at £35. 12s. od. in 1675, and this included '10 heads of all sorts of mountaine horses' worth £3. In the hills

18 *Ibid.*, p. 383; 'Montgomeryshire Horses, Cobs and Ponies', *Montg(omeryshire) Hist(orical) Coll(ectio)ns*, 22 (1888), pp. 19, 29; H. L. Squires and E. Rowley, eds., *Montg. Hist. Collns.*, 22 (1888), p. 284.
19 Blundeville, fo. 6v.
20 *C.S.P.V.*, VI, iii, 1557–8, appendix, pp. 1606, 1608–11, 1613–14.
21 J. S. Brewer and W. Bullen, eds., *Calendar of the Carew MSS (at Lambeth) 1515–1574* (1867), p. 255.
22 J. H. Long, 'Regional Farming in Seventeenth-Century Yorkshire', *Agric. H.R.*, 8 (1960), pp. 103–14; Shropshire inventories, *passim*; Derbyshire sample inventories.
23 Chell, 'Agriculture and Rural Society', table 5 between pp. 67–8.

of Monmouthshire, Edmund Richard of Gelligaer owned six horses in 1679 and their value, set at £1. 10s. 0d., was one-tenth (9.8 per cent) of his goods.[24] The largest herds were kept by members of the gentry and prosperous yeomen who possessed extensive rights of common on the wastes. Thus in the late sixteenth century John Whit, a yeoman from Bartley in the Hampshire parish of Eling, ran a large cattle-corn enterprise which also included the keeping of horses in the New Forest. His adult horses, apart from his stallion and ten cart horses, comprised six geldings on the common and 28 mares in the Forest and in Callmore. In addition he had six two-year-old colts and nine yearling colts. Elsewhere, John Price, a Devynock (Brecs.) gentleman, left six wild horses and seven wild mares on the hills in 1685.[25]

Large numbers of ponies were used in the carrying trade as pack-horses and this facilitated their distribution around the country. Horses were bought and sold as the need arose and examples of the distances travelled can be seen in the late seventeenth-century toll books of the markets at Chester and Oxford. At Shrewsbury, the centre of the North Wales textile industry, people bringing in consignments of wool or unfinished cloth sold their ponies to others who, for instance, required them to take wool to the Essex clothiers or cloth to Blackwell Hall in London. Similarly, horses in the South-west were disposed of at textile centres like Exeter where at the end of the seventeenth century Celia Fiennes observed the streets thick with carriers driving their horses loaded with cloth from the surrounding district.[26]

Of course, fairs located in or near the breeding grounds provided outlets for the horses and the important marts attracted custom from centres of trade and industry. In the North, Carlisle was prominent for the sale of galloways. Through the fair and that of Rosley Hill, some nine miles to the south, horses, largely brought in by local dealers, were in the mid-seventeenth century being moved further into England or driven over the Pennines to the North-east. In addition, dealers on both sides of the border were at Ripley (W.R.Y.) in the early eighteenth century supplying the West Riding textile industry with galloways. They even penetrated into lowland England, for in the post-Restoration period Lord Harley noted that whilst in the Doncaster area he had come across a party of Scotsmen from

24 N(ational) L(ibrary of) W(ales), Probate MSS transcribed by Frank Emery. I am grateful to Frank Emery for sending me information taken from the inventories he used for *Agrarian History*, V.

25 Hampshire R.O., Probate of John Whit of Eling, 1573 B Wills 143/2; N.L.W. Probate MSS.

26 Edwards, 'The Farming Economy . . .', pp. 192–5; Celia Fiennes, *The Journeys of Celia Fiennes*, ed. C. Morris (1947), p. 246.

Annandale on their way with stock to Leicester fair.[27] At Ripley and Adwalton near Bradford more local horses for use in the textile industry could be bought too.

Horses from Wales and the Welsh border were also widely sought and in areas of developing industry in the North mingled with those from the Scottish border. In the late sixteenth century some of the horses bought by dealers at Leominster (Herefs.) and Shrewsbury were taken to Chester, where they joined other animals brought directly from Wales. Two-fifths (42.5 per cent) of the 292 horses for which the residence of the purchaser is known, remained in the county, but of the others, two-thirds (65.5 per cent) were acquired by men from Yorkshire and the three north-western counties. Welsh border ponies, not unexpectedly, were in demand in the west Midlands and many dealers travelled to the Shropshire fairs at Bridgnorth, Ludlow and Shrewsbury for stock. Men from the Black Country were well represented, although others buyers came from a string of parishes stretching from north Worcestershire, through Birmingham and Coventry, to the coal mining area of north-east Warwickshire. At the turn of the sixteenth century the Rockes of the Stourbridge district were particularly active and between 1585 and 1626 thirteen members of the family, representing more than one generation, are recorded in the toll books of Shrewsbury fair, buying 321 horses and selling only 32. Another prominent family, the Dabbses of the Atherstone district of north-east Warwickshire, regularly came to Shrewsbury in the mid-seventeenth century, although like the Rockes they were interested in a variety of horses and travelled extensively around the Midlands. The trade connexion clearly continued to fulfill a need, for when the Dabbses disappeared from the records later in the century, their place was taken by dealers who lived in nearby Bedworth. Of these, the Frizwells and the Hanburys were the most important. By this time the run of toll books at Shrewsbury had ended but members of the group frequently travelled to Bridgnorth and Ludlow.

These men bought similar stock bred in the Forests of Arden, Feckenham and Kinver at Dudley, Kidderminster, Stratford-upon-Avon and Warwick. There, and in Shropshire too, they shared the market place with dealers from the West Country whose purchases stretched the trading links even further. The Somerset men lived in the eastern part of the county in or near Castle Cary, Shepton Mallet, Radstock, Frome and Bath; in Wiltshire they came from Devizes and the Chippenham area and in Gloucestershire their homes were located in a triangular section of the county with its base between Tetbury and Cirencester and its apex at

27　Portland MSS, VI, p. 90.

Swindon. Several dealers moreover lived in the neighbourhood of Bristol – at Bedminster in Somerset and at Barton Regis and St Philip's in Gloucestershire. It is not clear how far these people co-ordinated their activities but they did know one another and travelled to the same fairs, perhaps in one or two groups. The horses that they traded in varied in price and quality and it does seem as though they were concerned with the provisioning of a number of distinct markets. The smaller horses they acquired in the Midlands could have been used to carry cloth, and as some of the dealers were involved in the textile industry, they may have been helping to integrate the trade between centres in the West Country, the west Midlands and the Welsh border.

LARGER DRAUGHT AND SADDLE HORSES

When Henry VIII sent out his agents to look for suitable cart horses for his campaign of 1512–13, the most valuable ones came from Lincolnshire, Norfolk and Suffolk.[28] Many must have been bred in the fens where the availability of grazing land and the plentiful supply of hay encouraged farmers to breed them. In the early seventeenth century Robert Reyce, writing of Suffolk, said that the horses bred in the low-lying areas were best suited as draught and burden animals.[29] Like other animals, horses grew in weight and stature as a result of eating the lush grass. In the mid-nineteenth century the writer of the *Cyclopaedia of Agriculture* (1855) insisted that dray horses could only be reared on the richest pastures which are 'found in the fens of Lincolnshire in the greatest perfection'.[30] These animals, although fed with moor hay and grazed on the fens in summer, were basically kept on firmer land since, as noted above, they would have sunk into the boggy ground.

In the Lincolnshire fens horse breeding was well-established in the sixteenth century and as the average holding contained six horses, more than required on most farms, they were being bred for sale. Mares and young stock predominated, as can be seen in Table 2, which lists the horses recorded in the fen-edge parishes of Horbling in Lincolnshire and Mildenhall in Suffolk. In Yorkshire, farmers on the Ouse marshes and in the Holderness fens maintained breeding herds and took advantage of their grazing rights on the low-lying commons to obtain additional feed. Henry Best, describing the fair at South Cave (E.R.Y.) in 1641, commented that 'horses ... goe well of there and especially mares, because it is neare to

28 P.R.O., E101/56/24; E101/60/24; E101/107/17; E101/107/28.
29 Robert Reyce, *The Breviary of Suffolk*, ed. Lord F. Hervey (1902), fo. 42.
30 Quoted in D. Machin Goodall, *A History of Horse Breeding* (1977), p. 184.

Table 2. Types of horses listed in inventories of Horbling and Mildenhall

	Horbling (Lincs.)				Mildenhall (Suffolk)	
	1537–99		1660–1714		1660–1714	
Mares	131	43.7%	78	38.8%	105	47.1%
Fillies	22	7.3%	7	3.5%	5	2.2%
Foals	56	18.7%	29	14.4%	12	5.4%
Other young	22	7.3%	22	10.9%	2	0.9%
Colts	17	5.7%	18	9.0%	43	19.3%
Horses	49	16.3%	44	21.9%	53	23.8%
Geldings	2	0.7%	3	1.5%	1	0.5%
Nags	1	0.3%	—	—	2	0.9%
Total	300		201		223	

Walling:fenne, the greate common, and if a mare chance to fall lame, they putte her to the common and breede of her'. In Somerset, Defoe later observed that considerable numbers of very large colts were being bred on the Levels, a practice which by the time that he was writing in the early eighteenth century was already at least 100 years old.[31] The toll books of the fair held on Magdalen Hill outside Winchester survive for the early 1620s and they indicate that it was being supplied with large colts from the Levels brought there by Somerset dealers.

Horses were also bred in some mixed-farming areas, where the activity was normally associated with rearing. Farmers kept horses, colts and mares, disposing of surplus females and trained colts at local fairs. In the Severn Valley in Montgomeryshire and Shropshire the horses produced were larger than those bred on the surrounding hills and commons and if both sorts were sold at fairs such as Bridgnorth, Ludlow and Shrewsbury, they can be distinguished by differences in price and destination (Map 2). Breeding was also carried on in the Trent Valley, mid-sixteenth century inventories of the Southwell Peculiar (Notts.) revealing that local mixed farms were stocked with horses, mares and foals. Sample inventories from south Derbyshire, covering a number of decades between 1540 and 1719, indicate a similar pattern and show the persistence of the practice over a long period of time. A nineteenth-century historian of Derbyshire, quoting one of his sources, noted that the county had long been famous for its

31 J. Thirsk, *English Peasant Farming* (1957), p. 32; Lincs. A.O., Horbling inventories; West Suffolk R.O., Mildenhall inventories; Yorkshire sample inventories; C. B. Robinson, ed., 'Rural Economy in Yorkshire in 1641, being the Farming and Account Books of Henry Best of Elmeswell in the East Riding', *Surtees Society*, 33 (1857), p. 113; Defoe, *Tour*, p. 255.

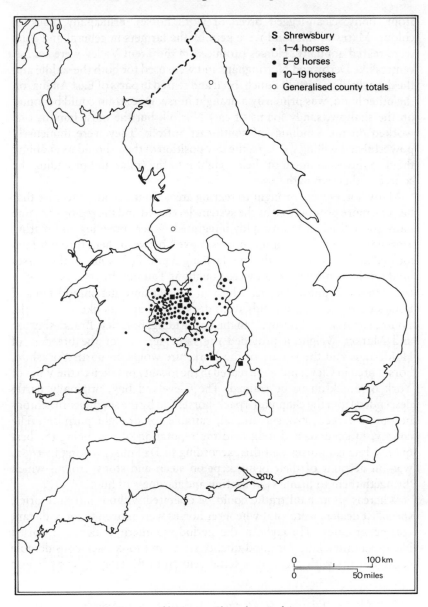

2 Buyers of horses at Shewsbury's fairs, 1647

stout, bony, clean-legged breed of work horses, principally black in colour. Mares of this kind were kept by the farmers in general and colts were reared annually. Horses produced in the Trent Valley were sold at centres like Derby and Nottingham and were used for both the saddle and the draught. The Suffolk Punch, bred and reared in parts of East Anglia, on the other hand, was primarily a draught horse. One strain could be found on the shallow, sandy loams of east Norfolk but the most famous one worked on the Sandlings of south-east Suffolk. They were immensely powerful and willing workers, the low position of their shoulders enabling them to throw so much of their weight into the collar and providing the source of their strength.[32]

Many horses were brought to rearing areas from outside, a feature that became more pronounced as the system developed and the regions became more specialised and thoroughly integrated. Where breeding and rearing areas lay close to each other, horses moved between them through fairs located at the junction of the two farming types. Thus some of the horses bred on the Somerset Levels were bought at Taunton by rearers living in the Vale of Taunton Deane, whilst in Lincolnshire marsh and fenland horses destined for the wolds were disposed of at fairs like Horncastle, Louth, Partney and Spilsby.[33] In the East Riding, Beverley, Brandesburton and Market Weighton provided the same service for the breeders of Holderness and the rearers of the Yorkshire wolds. In north Yorkshire, horses bred in Cleveland were reared in the locality or taken to the Vales of York or Stockton to be trained. The Cleveland Bay, originally partly descended from the chapman's pack-horse, had by the seventeenth century become a larger, stronger animal, suitable for draught purposes. The county, in general, had long held the reputation of producing the best quality English horses and this, according to Dr Fuller, writing in 1662, was on account of their being kept on steep and stony ground which 'bringeth them to firmness of footing and hardness of hoof'.[34]

Whereas short-haul traffic could be operated without intermediaries, specialist dealers were vital whenever horses were moved to more distant rearing grounds. Throughout the period, southern dealers patronised North Country fairs for good quality stock and took back considerable consignments with them. In a letter sent from Beverley in 1705 it was

32 T. Noble, ed., *History and Gazeteer of the County of Derby* (Derby, 1831), p. 188; E. Kerridge, *The Agricultural Revolution* (New York, 1967), pp. 79–80, 295, 301, 318, 320; Machin Goodall, *Horse Breeding*, p. 146.
33 Lincs. A.O., Massingberd of Mumby Colln., MM 6/1/5.
34 Robinson, 'Henry Best', pp. 112–13; J. H. Long, 'Regional Farming', p. 107; Machin Goodall, *Foals*, pp. 155, 165; Machin Goodall, *Horse Breeding*, p. 166; Thomas Fuller, *The History of the Worthies of England*, II, ed. P. A. Nuttall (1840), p. 395.

noted that the best horses had been bought up by local dealers who, after grooming them, returned the animals to the fairs where they were purchased by their counterparts from the South who came up six to eight times a year.[35] At the Shropshire fairs of Bridgnorth, Ludlow and Shrewsbury in the mid-seventeenth century a prominent group comprised dealers from the mixed farming area of south-east Worcestershire. In the South the large colts bred on the Somerset Levels were taken to more distant grounds as well as to local ones in the Vale of Taunton Deane. In the seventeenth century, Somerset dealers took horses to Winchester where they were sold to rearers from the Wiltshire, Hampshire and Sussex downs. In the years 1620–5 these men provided three-fifths (60.3 per cent) of the horses recorded in the toll books and of the ones described in detail, four-fifths (79.6 per cent) consisted of colts. Somerset horses were also driven westwards into Devon and Cornwall where they helped to make up for the local deficiency in large strong animals. As William Marshall later commented, 'The SADDLE HORSES at present in use, are chiefly, I believe, brought into the District (west Devon) from the Eastward'.[36]

When Defoe wrote in the 1720s many of the colts off the Levels were being moved northwards where they were bought by dealers in Stafford-shire and Leicestershire for rearing in the east Midlands. By his time the latter region had become the foremost rearing area in the country, for, as he said of Leicestershire,

The horses produced here, or rather fed here, are the largest in England, being generally the great black coach horses and dray horses, of which so great a number are continually brought up to London, that one would think so little a spot as this of Leicestershire could not be able to supply them.[37]

Of course, the county did not provide all the animals and local supplies were augmented by large numbers of horses brought in annually from far afield. Thus east Midlands dealers were prominent among the purchasers recorded in the toll books of Elizabethan Worcester, in those of Derby and Nottingham in the mid-seventeenth century, and in those of Warwick in the mid and late seventeenth century. William Eaton of Cottesbrook (Northants.), a leading dealer, together with his partners, also acquired stock at Spalding and Swineshead in Lincolnshire in September 1631, and if this were typical of the actions of such men, they were acquiring horses directly from the breeding grounds too.[38] Through the medium of fairs

35 *H.M.C.*, 13th Report, part 2, p. 188.
36 W. Marshall, *Rural Economy of the West of England*, I (1796; repr. Newton Abbot, 1970), pp. 238–9.
37 Defoe, *Tour*, pp. 255, 408–9.
38 Woodstock Town Hall, Portsmouth Book 1618–35. I am grateful to Mr D. G. Vaisey for this reference.

like these, rearers in the east Midlands gained access to stock from places as far apart as Yorkshire, East Anglia and the Somerset Levels.

At local fairs these horses were sold to rearers who returned them two or three years later as coach, carriage and cart animals. The fairs had a nation-wide reputation for the quality of their stock and one of them, Northampton, was counted the centre of the horse trade in the country. 'Here', Defoe wrote, 'they buy horses of all sorts, as well for the saddle as for the coach and cart, but chiefly for the two latter.'[39] Because of their prominent position in the trade, east Midlands fairs attracted the attention of both the upper classes and the metropolitan dealers. The horses bought by the gentry and the nobility moved in a number of directions, according to the location of particular estates, but overall surviving toll books indicate that a strong flow of traffic to the South and South-east developed during the course of the period. At the beginning of the seventeenth century dealers from London bought horses at Market Bosworth (Leics.) but the southerly drift of stock was more pronounced at Boughton Green near Northampton in 1627. Two-fifths of the stock left Northamptonshire and most of them were dispatched to London and the intervening counties. At Rothwell, a much superior fair, metropolitan dealers were very much in evidence at the turn of the seventeenth century for of the 562 usable entries in the period 1684–1720 one in three of the horses were acquired by Londoners. These men included George Arnold, Edward Horton and John Knight, three of the country's leading dealers, and they often bought horses in quite large lots (Map 3).

Other horses sold in the east Midlands were bought by dealers from Bedfordshire and Hertfordshire who used the fairs to stock up with horses for their own rearers at home. Farmers living in the southern fringes of Hertfordshire were preoccupied with breeding and rearing too, influenced by the demands created by the roads leading to London which ran through the area. Nearly every farmer of any standing in the mid-sixteenth century kept mares and colts which were reared at home and fed on oats. A century later Dr Fuller praised the horses of the county, observing that 'their Teams (oft times deservedly advanced from the Cart to the Coach) are kept in excellent equipage, much alike in colour and stature, fat, fair, such is their care in dressing and great feeding of them'. In Bedfordshire a collection of inventories for the years 1617–19 shows that the horses consisted predominantly of mares, stallions and colts and this presumes a combination of breeding and rearing on the holdings. These horses, when trained, were sold at places like Biggleswade, Dunstable and Elstow,

39 Defoe, *Tour*, p. 406.

3 Buyers of horses at Rothwell Fair, Northants., 1684–1720

where the fairs had a reputation second only to the ones in the east Midlands.[40]

Whilst horses, colts and geldings tended to move by stages towards the South or South-east, mares, fillies and foals were taken in the opposite direction. Fairs like Derby and Nottingham in the north Midlands or Warwick and Stratford-upon-Avon in the west Midlands, located at the junction of mixed farming and pastoral areas, acted as pivotal points in the trade, sending horses of one type one way, and others elsewhere. Thus at Derby, Nottingham and Market Bosworth, dealers from the west Midlands and the Welsh border mixed with others from the east Midlands. Shropshire men, living in parishes on or near the eastern border, travelled regularly to Derby and Market Bosworth, often in company with people from the adjoining part of Staffordshire. At both fairs their purchases consisted almost exclusively of mares and fillies. The westward flow of breeding stock was increased by the activities of dealers from elsewhere, among whom two groups who lived in the north Midlands and who had easy access to the fairs at Derby and Nottingham were particularly prominent. One group was based at Mickleover near Derby and was led by the Bratt and Pegg families. In the mid-seventeenth century they bought mares and fillies at Nottingham and Market Bosworth, selling them locally at Derby or further afield at Bridgnorth and Shrewsbury. A much larger group lived in a number of parishes in the mixed-farming area of east-central Nottinghamshire. They bought much of their breeding stock at Nottingham and Derby, although they also disposed of a considerable number of mares and fillies at Derby. Others were taken to Shropshire, especially to Bridgnorth, where between 1659 and 1677 various members of the group sold a recorded total of 98 horses, at least 82 of which were either mares or fillies.

IMPROVEMENTS IN THE BREEDING OF ENGLISH HORSES

In the early part of the period under review England's stock consisted largely of small work horses, light saddle mounts and some larger animals suitable for the draught. From the government's point of view, however, it soon became apparent that the country could not provide the sort of horses which it really wanted, namely large cavalry and draught horses for the army. In fact, very few serviceable war horses could be found. According to Annibale Litolfi, who wrote to the Duke of Mantua in 1557,

40 *Agrarian History*, IV, p. 50; Fuller, *Worthies of England*, p. 37; F. G. Emmison, ed., 'Jacobean Household Inventories', *Beds. Hist. Rec. Soc.*, 20 (1938), *passim*; Camden, *Britannia*, I, p. 324; W. Ellis, *Modern Husbandman*, III, iii (1744–5), pp. 87–8.

the dissolution of the monasteries had caused the decay, since the secular lords were far less concerned with breeding than the abbots and bishops had been. The Wars of the Roses had already had an adverse effect and the situation was exacerbated by Henry VIII's numerous military adventures. Exports abroad had also depleted the stock. In consequence, Giovanni Michiel, the Venetian ambassador, reporting on the state of England in 1557, observed that the only horses available came from Wales and the royal studs. Michiel similarly criticised the light cavalry horses which he said were plentiful in number and courageous by nature but weak and in poor condition.[41] In Henry's campaigns, home-bred draught horses proved inadequate too. In the war against France in the 1540s it was found that four Dutch horses could do the job of seven English ones, whilst in the field the latter showed themselves to be so weak that often fourteen or fifteen were needed. One reason for this seems to have been the lack of care with which Englishmen treated their horses. Polydor Vergil in 1511 attributed this to the abuse done to young horses, being worked too strenuously too early in their lives. Litolfi later commented that England was a paradise for women but a purgatory for servants and a hell for horses. If they were fed largely on grass, as Michiel suggests was the custom in England, this would also have limited their ability to pull heavy loads.[42]

One solution adopted was to import foreign stock to improve particular qualities in the native breeds. For heavy draught purposes Flemish horses were reputed to be the strongest. Blundeville wrote of Flemish mares that they 'will endure great labour as is well seen for that the Flemings do use none other draught, but with those Mares in their Wagons, in the which I haue seen two or three Mares go lightlie awaie with such a burthen, as is almost incredible'. German horses were similar in shape, disposition and pace, although probably not as large or so powerful. They were used for the heavy cavalry, but being tractable by nature, they made good draught animals too. The Frisian breed was smaller than either of these two; Blundeville describes them as being of medium height but strong and compact, with very good legs but devilish and stubborn in temperament. The Duke of Newcastle noted that Denmark produced an excellent breed of horse, very similar to the Frisian but lighter and more intelligent. Depending upon size, pace and shape these draught horses not only pulled the plough and the cart but also drew coaches too. Many had a varied

41 *C.S.P.V.*, VI, iii, 1557–8, appendix, pp. 1672, 1049; K. Chivers, *The Shire Horse* (1978), p. 33; R. Longrigg, *The English Squire and his Sport* (1977), p. 54; Thirsk, *Horses*, pp. 8–12; Preamble to 11 Henry VII c. 13.
42 *L & P Henry VIII*, XIX, i, nos. 271–6, and esp. pp. 14–18, 545, 465. Quoted in Thirsk, *Horses*, p. 10; *C.S.P.V.*, II, 1509–19, p. 51; *C.S.P.V.*, VI, iii, 1557–8, p. 1672.

experience, being trained in the one before moving on to the other.[43]

In the early part of the period the coursers of Naples enjoyed a reputation throughout Europe as heavy cavalry mounts. Marcus Fugger, a member of the German banking family, wrote that they were not only much sought-after in foreign countries but were also highly regarded by Italians, the acknowledged experts, as better than other breeds. In England, Blundeville advised breeders to obtain one for a stallion, commenting that 'The Napolitan ... is a trim horse, being both comelie and stronglie made, and of so high a coureage as anie Horse is, of what countries soever he be.' Although he admits that they were reputed to be less strong than they once had been, considering

> their gentle nature and docilitie, their comelie shape, their well reining, their loftie pace, their cleane toothing, their strong galloping, and their swift running ... they excell numbers of other races, even so farre as the faire greihounds the fowle Mastiffe curres.

According to the contemporary account of Holinshed, cross-bred English Neopolitans out of native mares were as strong and as brave as both the parent stock and the jennets of Spain. By the end of the sixteenth century, however, as chargers their day had passed, and as they were superseded by lighter, more mobile horses, they were increasingly relegated to ceremonial occasions or more prosaically to the cart. 'Dull heavy Jades, fitter for a Brewers-Cart than the saddle', was the Duke of Newcastle's opinion, made in the mid-seventeenth century.[44]

For the changing needs of the cavalry, the jennets of Spain were the most highly regarded and were valued by contemporaries for any task in which lightness, speed and courage were important. The Duke of Newcastle thought them the best stock from which to breed for all purposes except the cart. Eastern and North African stock – arabs, turks and barbs – were also used and if the former two breeds were often under fifteen hands high, they were fast and nimble and ideally suited to carry out the new cavalry manoeuvres. The Duke of Newcastle, in fact, recommended horses of a middling size since they possessed both strength and agility.[45] Prince Rupert rode a barb in the Civil War, as did Sir Thomas Fairfax, the commander of the New Model Army. Captain Richard Atkyns, a Royalist officer under Prince Maurice, also owned some,

---

43 Blundeville, *Horsemanship*, fo. 6; William Cavendish, *A New Method and Extraordinary Invention to Dress Horses* (1667), p. 65.
44 Machin Goodall, *Horse Breeding*, p. 156; Blundeville, *Horsemanship*, fo. 4v; F. J. Furnivall, ed., *Harrison's Description of England*, The Supplement (1881), p. 271; Cavendish, *A New Method*, p. 68.
45 Cavendish, *A New Method*, pp. 50, 78.

perhaps an indication of the number that had already been imported.[46]

Such horses were also raced and the modern thoroughbred evolved through cross-breeding them with the finest English mares. In the early sixteenth century the foundations of the royal racing stables were laid as a result of gifts of barbs that Henry VIII received from the Marquis of Mantua.[47] For those wanting race horses Blundeville recommended the importation of barbs or turks as stallions to serve English mares of a similar stature. Barbs, he wrote, were particularly swift but also hardy and needed little attention, whilst turks were very light and swift runners and full of courage. Gervase Markham preferred arabs to barbs, both of which he placed higher than turks and jennets, although he may have been influenced by the fact that as a young man he had been given an arab to look after by his father.[48]

It was in the reign of Henry VIII that foreign horses once more started to come into the country in any number. Some were received by the King as gifts from foreign rulers. Henry and the Marquis of Mantua, who had a particularly fine stud, regularly exchanged horses, Henry sending mainly hobbies and in return receiving barbs, coursers and jennets.[49] Of his purchases abroad, however, draught horses from the Low Countries were the most numerous; in 1525, for instance, he bought 300 horses in Holland and in 1544 he acquired 200 Flanders mares for his own use.[50] In order to make best use of these horses for breeding he created or developed a number of studs. His efforts clearly impressed Marillac who reported to Francis I in 1542 that the King had two stables of 100 horses and obtained 150 animals a year from his studs in Wales and Nottinghamshire.[51]

He used some of his parks for breeding purposes and after the dissolution sent surveyors around monastic estates to look for further sites. The property belonging to Wigmore Abbey (Herefs.) was surveyed but rejected because the air was unwholesome and the horses would not eat the hay. At Jervaulx Abbey near Ripon conditions looked more promising, for not only could the King draw upon the tried breed of the North but

---

46 Brereton, *The Horse in War*, pp. 41, 43. It is difficult to know the origin of many of these Eastern horses as they came from a number of sources. Arabs, for instance, were often shipped through ports in the Turkish empire. The term 'barb', moreover, was used in a general sense to denote a swift horse (private communication from D. Machin Goodall).

47 *C.S.P.V.*, II, 1509–19, p. 174, for example; Machin Goodall, *Horse Breeding*, pp. 231, 234–5.

48 Blundeville, *Horsemanship*, fo. 3v; Markham, *Cavelarice*, VI, fo. 2; G. Markham, *How to chuse, ride, traine and diet, both Hunting-horses and running Horses* (1599), fos. A3–A4.

49 *L & P Henry VIII*, I, 1509–14, p. 930, for instance.

50 *C.S.P.V.*, III, 1520–6, p. 435; *L & P Henry VIII*, XIX, i, pp. 518–21.

51 *L & P Henry VIII*, 1542, p. 80; C. M. Prior, *The Royal Studs of the Sixteenth and Seventeenth Centuries* (1935), p. 3.

also on good summer and winter grazing grounds. Such considerations were put forward when at the same time it was proposed that the King should establish a stud at Caersws (Montgs.). His two principal studs, however, were set up at Tutbury (Staffs.) on Duchy of Lancaster land and at Malmesbury (Wilts.) on old monastic property. Stocked with high-class brood mares and served by imported stallions, they provided a source of excellent horses for the stables of Henry and his successors.[52]

The Crown continued to take the lead in the breeding of horses, and its studs contained some of the finest stock in the country. Horses still came in from abroad, and after the appointment of the Duke of Buckingham as Master of the Horse in 1616 imports became more numerous. In about 1621 James I wrote to Buckingham to express his gratitude for the work he had done to improve the breed, 'God thanks the maister of the horse for provyding me such a number of faire usefull horses, fitte for my hands; in a worde I proteste I never was maister of such horses'.[53] After the execution of Charles I in 1649 the Tutbury stud fell into the hands of Parliament and the State Papers reveal the concern of the Council of State to prevent such a valuable breeding centre being lost, especially after the destruction caused by the Civil War. The Duke of Newcastle thought that the upheaval had led to a decline in breeding standards but this seems to have been an over-pessimistic view. The horses at Tutbury and the other studs may have been spread around the country but they were not lost and interest in horse breeding persisted. Oliver Cromwell was himself a keen and knowledge-able breeder and used foreign stock to improve the quality of his horses.[54]

If its policy were to succeed, the Crown needed the support of others, especially the upper classes, and this was done partly by legislative action and partly by encouragement. In 1540, as has been noted above, Henry VIII attempted to exclude small horses from the commons and this followed on a more positive measure passed in 1535–6, designed to promote the breeding of serviceable animals. By its provisions all owners of parks throughout the country, except in the four northern counties, had to keep in them, according to size, a certain number of brood mares at least thirteen hands high. Six years later the nobility, gentry and clergy were asked to maintain a stable of stallions, the number of which ranged from seven for dukes and archbishops down to one for clergy with an income of

---

52 Prior, *Royal Studs*, p. 3; Thirsk, *Horses*, p. 14; quoting *L & P Henry VIII*, XII, ii, p. 21, and *L & P Henry VIII*, XIV, ii, pp. 131, 133; 'Montgomeryshire Horses', *Montg. Hist. Collns.*, 22 (1888), pp. 28–9.

53 Prior, *Royal Studs*, pp. 73, 39–40, 44, 55, 74.

54 *C.S.P.D.*, 1649–50, pp. 256, 451; *ibid.*, 1650, p. 67; *ibid.*, 1651, p. 4; Cavendish, *A New Method . . .*, p. 61; R. Sherwood, *The Court of Oliver Cromwell* (1977), p. 57.

£100 to 500 marks (£333. 6s. 8d.) and for gentry whose wives wore silk gowns, French hoods or velvet bonnets.[55] Apart from the 'stick', various 'carrots' were also used. Good quality stallions were made available to the upper classes – in 1540 Thomas Cromwell sent one to John Uvedale, secretary to the Council of the North, who intended to run thirteen mares with it that summer. Gentlemen-pensioners, as members of the royal household, were expected to set an example in their own counties by keeping a good stud. One of them, Nicholas Arnold of Highnam (Gloucs.), imported horses from Flanders and kept fine Neapolitan horses for use as heavy cavalry mounts. Works on horsemanship which started to appear in the late sixteenth century also had a profound effect upon the consciousness of the upper classes, and if the influence of the Crown is not immediately discernible, it surely is no coincidence that three of the four earliest authors on horsemanship emerged out of the circle of gentlemen-pensioners.[56]

Many members of the gentry and the nobility did in fact involve themselves in the business, importing stock from abroad and breeding good quality animals. In Yorkshire, traditionally the home of good horses, inventories indicate the important contribution made by the gentry. Ninian Stavely esquire of Ripon Park typified their activities. He bred and reared horses and when he died in 1559 he left a herd of 41 head that consisted of five mares, six young horses, nineteen young colts, three foals, six nags and two geldings. Henry Broughton was another Yorkshire landowner interested in breeding, as were his contemporaries, Sir George Reresby of Thrybergh Hall and Sir Richard Cholmondeley of Whitby. According to his descendant, Sir John Reresby, Sir George's pastime 'was sometimes haukes, but his cheefest was his breed of Horses, in w[hi]ch he was very exact'.[57] Such men were often associated with other like-minded people, passing horses amongst themselves and loaning out their stallions to service each other's mares. Sir Richard Cholmondeley's cousin, Sir Richard Cholmondeley of Brandsby, belonged to one such circle, as did the Pelhams of Halland (Sussex) later in the seventeenth century. In the post-Restoration period other groups can be seen at work in Lincolnshire and in the Shropshire/Staffordshire area.[58]

55 32 Henry VIII c. 13; 27 Henry VIII c. 6; 33 Henry VIII c. 5.
56 Thirsk, *Horses*, pp. 13, 17–20; Blundeville, *Horsemanship*, fo. 7.
57 P. C. D. Brears, ed., 'Yorkshire Probate Inventories 1542–1689', *Y.A.S.*, 124 (1972) *passim*, pp. 3–8 for Ninian Stavely esquire of Ripon Park; J. T. Cliffe, *The Yorkshire Gentry from the Reformation to the Civil War* (1969), pp. 376, 121; B. L., Harleian MS 29, 443, fo. 3v.
58 North Yorks. R.O., Commonplace Book of Richard Cholmeley of Brandsy (no ref.); B.L., Add. MS 33,146; A Fletcher, *A County Community in Peace and War: Sussex 1600–1660* (1975), pp. 49–53; S. Robertson, ed., 'The Expense Book of James Master

Breeding good quality horses was an expensive business however, requiring a considerable outlay in terms of time, money and facilities and not every enthusiast enjoyed the full support of his family. According to his son, Sir Richard Cholmondeley of Whitby's horses ran over most of the demesnes and the business was altogether 'vain and unprofitable'. Sir George Reresby of Thrybergh Hall was also said to have kept too much of his ground at Thrybergh and Ickles reserved for his horses which, if they had been kept at good rates, would have brought in more income.[59] Breeders like Sir Roger Pratt of Ryston Hall (Norfolk) and Sir Richard Newdigate of Arbury Hall, who carefully counted the cost of their enterprises, would have vigorously refuted these allegations. In January 1673/4, for instance, Sir Roger showed his concern to balance his books when he stated that apart from keeping the best colts for the saddle and the cart, the others were to be sold at the age of three since thereafter they would cost more than they were worth. In 1682 moreover he calculated that the work done by the horses in use repaid the cost of their feed (though earlier in the century the accounts of Robert Loder of Harwell on the Berkshire Downs indicate a considerable deficit). The sale of some of the horses every year brought him in extra income and both he and Sir Richard Newdigate emphasised the savings made by breeding their own stock. Sir Roger prided himself on being self-sufficient in saddle and cart-horses, whilst Sir Richard in 1691 observed, 'Value not Selling. Wee breed to save Buying'. Nonetheless, other comments made by Sir Richard show that he did not hesitate to sell horses in order to improve his stock. 'Take Care not to be overstockt ... Keep few Idle horses'. That year he earmarked 22 horses for sale, namely eight mares, two stallions, six geldings, two coach mares and four cart horses (see Appendix 2). Clearly, circumstances varied from individual to invidual but as has been noted in the Introduction, non-economic criteria had a considerable influence on the decisions of the upper classes, even upon those made by men such as Sir Roger and Sir Richard, and with regard to horses their calculations were based upon their interest in the animal and their assumption that it was necessary to have a large and varied stock. Sir Roger, for instance, included the value of the land set aside for the horses as well as the costs of keeping and maintaining them but he did not consider alternative and perhaps more profitable uses for it.[60] Because they were concerned with producing good

Esquire A.D. 1646 to 1676' (in four parts) *Arch(aeologie) Cant(iana)*, 15 (1883), pp. 179, 181, 183, 188, 213; Massingberd (M) Colln., MM 6/1/2–3, 5; Lincs. A.O., Ancaster Colln. ANC 10/356/2; Staffs. R.O., HM 27/2.

59 Cliffe, *Yorkshire Gentry*, p. 120.
60 Norfolk R.O., Pratt of Ryston Hall Colln. m/f reel 218/7; Newdigate Colln. CR 136/V/142; G. E. Fussell, ed., 'Robert Loder's Farm Accounts 1610–1620', *Camden Society*, 3rd ser., 53 (1936), pp. 20–2, 49, 53–4, 56, 76.

quality horses for an essentially high-class market, such men could obtain top prices for their animals and thus their enterprises could show a return on their investment. At the same time, however, they possessed a similar set of attitudes as others of their class and their enthusiasm for horses may even have led them to make extra expenditure on them. This could take the form of imposing stable blocks – Sir Richard Newdigate's at Arbury Hall, for instance – large and fancily clothed staff; and heavy outlays on feed and maintenance.

The upper classes through their breeding activities, purchases and imports made available a large and growing pool of serviceable animals for use in time of war. The country thus benefited from their interest in horses but in spite of the exhortations of the government, the motives of the upper classes were personal rather than patriotic and it was fortunate that the national interest coincided with the dictates of fashion and status. Non-gentle horse breeders and keepers, on the other hand, were more concerned with the economics of the business, but here too circumstances enabled them to increase the nation's stock of horses, especially for the draught. With a sufficient supply of grass, breeders could make a profit on the animals they bred, selling them off to rearers at the age of two or three. Rearers, normally based in mixed-farming communities, found the business worthwhile too, since they needed draught animals and the training up of young stock provided them with horses at comparatively little cost.

The upper classes, of course, were not the only people who bred good quality horses but they did take the initiative in improving the stock of native breeds, especially through the importation of foreign animals, and their role in this regard has to be emphasised. Gradually, the improvements worked their way through to the horses kept by a wider section of the population, and although it was by no means completed by the end of the period, greater advances were made than perhaps has hitherto been thought. Improvements were made in a number of ways. First, landowners allowed their tenants the use of their stallions to service their mares, as did Sir Richard Cholmondeley of Brandsby.[61] The local population would also have been able to purchase off a nearby estate horses surplus to requirements – even if old or lame, they could produce valuable offspring. Others were sold at market at fairs, especially at those which had acquired a reputation for the sale of good quality horses. In Yorkshire, Malton and Ripon were on the Duke of Newcastle's exclusive list, but the activities of the gentry ensured that there were many centres in the county where such horses could be obtained.[62] In the Midlands, Penkridge (Staffs.) and Lenton (Notts.), both recommended by the Duke of Newcastle, sold

61 Richard Cholmeley's Commonplace Book.
62 Cavendish, *A New Method* . . ., p. 60.

saddle horses and those on offer at the former fair were reputed the best in the country. Visiting the fair in the 1720s Defoe records,

We expected nothing extraordinary; but was I say surprised to see the prodigious number of horses brought hither, and those not ordinary and common draught-horses, and such kinds as we generally see at county-fairs remote from London. But here were really incredible numbers of the finest and most beautiful horses that can any where be seen . . .[63]

As at the leading northern fairs, the gentry sold horses as well as buying them and thus gave other social groups a chance of acquiring them. Defoe remarked on the large number of London dealers who travelled to the fair to buy horses, a feature that had become established by 1640, when at least 31 and possibly as many as 40 of the 80 horses tolled for on 23 September were bought by London men, mainly living in and around Smithfield, the celebrated livestock market. For draught horses, as noted above, one had to go to the east Midlands and of the numerous fairs there, those at Market Harborough and Melton Mowbray in Leicestershire and Northampton and Rothwell in Northamptonshire were accounted the best by the Duke of Newcastle.[64] Of course, good quality horses could be obtained elsewhere and many other centres appear in estate accounts as places where the upper classes sold their stock.

THE EXPORT OF ENGLISH HORSES

Because of the strategic value of a good supply of serviceable horses in times of war, it was inevitable that the government would not only try to improve the quality of the horses bred at home but would also try to prevent them leaving the country. In 1495, Henry VII banned the export of serviceable horses – henceforth, no-one was to export any horse or mare worth more than 6s. 8d. without a special licence from the King, which could be obtained for personal mounts of those travelling abroad. The measure clearly had little effect, for when it was re-enacted by Henry VIII in 1530–1, the preamble noted,

Sith the makynge of which Acte great nombres of horses and mares have ben secretly and otherwyse conveyed out of this Realme . . . wherby the Horses . . . apte and mete for the waye and for other necessary uses be . . . moche derer . . . and . . . the good brede of Horses . . . is greatly decayed; whych is a nother cause of derth and scarcyte of the . . . horses.

The offence was now made a felony, although officers of the Crown such as the governor of Calais and the wardens of the Scottish Marches were

63 *Ibid.*, p. 60; Defoe, *Tour*, p. 400.   64 Cavendish, *A New Method . . .*, p. 59.

empowered to grant licences to persons using their horses on legitimate business. Export to Scotland was specifically barred the following year.[65]

The government was particularly concerned about the movement of horses into Scotland, the traditional enemy, since they helped to make up for the chronic shortage of serviceable animals bred there. This in turn went some way towards cancelling out the military advantage enjoyed by England. The measures did not tighten up control however and to improve the deterrent effect the punishment, increased to a fine of £40 in 1547 and to a year's imprisonment in 1559, had by 1580 been made a March treason and a capital offence. Nonetheless, in 1562 Elizabeth's government had to re-enact the prohibition against travellers taking horses out of the country without licence.[66]

In 1606, three years after James I had become King of England, official restraints on the trade with Scotland were lifted, but it is evident that before then many horses by one means or another had crossed the border. In times of peace, improvements in the relationship between the two Courts enabled the Scottish king to acquire much needed stock. In a letter written in 1535 to Thomas Cromwell on behalf of James V of Scotland, the King's advocate asked for the end of the prohibition in this 'tyme of lufe and kyndness'. As a token of friendship, he suggested that Henry VIII could grant permission for James's servants to buy horses in England and for Englishmen to sell horses to them. Four years later James V made a personal request to Henry VIII for 24 suitable geldings, sixteen of which were to be 'swift trottand' and the rest 'well goying hacknayis'. Perhaps he felt that as he had asked for geldings, the King would be more willing to agree.[67]

A regular stream of horses also entered Scotland by more devious means. Apart from cross-border raiding which, as will be shown in a later chapter, accounted for thousands of animals, many others were acquired as a result of illegal deals.[68] This practice, which simultaneously increased the supply of horses to the Scots whilst reducing the number available to Englishmen, was a matter of constant concern to the government, especially in the late sixteenth century when it was held to be a chief cause of the decay of the border. In 1579 the Privy Council wrote a letter to Lord Scrope, warden of the West March, complaining of the number of horses

---

65 11 Henry VII c. 13; 22 Henry VIII c. 7; 23 Henry VIII c. 16.
66 1 Edward VI c. 5; Machin Goodall, *Foals*, p. 140; S. W. Watts, *From Border to Middle Shire: Northumberland 1586–1625* (Leicester, 1975), p. 104; L. Boynton, *The Elizabethan Militia 1558–1638* (Newton Abbot, 1971), p. 77.
67 Quoted in Machin Goodall, *Foals*, pp. 145–6; D. Hey, ed., *The Letters of James V* (Edinburgh, 1954), p. 385.
68 *Infra*, pp. 135–7.

that had been sold to the Scots, whereby 'they are growen to be verie well horsed, and her Majesties subjectes eche where on the Borders greatelie unfurnished'. Lord Scrope was ordered to search for the culprits and punish them. He also had to maintain a surveillance over the markets and fairs in his wardenry to prevent any horses being bought and taken to Scotland.[69] Needless to say, the practice continued and in 1595 it was reported that the supply of geldings in the North, usually plentiful, was being impaired by the presence of Scots at local fairs who were buying up all the stock under the pretence of a licence to do so.[70] The situation was not helped, according to a governmental view of 1592, by the widespread abuse of regulations and a reluctance to punish offenders. Local gentry were among those implicated. In 1580 Lord Hunsden even had to write to Lord Burghley about the activities of Sir Cuthbert Collingwood, a possible warden of the East March, whom he claimed had sold horses to the Scots.[71]

There was also a thriving export trade in southern England through the Kentish and Sussex ports in particular, for although until 1657 the shipment of horses abroad was barred by legislation, passes could be obtained and others left the country either as gifts to foreign rulers and noblemen or illicitly as contraband. The trade seems to have developed in the second half of the sixteenth century when the records of south coast ports indicate that ships were carrying large consignments abroad. In a letter sent by the Privy Council to the customs officers at Dover in August 1562, it was observed that many horses and geldings had been exported that month and the port continued to play a leading role in the trade throughout the rest of the period. Other ports involved included Gravesend and Hythe in Kent, and Rye, Chichester and Hastings in Sussex. Dover and Rye in general acted as ports of embarkation for horses sent to France, whereas Gravesend was a major outlet for animals destined for Holland and northern Europe.[72]

The development of these commercial links suggests that as time went by the measures taken to improve the quality of English horses were beginning to take effect, especially as many of the people who wanted the animals were foreign rulers and other dignitaries. In 1607, for instance, the Holy Roman Emperor expressed a desire to have some English trotting horses which he had heard were both swift and of excellent quality. Others

69 C.S.P.D., Addenda, 1580–1625, p. 123; A.P.C., N.S., 11, 1578–80, pp. 131–2.
70 H.M.C., Marquis of Salisbury MSS, V, p. 414.
71 Watts, *Northumberland*, p. 104.
72 R. F. Dell, 'Rye Shipping Records 1566–1590', *Sussex Record Society*, 64 (1965–6), p. xxxii, is based on material gathered from the Port Books. Other relevant information is to be found in this class of documentation, esp. *vide* P.R.O., E 190/737/3, 18–19, E 190/738/ 10; for the Dover ref. of 1562, *vide* A.P.C., N.S., VII, 1558–70, p. 127.

petitioned the government to allow them to take their purchases abroad with them and the State Papers are full of such requests. In the six months between 20 February 1622/3 and 1 September 1623, 187 horses passed through Dover under licence from the King or the Duke of Buckingham and of these, 99 had been bought by foreigners, often in large lots.[73]

If passes could not be obtained, customs officers could be bribed or the animals smuggled out and this illicit traffic, although unquantifiable, greatly added to the number of horses passing out of the realm. From time to time the Privy Council, concerned about the practice, intervened in an attempt to eliminate the abuse but all to no avail. In August 1587 it was reported that choice geldings were regularly being smuggled to France from the Hampshire coast, where ten years later a party of Frenchmen, intending to buy horses worth £40 to £50 each, were apprehended. Sometimes officials at the ports connived at the practice but even if honest, it was difficult for them to take action because of the strength of the opposition. In 1656, for instance, the Customs Commissioners, in response to a directive from the Council of State to stop the illegal trade, wrote to say that they had done their best but because of their limited resources had been unable to eliminate it. The smugglers, they reported, had organised themselves into large companies and this had placed their officials in great danger. In one incident on Shoreham cliff in September 1656, John Carter, a customs officer at Dover, had confronted a gang of masked men, well armed with pistols and pike staffs. In the ensuing fight Carter was knocked to the ground and two of the people with him seriously wounded.[74]

Whilst the government tried to exert some control over the trade with the Continent, it increasingly found itself involved with the problem of supplying colonists in the Americas with horses. An early indication of its attitude towards the business can perhaps be gauged from a draft of a proclamation included in the papers of Sir Richard Graham, Gentleman of the Horse to the Duke of Buckingham, and probably written in the 1620s. It is interesting to note that only geldings were to be sent, making the colonies permanently dependent upon imports and providing the mother country with a steady income. Merchants however were to be allowed to transport as many horses as they liked – 'they are a slovenly kind of beast for draught for sugar mills that are carried' – paying a small customs duty on them and giving security that they would be landed in the stated place.[75] In the period of the Commonwealth, a time when Barbados was

73 Salisbury MSS, XIX (1965), p. 23; Norton Conyers MSS.
74 Salisbury MSS, III, p. 278; C.S.P.D., 1649–50, pp. 310, 331; *ibid.*, 1650, p. 161; P.R.O., S.P. 18/130/30.
75 Norton Conyers Colln.

being developed, the State Papers record the shipment of numerous draught horses there.[76]

The development of these commercial links with the colonies occurred when the climate of opinion was becoming more favourable to the export of horses. Merchants had always been able to pay for a licence to export stock, indicating the element of fiscalism present in many of the government's economic and social measures, but under the Commonwealth and the Protectorate the financial advantages to be gained from liberalising commerce in general, and the trade in horses in particular, came to be more plainly seen. Horses were evidently in great demand abroad and with the ending of the Civil War (once the losses had been made up) there was surplus capacity at home. From 1 January 1657 therefore, horses, on the payment of specified duties, could be exported freely from the country.[77]

SUMMARY

By the end of the period not only were more people using horses, but they were better able to choose one that was suited to their particular needs. This situation had been brought about by a growing interest in horse breeding at home, the organisation of the market on a national scale and, to a greater extent, by the admixture of foreign blood. Because of the costs involved, the upper classes were inevitably pre-eminent in bringing in stock from abroad and the effect was first of all seen in the kinds of horses which interested them. If the original impulse had been the desire of the Crown to maintain an adequate supply of war horses, the growing concern for high standards influenced the quality of animals used for many other purposes. Gradually, as these horses and their progeny spread over the country, the benefit worked its way through to the stock belonging to a wider section of the population.

This development was particularly noticeable in the breeds of draught horses. By the time that Defoe wrote, central England from Staffordshire to Lincolnshire had been penetrated by foreign stock drawn mainly from the Low Countries which when mixed with local horses produced heavier and much stronger animals. Characteristically black in colour, they formed the basis of the heavy 'Old English Black' draught horses of the eighteenth century. The impact of this cross-breeding can be seen in the coat colours of horses sold at fairs in the east Midlands, where the centre of the trade was located. At the fair held at Boughton Green near Northampton in June 1627 there were more bays and greys than blacks, whereas at Rothwell (Northants.) at the turn of the seventeenth century over two-

76 *C.S.P.D.*, 1651–2, p. 566, for instance.   77 Thirsk, *Horses*, p. 27.

thirds of the animals were black. At the two fairs held at Hallaton (Leics.) in 1720 almost three-quarters of the 101 horses were black. At Derby too, black horses were more numerous at the end of the seventeenth century than they had been fifty years earlier.

Inevitably there were one or two people at the time who felt that things were not getting better. Both William Harrison and Nicholas Morgan, writing in the reigns of Elizabeth and James I respectively, minimised the importance of foreign stock. Morgan, in particular, condemned the uncritical attitude of many horsemen and breeders who 'doe much insist herein, so as if a Neapolitan, Arabian, Barbarie or such like bee brought into England, how inestimable hee is valued, prised, and solde, and how all men desire him, who can doubt'.[78] Whilst it is true that a careful and systematic approach to breeding evolved only slowly during the course of the period under review and was nowhere complete by the end of it, in practice groups of breeders soon came to know which were the good horses and either bred from them or used them to service each other's mares. Moreover, individuals such as Sir Richard Newdigate clearly understood the finer points of good breeding practice and acted upon them. English horses in fact were being recognised as among the best all-purpose breeds as the seventeenth century progressed. The Duke of Newcastle, a highly discriminating judge of horseflesh and one who had seen foreign horses at first hand, was of this opinion. They were the 'best horses in the world for all uses whatsoever, from cart to manege and some are as fine as any, as bred out of the horses of all nations'. This comment was echoed by Richard Blome and Daniel Defoe and by the numerous foreigners who bought English horses.[79]

78 *Harrison's Description*, p. 271; Nicholas Morgan, *The Perfection of Horsemanship* (1609), p. 18.
79 Cavendish, *A New Method . . .*, p. 58; Richard Blome, *The Gentleman's Recreation* (1686), 2nd part, p. 2; Defoe, *Tour*, p. 515.

2

HORSE FAIRS, MARKETS AND PRIVATE DEALING

Throughout the Tudor and Stuart period, horses continued to be sold privately and at markets and fairs, although the relationship between the three varied from area to area and over the course of time. In the North, fortnightly horse 'markets' often performed the function carried on elsewhere by annual fairs, while all over the country the growth of private dealing affected the viability of some outlets. Nonetheless, the impact of changes in marketing techniques was probably less severe in the livestock trade than in other branches of commerce; smaller centres suffered as the trade was rationalised but this was off-set by the development of a hierarchy of specialist horse fairs. The agents of the change, the middlemen horse dealers, increasingly made use of private contracts to bypass the traditional institutions, but at the same time continued to do a good deal of business there. Thus, the decline in importance of the markets and fairs was a slow one and many continued to thrive throughout the eighteenth century.

SPEED OF SALE AND THE EXCHANGE OF STOCK

One of the most remarkable features of the trade in this period was the ease with which horses were bought and sold and the speed of turnover. Depositions taken in horse stealing cases often record the repeated sale of a particular animal, sometimes in a short space of time, a practice that was not solely due to the desire to dispose of 'hot' property as quickly as possible. Whilst such a consideration may have determined the actions of the thief, the new and unsuspecting owner did not have the same motivation. Sometimes the horses were sold at markets or fairs, if there were one convenient, and on other occasions they were sold privately. In a somewhat unsystematic sample of depositions drawn from Quarter Sessions and Assize records from which those containing the unsubstantiated stories of suspects have been weeded out, of the 126 animals referred to in the period 1600–1714, 46 changed hands at markets or fairs and 80 privately.

In one instance, in the East Riding in 1671, fairs were used. On 12 June the thief, William Agar of Howden, stole a colt from the town fields of Hunmanby some 40 miles away and headed home with it. Seven days later he disposed of the colt at the nearby fair at South Cave to John Dunn, a draper from Howden, who immediately sold it to Richard Simpson, a labourer from the same town. On 25 July, Simpson took the animal fifteen miles to Pocklington fair where he exchanged it for a filly belonging to George Skipwith, a Spaldington brewer. There, at Spaldington, Richard Blackburn of Hunmanby found his stolen horse. A more extended case in the North Riding in 1696–7 involved the stolen animal passing through a number of hands in a succession of private deals. On 16 April 1696, Richard Gibson (alias John Dixon) stole a bay gelding from William Bernard of Yarm, selling it two days later to Henry Soar of Brotton, twenty miles away. Soar kept the gelding for a year before giving it (sometime in mid-May 1607) to William Simpson, a butcher from Eston, in exchange for a sorrel colt. Simpson, in company with Robert Mann, also of Eston, had been travelling to Sandsend near Whitby and may have met Soar by chance as they passed through Brotton. Eight or nine days later Mann bought the gelding but very quickly exchanged it with Francis Thompson, a Stockton cooper, for a little sorrel gelding and 5s. od. to boot. Between 24 and 27 June 1697, however, Robert Mann, who surely did not know of the original theft, acquired the animal again (plus £1. 10s. od.), giving Thompson a little sorrel gelding in exchange.[1]

This case illustrates another interesting feature of the horse trade; that is, the exchange of animals rather than their outright sale. An analysis of a number of toll books suggests overall a relatively low figure but the proportion varied considerably, and could on occasions be quite high – at Ripley (W.R.Y.) exchanges formed one half of the 136 transactions listed in the toll books in the 1720s. This practice was not merely a development of the post-Restoration period, however, for the records of some earlier fairs also indicate a relatively large number of exchanges. At Penkridge in 1558, twenty took place, some three or four per cent of total sales, but in 1579 the figure went up to 52, one in four of all transactions.

It is clear there was a certain amount of variation and this could change the picture year by year. Nonetheless, certain generalisations can be made about this practice, the first being to note its popularity among dealers. In an assize case in Cumberland in 1690 one of the suspects recounted a meeting with a party of horse coursers at Warcop (Westmorland).[2] His companion, whom he said he had met on the way, bargained with them but as they wished to exchange horses and he wanted to sell his, the deal

1 P.R.O., ASSI 45/10/1/1, ASSI 45/17/2/37.   2 P.R.O., ASSI 45/16/1/6.

fell through. More specifically, the toll books record business done at a number of fairs. At Penkridge in 1579, large scale and long distance traders were particularly prominent and included people from as far afield as Gloucestershire, Nottinghamshire and Rutland. Richard Harrison of Birmingham made nine transactions at the fair, eight of which involved exchanges. At the turn of the seventeenth century many of the exchanges that took place at such fairs as Ludlow, Bridgnorth, Warwick, Kidderminster and Dudley were due to the activities of groups of dealers, among whom those from north-east Warwickshire and the West Country were particularly prominent.

The practice of exchanging animals was evidently an attractive one to many people apart from thieves who used this method to fence stolen animals. To horse dealers it could increase the range of animals they had at their disposal and provide a two-way trade between fairs they visited. Perhaps they even made prior arrangements with fellow-dealers from elsewhere. At the same time, they maintained their stock and, especially in their dealings with non-specialists, may have hoped to use their knowledge to good effect. Even if they did not practise the open deceits remarked upon by Thomas Dekker and others,[3] their greater understanding of the market and wider range of contacts would have enabled them to find outlets for any acquisitions. For others, an exchange could offer a means of improving the quality of their stock without too much expense. One suspect in an Assize case in 1617 confessed that he had been at Penkridge fair at Michaelmas 1616. He had taken three nags, two of which were small and of little value, and whilst there had bought or exchanged about a dozen horses in a succession of deals. When he left he had two (better quality?) nags with him, one grey and the other black.[4]

Exchanges could also help people to acquire a little money without the loss of a horse, and this concern for small profit margins is typical of low-income agrarian societies like that of Tudor and Stuart England. Thus evidence heard in a Quarter Sessions case in Wiltshire in 1609 reveals the two parties in an exchange haggling over small amounts. One examinant, William King, stated that he had met a man on the road while on the way to market at Devizes who asked him if he would exchange horses. 'What will you give me to boot?', asked King, to which the other man replied, 'Nay . . . what will you give me'. In the end, King gave him 4d. and half a bushel of wheat. Many dealers operated in the same way, especially if selling ordinary horses to the population at large. In 1587, for instance,

---

3 *Infra*, pp. 99–103.
4 N(ational) L(ibrary of) Wales, Great Sessions, Montgomeryshire, Wales 4/144/2(i)/93.

John Hooper of East Brent (Som.) sold eleven colts, making £2 profit on the transaction for himself and his partner – just over 3s. 7½d. a horse. Another colt was sold for £1. 16s. 8d. and if this represented a typical price for one of their horses, they received a gross return on their investment of 10 per cent. Considering the cost of feeding and maintaining the stock while in their possession, this was hardly excessive.[5]

THE SOURCE MATERIAL: TOLL BOOKS

The toll books which provide so much information about the horse trade of Tudor and Stuart England were introduced by Act of Parliament in 1555 and extended in scope in 1589.[6] The legislation was specially aimed at reducing the incidence of horse stealing but as its provisions also helped to give the authorities greater control over the trade, it should really be seen in the context of the government's overall policy of regulating the social and economic life of the country. It is significant that the first measure was passed in the critical years of the mid-sixteenth century, a period that also saw the government intervene in such important sectors of the economy as agriculture and the wool and leather industries, take action to control the supply of labour and begin to deal with the growing problem of the poor. Of course, many of the measures had medieval antecedents but the flurry of activity at this time reflected contemporary concern over changes that were threatening the stability of the country, and the government's determination to preserve order.[7] No one at the time seriously questioned the right of the government to intervene; indeed it was widely felt that its role as arbitrator between conflicting groups and in particular its duty to act as the protector of the consumer became more necessary as the traditional forms of social and economic relationships broke down.[8]

The motives behind the measures to control the horse trade – social concern, economic conservatism and the desire to preserve resources – were those which inspired so much of contemporary legislation. On one level, the Act of 1555 indicated the government's concern over law and order at a time of economic hardship and social unrest, a concern which

5 P.R.O., PROB 11/71 PCC 42 Spencer. I am grateful to Dr Patricia Croot for this reference.
6 2 and 3 Philip and Mary, c. 7; 31 Elizabeth 1, c. 12.
7 Chartres, *Internal Trade*, pp. 60–1; W. R. D. Jones, *The Tudor Commonwealth 1529–1559* (1970), pp. 2–4; L. A. Clarkson, *The Pre-Industrial Economy in England 1500–1700* (1971), pp. 163–78.
8 Palliser, *Age of Elizabeth*, p. 316.

found simultaneous expression in anti-vagrancy measures. Similarly, the 1589 Act was passed during years of depression when the evidence suggests that criminal activity of all sorts, and especially that of theft, was rising.[9] At the same time the initial impulse must have owed a good deal to the need to maintain an adequate supply of such a vital commodity put at risk by losses inflicted by the campaigns of the 1540s and 1550s and constantly threatened by the growth of horse stealing and illicit trafficking. By insisting, moreover, that all horses to be sold had to be openly displayed in the market place for at least an hour, the government also sought to maintain the viability of the traditional marketing institutions, the market and the fair, under attack from the growth of private dealing. In particular, the 1555 Act was aimed as much against the agents of change, the middlemen, as against the stealers of horses, and thus formed part of a general assault on such people, other elements of which included measures taken against dealers in corn and other victuals in 1552 and 1563, the wool broggers in 1552 and the currier-middlemen in 1563.[10]

According to the provisions of the Statute of 1555, all transactions had to be recorded by a specially appointed toll gatherer who had to 'write or cause to bee written in a Booke to bee kept for that purpose, the names, surnames and dwelling places of all the said parties, and the colour, with one speciall marke at the least of every such Horse Mare Gelding or colte'. At the open fair held at Chester on 24 June 1571, for instance, it was recorded that 'John White of Lauton in the Countie of chest(er) gent hath sold to W(illia)m pary of eton in the county of hereff(ord) yeman one bay gelding for v^{li} w(i)th cut eares and whit fite'. After 1589 even more detail had to be written in the book, the act stating that all sellers henceforth either had to be a personally known to the toll gatherer or had to bring 'one sufficient and credible person' who would guarantee their honesty. Most of the entries merely give the bare details, but as in the following example, some are more informative. Pinned to the list of tolls taken at Bridgnorth in June 1670 is a note written by John Brown, a noted Nottinghamshire dealer, who proclaimed

Know all men by these p[re]sents or to whom it shall appeare that I: John Browne of Halam in the Cownty of Notingham did sell and uoghtsafe the sale of a bay mare to Mr. Thomas Wheeler then Bayliff of the corporation of Bridgnorth which further markes are a star in the forehead with a fier brand on the nere buttock (*it is 'A'*)
She the sayd mare is thought to be fiue years old: the mare is ciuily bought and honestly payd for before us subscribed the prise was six pownd honestly payd:

9 *Infra*, p. 109.
10 5 and 6 Edward VI, c. 14; 5 Elizabeth I, c. 12; 5 and 6 Edward VI, c. 7; 5 Elizabeth I, c. 8.

vouchers for the same John Stockall of Bridgnorth and Nicolis Dunn of Allchurch in the County of Woster

Witness
Richard: Addams[11]

This example illustrates the value of the source but the books do have a number of shortcomings which have to be borne in mind when using them. Inevitably, many have been lost over the passage of time and all that has survived is a random sample, often fragmentary and with many gaps. Few really long runs exist and those that do are biased towards the Midlands and the last third of the period. Sometimes it is possible to discern the reason for a break in the run. In places such as Derby, Nottingham and Shrewsbury interruptions were caused by the Civil War and at Warwick the fire of 1694 was possibly the occasion when the recording of tolls ceased. A common explanation was the leasing out of the tolls.[12] A widespread practice at the time, it was more likely to lead to the loss of records, either because they were less well kept or, since they were in private hands, had less chance of survival. The existing books at Banbury run from 1753 to 1767 but in the following year the tolls were leased and the documentation ends.[13]

Other defects are of an institutional nature and like so much of Tudor and Stuart legislation, highlight the gap between the intentions of the legislators and the way in which the measures actually worked.[14] Not all market officials complied immediately with the terms of the Acts. One might have expected a number of toll books to have begun in 1555, but, according to the available evidence, this was not the case. Only stray documents for Leominster (1556–7) and for Penkridge (1558) may possibly indicate the impact of the legislation. Tolls on items coming to markets and fairs had long been a source of income, and local peculiarities in accounting may have survived the passing of the statute. Those for the horses and cattle fairs at Shrewsbury begin in 1524–5 and 1552 respectively, and whilst the care with which they had been kept encouraged the continuation of good practices, officers at other places may not have been so meticulous. It is probable, therefore, that many books were not started on time and were badly kept. At Ludlow the corporation on 17 August

11 Bridgnorth tolls.
12 J. A. Chartres, 'Markets, Fairs, and the Community in Seventeenth and Eighteenth Century England', *University of Leeds, School of Economic Studies, Discussion Paper Series*, no. 6 (Leeds, 1974), p. 12. I am grateful to Dr John Chartres for sending a copy of the paper to me.
13 W. Thwaites, 'The Marketing of Agricultural Produce in Eighteenth Century Oxfordshire', Unpublished Birmingham University PhD Thesis (1980), p. 356.
14 Palliser, *Age of Elizabeth*, pp. 315–18.

1607 ordered the keeping of a toll book of beasts sold in the town, an instruction, moreover, which they had to repeat two months later. In 1614 a book still had not been provided.[15]

Another problem is one of accuracy. Dr Thwaites suggests that at Banbury in the mid-eighteenth century the authorities may not have kept a full record of all transactions, especially those involving local people.[16] Friends and neighbours were known to the market officers and this made it less necessary to keep an account of their sales. In this way too they could avoid the payment of toll, perhaps with the connivance of the toll keeper. In corporate towns, burgesses were normally exempt, a concession shared by citizens of other towns with special privileges, and as their deals did not bring in any revenue they were perhaps ignored. Some books do indicate a surprisingly small proportion of business being conducted by local inhabitants – at Taunton between 1621 and 1625 only seven purchases and two sales were carried out by the townspeople – and although this is partially accounted for by the greater use which the residents made of their weekly market, a certain amount of under-registering occurred. Registration was also affected by the development of private marketing, which if it did not take such a hold of the horse trade as it did some other branches of commerce, still proceeded apace. As early as 1571 the sheriff of Chester exhorted all buyers and sellers at the fair to

repaier to the same sheriff or to such other clerk whom in this place they have appointed ther to enter all such their contracts sales and bargaines and towle for the same according to the statut in that case p[ro]vided. As they and eu[er]y of them [blank] to meane to avoid the danger of the [blank] and will answer to the contrary at ther p[er]ill.[17]

In spite of its failings, when compared with other measures of economic control undertaken by the Tudors and Stuarts, the toll book system must nonetheless be adjudged a qualified success. It operated much more effectively and more consistently than the licensing of corn badgers and cattle drovers, for instance, trades in which similar provision was made for the keeping of a register of authorised dealers. Here the enforcement of the Act seems to have fluctuated according to the state of the economy and bouts of intense activity tended to coincide with years of crisis. This feature was typical of much of the economic and social programme of the Tudors and Stuarts (especially with regard to those measures designed to prevent social discontent), with the result that in critical years anti-enclosure acts, food and market controls and the apprenticeship laws were applied with

15 Shrops. R.O., Ludlow Corpn. Records, 356/2/Box 2, Minute Book 1590–1648.
16 Thwaites, 'Agricultural Produce', p. 357.   17 Chester tolls.

renewed vigour.[18] The system was also more successful than controls in the leather and textile industries where legislation reflected the lobbying of sectional interests as well as the government's ignorance of the structure of the industries and the ways in which they operated: as a result the measures not only failed to maintain standards of workmanship or to control the activities of middlemen, but also did little to protect the consumer.[19] The registering of horses, on the other hand, did not conform to this general pattern. The evidence of Quarter Sessions and Assizes' records shows conclusively that after a faltering start the system did become operational, that market centres, by and large, did keep their books, and that they were used by buyers and sellers of horses. Unlike many other regulations, the measure had a certain amount of utility and helped generate business at market and fairs. As will be shown in Chapter 4, it did have some effect in controlling horse stealing even if it did not eradicate it. Moreover, since horse thieves were treated with particular severity by the authorities, it was essential that owners of horses could prove that they had acquired the animal lawfully. In this respect, therefore, the toll book acted as a sort of early modern log book, facilitating the transfer of ownership and helping to protect people who were dealing openly and honestly. In consequence, even in private deals, there was pressure to have the transaction recorded, especially when dealing with strangers or suspicious persons, since it enabled the purchaser to gauge the honesty of the seller and obtain greater security against arrest. Transactions involving friends, neighbours or known dealers were probably not entered to the same extent, but many were written down. As a result toll books, in spite of a certain decline in registration from the late seventeenth century, continued to be maintained at numerous centres during the course of the following century; books survive for fairs held at such places as Banbury, Bridgnorth, Hallaton, Ripley and Sutton Coldfield but others were kept elsewhere too. In an Assize case heard in the East Riding in 1725, for instance, John Hough of Hutton Pannall (W.R.Y.) in whose possession a stolen mare was found, was said to have told the owner, Thomas Fallowdowne of Tickton (E.R.Y.), that he had bought it at Pontefract fair, and that it had been tolled and vouched for. On examining the book there, Fallowdowne found that it had been sold by Thomas Witting of Howden (E.R.Y.) and vouched for by Thomas Pickardyke, reputed to be Whitting's servant.[20]

18 A. M. Everitt, 'The Marketing of Agricultural Produce', *Agrarian History IV*, p. 580; Clarkson, *Pre-Industrial Economy*, p. 177; Chartres, *Internal Trade*, p. 60; E. Moir, *The Justice of the Peace* (Harmondsworth), p. 62.
19 Chartres, *Internal Trade*, pp. 59–60; Clarkson *Pre-Industrial Economy*, pp. 173–6.
20 P.R.O., ASSI 45/18/2/70.

The enrolment of private deals in the toll books could impair their accuracy as indicators of the catchment areas of particular markets and fairs, but fortunately the problem does not appear to be a serious one. Most of the sales were concluded in the locality and thus do not distort the picture of the longer distance trade. Another difficulty in defining accurately the sphere of influence of particular centres is created by the task of identifying individual buyers and sellers and assigning them to the correct parish. Some of the books are difficult to read and others, even if they have been neatly written, may not have been the original record but rather fair copies made later and full of inaccuracies. At Chester an undated list, probably of the mid-1560s, appears to record the sale of some of the horses in duplicate, perhaps the result of binding together two separate drafts of the same tolls. At Shrewsbury, as I have written elsewhere, 'one not only has to place the host of Joneses and Davieses in the correct parish but also has to try to decipher the attempts of semi-literate Englishmen at spelling Welsh place names'.[21] The same situation can be found on the Scottish Border, where the predominance of particular surname groups and the duplication of certain place names make some entries difficult to disentangle. In the Carlisle toll book of 1653–4 three separate John Fosters are recorded coming from different townships in the parish of Arthuret!

MARKETS AND FAIRS

Although markets and fairs shared a common origin and continued to exist in the early modern period as centres of distribution, in practice certain distinctions can be made between the two. Whereas market towns normally had the right to hold one or more fairs during the course of the year, many fairs were held outside and independent of such centres. Some were of considerable antiquity, having developed from heathen festivals or from customary tribal meetings, and the christianisation of this phenomenon can perhaps be seen in the number of fairs which were held on the patronal day of the saint to whom the parish church was dedicated. In terms of timing, markets were based upon a weekly cycle, while fairs had an annual one. To Margaret Hodgen this difference reflected the contrast between the market as a retail outlet for local people and the fair which, as a centre of both retail and wholesale business, attracted custom from further afield.[22] Significantly, the staple commodity sold at markets

---

21 P. R. Edwards, 'The Horse Trade of the Midlands in the Seventeenth Century', *Agric.Hist. Review*, 27 (1979), p. 90.
22 Everitt, 'Marketing', pp. 532–3; M. T. Hodgen, 'Fairs of Elizabethan England', *Economic Geography*, 18 (1942), p. 389.

4 Horse markets and fairs mentioned in the text

was corn and the maintenance of a regular supply at a reasonable price became a matter of growing concern to both national and local authorities, as rising population from the mid-sixteenth century increased demand. Fairs, conforming more closely to the rhythm of the farming year, were the normal outlets for livestock. Animals could be driven there on the hoof and this facilitated the movement of stock over greater distances than was feasible for the weekly market. An indication of the difference in the distance travelled to markets and to fairs is given in an undated, sixteenth-century document found among the Ludlow corporation records.[23] Although the information should be treated with care because of the element of special pleading, the petitioners clearly felt that it proved the point. At issue was the long-standing practice in the town of holding the markets and fairs on other days than the ones granted by the charter. On the nominated day, Thursday, the corporation argued, markets were also being held at Knighton (Rads.) and Kidderminster (Worcs.) which lay within ten and fifteen miles respectively of the town, whereas on Monday the only other markets kept in Shropshire, Herefordshire, Radnorshire or Worcestershire were located at Oswestry (32 miles) and at Evesham (36 miles). On the other hand, Evesham held its fair on the same day (the feast of St Philip and St James the Apostles) as that granted to Ludlow and for this event the 36 miles between the towns was not enough. The fairs were actually being kept in Ludlow on 10 August and 25 November, much better dates, the petitioners claimed, since they did not clash with any other mart within a fifty mile radius.

Horses ranked among the most important items sold at fairs and, according to Professor Everitt, took third place behind cattle and sheep.[24] They could be obtained at markets as well, but for those people whose prime intention was to buy or sell an animal, the fair offered a wider choice and a greater number of customers. Some sales, it is true, involved persons whose presence there was due to other factors – dealers in a variety of commodities for instance, who acquired stock or disposed of it, according to need – but such deals occurred with greater frequency at the weekly markets. This distinction, as I have already noted elsewhere, was certainly apparent at Chester. 'Chester's fairs in the 1560s were already being provisioned by specialist horse dealers. Many of the horses sold in the later seventeenth-century markets, however, were brought by persons whose business was only incidentally connected with such transactions.'[25]

Horses formed a regular part of the stock sold at fairs and could be

23 Shrops. R.O., Ludlow Corpn. Records, 356/297.
24 Everitt, 'Marketing', p. 535.
25 P. R. Edwards, 'The Horse Trade of Chester in the Sixteenth and Seventeenth Centuries', J(ournal of the) C(hester) A(rchaeological) S(ociety), 62 (1979), p. 98.

obtained at many centres. According to Owen's list of fairs (1756 edn.), a compilation which in spite of certain weaknesses and omissions remains an essential source for analysing the fair as an institution, some counties were well served with outlets and only three counties in England and Wales (Caernarvonshire, Flintshire and Glamorgan) possessed no horse fairs.[26] Yorkshire, an important horse breeding area, led the list with some 150 separate meetings during the course of the year. Next came Cornwall (114 entries), followed by Lincolnshire in third place (56 entries).

These outlets, however, varied in size, importance and sphere of influence, a point which Owen occasionally recognised. All four of the fairs held at Northampton were 'great horse fairs' but the two at Halt-whistle (Northumb.), on the other hand, had 'few horses or sheep'.[27] The creation of this hierarchy of horse fairs mirrored the general trend in marketing in the early modern period; attempts were made to rationalise the nation's resources by developing regional specialisations and this led to the growth of certain centres which distributed goods over a wide area. Thus the development of dairy farming on the North Shropshire Plain, so apparent during the course of the seventeenth century, was already underway by the end of Elizabeth's reign, prompting a speaker in the enclosure debate in the House of Commons in 1597 to state that Shrop-shire consisted

wholie of woodland, bredd of Oxen & Dairies . . . yt one fayer daie in Shropshire there is aboue 10000 li. worth of Cheese and butter sold . . . at Bridgnorth, and hee said, hee hoped that as Hereforeshire and other Countries adioyning, were the Barnes for the Corne, soe this Shire might and would bee the Dayrie howse to the whole Realme.[28]

In the horse trade, this principle of regional specialisation could be seen at work in the growing integration of breeding and rearing areas and the movement of stock over considerable distances.[29] Consequently, fairs like Northampton and Rothwell became leading centres for the sale of coach and cart-horses not only because of the excellent training facilities to be found locally but also because they were patronised by the metropolitan dealers who bought large numbers of such horses there.[30] Naturally,

26 W. Owen, *An Authentic Account published by the King's authority of all the Fairs in England and Wales* (1756), *passim*.
27 *Ibid.*, pp. 64–5.
28 P. R. Edwards, 'The Development of Dairy Farming on the North Shropshire Plain in the Seventeenth Century', *Midland History*, 4 (1978), *passim*; A. F. Pollard and M. Blatcher, eds., 'Henry Townshend's Journal', *B(ulletin of the) I(nstitute of) H(istorical) R(esearch)*, 12 (1934–5), p. 16.
29 *Supra*, chapter 1, *passim*.
30 *Supra*, pp. 36–7.

suppliers, in turn, tended to concentrate their efforts on the more important outlets where they knew they could find a good market for their
animals. Of course, many of the smaller centres continued to operate, if in
a modest way, catering for the general needs of the local population, and as
Dr Dyer has shown, the second half of the seventeenth century saw 'a very
substantial increase in the total number of markets'.[31] Nonetheless, the
real expansion occurred among the more prominent fairs which, less
vulnerable to the competition posed by the growth of private marketing,
took an increasing proportion of the business.

Additional fairs, when granted, were mainly general ones, selling a wide
range of goods, although horse sales formed an important element of the
trading activity. These grants helped to fill out the calendar but nonetheless fairs continued to be spread unevenly throughout the year, peaking in
May and October but with a low level of activity in winter. May was the
most important month, according to Dr Chartres, who, if he based his
figures on Owen's work (1792 edn), had his findings corroborated by
reference to Rider's *British Merlin* from 1660 onwards. This pattern had
also been true of southern England in the second half of the sixteenth
century, although in the North the shorter trading season had led to a peak
in August. Dr Chartres similarly observed regional differences in the
incidence of fairs, drawing his examples from Shropshire, Hampshire and
Yorkshire.[32] Horse fairs conformed closely to the general picture, after
allowance has been made for the vagaries of the compiler and the problem
of fitting Lent, Easter and Whitsun fairs into the right month. Owen's list
of 1756 shows up the spring and autumn peaks, with events clustering
around May and, to a lesser extent, October (Table 3).[33]

Counting numbers, however, only answers some of the questions and
more detail is needed to discern those occasions when individual fairs were
at their most active. To a certain extent this can be provided for by an
analysis of surviving toll books, augmented by evidence gleaned from
estate records and contemporary accounts. In the Midlands the records of
a number of fairs include accounts of tolls paid at different times of the
year and thus enable a comparison to be made between the separate
meetings. While the results of such a survey may not be applicable to other
regions, the sample is a varied and wide-ranging one with an influence that
extended well beyond the Midlands.

31 A. D. Dyer, 'The Market Towns of southern England 1500–1700', *Southern History*, I
   (1979), p. 123.
32 Chartres, 'Markets, Fairs . . .', pp. 5–6.
33 An analysis of the dates of Easter Sunday during the period under review (1485–1714)
   indicates that 8 April, the median date and the mid-point in the range, was the best base
   point.

Table 3. *Number of fairs per month, according to Owen,* Fairs in England and Wales *(1756 edn) (for the dating of the movable fairs, see n. 33)*

January	18
February	54
March	75
April	95
May	256
June	111
July	120
August	110
September	138
October	161
November	118
December	53

In spite of Dr Chartres's view that the trade in horses was markedly less seasonal than the traffic in other commodities,[34] the toll books confirm the importance of the spring fairs, beginning at Easter and rising to a peak of activity in May and early June. Kidderminster, Ludlow, Shrewsbury and Warwick all had well-attended Whitsun Fairs and the one held at Derby was particularly prominent. Turnover, it is true, remained at a reasonably high level throughout the summer, as did the number of horse fairs, with one concentration occurring around Midsummer and another on St James's Day (25 July). Trade improved around Michaelmas, however, even if in the Midlands this peak appears to have been a lesser one than that occurring at Whitsuntide. The Michaelmas fairs at Ludlow and Warwick were important outlets but nonetheless fewer horses were sold then than earlier in the year, and even at Bridgnorth the October fair was not as pre-eminent at the end of the seventeenth century as it had been fifty years earlier. During the winter quarter, commercial activity tailed off, but in contrast to the North with its shorter trading season, did not disappear altogether. Business began to pick up again in February, and this build-up continued through March to Easter. At Bridgnorth, Kidderminster and Shrewsbury, trade fluctuated between two adjacent fairs, sometimes one being more important, sometimes the other. Other fairs elsewhere, placed close to one or between two more popular events, suffered a more permanent disadvantage. At Hallaton in the early eighteenth century the Ascension Day fair (May / early June) predominated over the one held on

34 J. A. Chartres, 'The Marketing of Agricultural Produce', in *Agrarian History*, V, ii, pp. 436–7.

Corpus Christi Day some three weeks later. This pattern was repeated at Taunton where a century earlier the St Botolph's Day fair (17 June) consistently did more business than was transacted at the St Thomas's Day fair (7 July).

As Dr Chartres has observed, horses were required at all times of the year,[35] but the spring and autumn peaks do reflect the natural seasonal rhythms of horse breeding and rearing. In the fenlands, brood mares were brought in early in the year and young stock was sold off around Michaelmas, whilst a contrary movement took horses into wood-pasture areas in the autumn for over-wintering and brought them back again in spring. In mixed-farming areas too, horses were disposed of after the spring sowing or bought in at Michaelmas in preparation for the autumn ploughing.

In the North the situation was complicated by the existence of so-called weekly or fortnightly fairs. At Rosley Hill (Cumbs.) they were held every two weeks from Whit Monday to Michaelmas and specialised in horses, cattle and yarn. According to Owen, 'These meetings are much regarded by the Breeders of Catle in this County; and are held at many other Places in this County, and are here called Fortnight Fair-Days.' Surviving toll books for Carlisle in the 1630s and 1650s record sales there at weekly horse markets, a pattern that was repeated at Cockermouth. In 1638 a new charter granted to the Earl of Northumberland by Charles I enabled the town 'to keep a fair . . . every Wednesday from the first week of May til Michaelmas'. In Yorkshire the same facility was provided at a number of centres, including those at Skipton, Hull, Adwalton and York.[36]

Fortunately, a number of seventeenth-century toll books have survived for Carlisle (1631–4, 1653–5) and for Rosley Hill (1650) which can be used for comparison with the more normal pattern of periodic fairs. At Carlisle, graphs of horse sales in the three years from 1631 to 1634 are remarkably similar. Twenty years later (1653–4) the slight shift in emphasis seems to mark a rationalisation of the earlier trend. Beginning at Michaelmas, a certain amount of business was conducted in October (even reaching a minor peak in October 1653), before falling away sharply to end by December. In the 1630s no trading took place between mid-November and the end of January, although in 1653–4 the gap was shorter and the preceding decline less steep. February and March saw a

---

35　*Ibid.*, p. 437.
36　Owen, *Fairs*, p. 17; R. Milward, 'The Cumbrian Town between 1600 and 1800', in C. W. Chalklin and M. A. Havinden, eds., *Rural Change and Urban Growth 1500–1800* (1974), p. 222; E. Gillett and K. A. McMahon, *A History of Hull* (Oxford, 1980), p. 133; K. L. McCutcheon, 'Yorkshire Fairs and Markets to the End of the Eighteenth Century', *Thoresby Society*, 39 (1940), pp. 76, 64–5; Owen, *Fairs*, pp. 96, 104.

resurgence of activity, but in 1654 not to the same level as that in October of that year. April and May were quiet months and numbers only picked up again in June to reach a new high point in July. The year then ended in dramatic fashion with two bursts in August and September occurring four weeks apart, which overshadowed all the business that had gone on before.

If any difference can be discerned between the 1630s and 1650s it lies in the greater importance in the earlier period of the summer fairs. More horses were sold then and the earlier minor peaks were not as pronounced. In 1653–4 the cyclical pattern is clearer to see. In all cases, sales peaked in July, August and September, but in 1653–4 the wider distribution of transactions increased the number of high points by three. In fact, apart from the dead periods of December–January and April–May the fairs normally worked on small fortnightly and larger monthly cycles.

At Rosley Hill, on the other hand, the situation was somewhat different. Tolls were taken for the fortnightly fairs for the period 3 June to 23 September, and in 1650 reached a high point on 1 July. Thereafter, the number of horses sold dropped rapidly throughout the rest of the month, levelled out in August, only to fall once more in September. It is possible that a higher peak had occurred in May, if the evidence of the receipts for horses, cattle and small tolls in 1649 can be accepted. However, this assumption is based upon the shifting relationship between the three items, the possibility that the number of horses was under-recorded and the certainty that numbers of cattle were. At the end of the 1650 toll book is a note which states that 'These names which Alledge that my lord hath no due to take toole on Rosley Faire and so Reffuse to pay any toole for beastes'. Underneath are written a number of names who collectively were responsible for 892 beasts!

An analysis of the toll books of the two places reveals that a certain amount of periodicity occurred in this arrangement too. Although many of the weekly/fortnightly markets sold more horses than the average market elsewhere in the country, only a few stand out from the rest. In many ways these occasions were more like normal fairs, attracting a much larger clientele and marked out as particularly important dates on the calendar. Both the peak August and September fairs seem to have done business on two separate days and this set them apart from the others. The timing of the peaks and troughs at Carlisle and Rosley Hill is also informative, conforming only partly to the general pattern noted at fairs. Rosley Hill may have had a May peak but its trade in September was negligible, while at Carlisle the opposite was true. This may be accounted for by a certain amount of integration between the two fairs; they lay some ten miles apart and local horse dealers were active at both. It is also interesting to note that although there was a two months' gap over Christmas at Carlisle, trade, especially in 1653–4, did not languish for months on end as Margaret Hodgen has suggested.[37]

At Chester, Wednesday and Saturday horse markets were granted in 1650 and 1677 respectively and when the toll books begin in 1658, they list at the most the sale of one or two horses at a time. Shortly afterwards (Saturday, 28 November 1663) a horse market was started at Newport in the neighbouring county of Shropshire. Nothing is known of its progress, although the source of information, the parish register, also records an earlier transaction made at a market in the town. Newport at this time possessed five fairs specialising in the sale of livestock, and as at Chester, it is likely that these periodic meetings continued to do more business. A similar relationship probably existed between the various fairs held in Banbury and the Thursday horse market established in 1608.[38]

Outside the North, markets were less important outlets for livestock in general and for horses in particular. The stock sold there tended to be few in number and unremarkable in quality and was often brought by people whose presence in town was unconnected with horse dealing.[39] Thus, many of the sellers were merchants, tradesmen and farmers from outside. Local people played a much greater part in the business that was conducted than they did at fairs, since the nature and scale of the trade was hardly likely to attract long-distance dealers. In the period under review very few specialist-middlemen are recorded in the surviving market toll books. Inhabitants of the town and its neighbourhood were particularly prominent as buyers but they also sold many of the horses too. Perhaps they felt that for ordinary horses the prospect of waiting for a fair to be held or of travelling to another one elsewhere was not worth the effort. In the market if there were fewer customers, it was always possible to sell an animal to one of those fellow-inhabitants who casually visited the market to see what they could find.

Toll books of markets therefore are less useful than those of fairs in determining the movement of people specifically interested in the purchase or sale of horses, but as they often include details of the occupations of the parties involved, they do indicate the broader economic links between the town and the outside world. At Chester, sellers travelled from virtually every English and Welsh county and represented a wide variety of trades

---

37 Hodgen, 'Fairs of Elizabethan England', pp. 393–6.
38 Shrops. R.O., Newport Parish Register, microfilm 412; J. S. W. Gibson and E. R. C. Brinkworth, eds., 'Banbury Corporation Records: Tudor and Stuart', *The Banbury History Society*, 15 (1977), p. 43.
39 Edwards, 'Chester Horse Trade', p. 98; Chartres, 'Road Carrying', p. 82; Thwaites, 'Agricultural Produce', p. 358.

and crafts. The largest groups, apart from those from Chester, came from London and Ireland and included a high proportion of gentry, merchants, wholesalers and distributors.[40] The contemporary records of Oxford market (1673–1745) reveal a similar pattern, although not surprisingly, there were fewer Welshmen and only one man came from Ireland. People from all over England sold horses in the market, with Londoners, once again, leading the out-county sellers.[41] Slighter lists exist from Bridgnorth (1631–51), Bristol (1705–14, 1735–58), Harton (Devon) (1617–1713), Plymouth (1590–1606), Portsmouth (1623–63) and Worcester (1635–56), and even if the samples are small, in general they reflect the same trend.

Most of the places cited above were important urban centres and inevitably drew a large and varied commerce to them. In the horse trade such links can be revealed by the number of transactions which involved persons of the same calling who had presumably met one another during the course of business. At Chester in September 1669 three tallow chandlers – two from Dublin and one from Chester – were involved in the sale of a horse in the capacities of seller, voucher and buyer respectively. At Oxford six years later John Nash, a local currier, bought a mare off Robert Catchpole, a saddler from Sandon (Essex). Another saddler, Edward Dowdall of Oxford, stood as his voucher. Often the links were personal ones, a characteristic of internal trade in general.[42] When Hugh Calcott sold a horse at Shrewsbury in 1590, he was working as a skinner in London, but the entry also records that he had been born in Shropshire – at Plealey, a village some ten miles south-west of the town.

An analysis of the relationship between sellers and their vouchers ought to cast further light upon the range and scope of extra-urban economic links, since by law they had to know one another. This was by no means certain, as a more detailed discussion in Chapter 4 will reveal, but perhaps in normal, non-suspicious transactions the situation was more straightforward.[43] Many of the sellers were regular visitors and experienced little difficulty in finding a local man to vouch for them. At Plymouth in April 1598 William Downman, a local merchant, bought a white gelding off Henry Lee, a merchant from London and 'a manne very well knowen to John Whyting of this Towne'.[44] At Oxford less than one voucher in seven came from the same county as the seller but nearly three-quarters lived in the city. Among these vouchers were individuals who seem regularly to have acted in this capacity. In the 1660s and 1670s Robert Giles, an

---

40 Edwards, 'Chester Horse Trade', pp. 98–9.
41 Edwards, 'Midlands Horse Trade', p. 129.
42 Everitt, 'Marketing', pp. 557–9.
43 *Infra.*, pp. 109–10.
44 Plymouth tolls.

Oxford farrier, stood surety at the local market for a number of men not only from the city but also from Oxfordshire and other counties. Of course his job would have brought him into contact with many people coming into Oxford or passing through.

PRIVATE DEALING

Many horses were sold privately and although this aspect of the trade is a difficult one to quantify, it clearly occupied an important position in it. Dealers struck bargains outside the market place, whilst innumerable sales were made among friends, neighbours and relatives or more casually between people meeting on the road, and although many were recorded in the toll books, others were not. Whilst much is known of the activities of the upper classes, transactions made by other people tend only to be revealed through the records of the various judicial bodies if, and when, they became a matter of dispute – non-payment of all or part of the purchase price and mis-representation of the quality of the animal were among the more common items found there. Details of horse-stealing cases provide valuable material too, often giving a great deal of incidental information concerning the way the trade was organised in general.

Dealers and others who went outside the markets and fairs to do business were liable to fall foul of the market regulations, the aims of which were to channel goods through the traditional outlets and to proscribe such crimes as forestalling, regrating and engrossing. The needs of an expanding population may well have necessitated new and more flexible methods of increasing supply but the government, especially at times of crisis, acted positively to check the opportunities for abuse which it felt such methods presented. Numerous instances of infringements can be found in the central records of the courts of Chancery, Exchequer, Requests and Star Chamber or more locally in Quarter Sessions' rolls or court of Piepowder presentments, and their bulk reflects the difficulties of bringing about change in the organisation of internal trade.

The horse trade was subject to many of the same regulations that affected other branches of commerce within the country and, as has been claimed above, the anti-horse stealing Acts of 1555 and 1589 were partly designed to improve their effectiveness.[45] Horse dealers were involved in private trading and from time to time local officials felt it necessary to remind them of their obligations. At Beverley, probably in the early seventeenth century, the mayor and governors of the town proclaimed that horses were to be bought and sold in the fair between ten o'clock in the

45 *Supra*, pp. 55–7.

morning and sunset and not 'in houses, stables, backsides or other secrett or private places'. In 1655 a similar exhortation was made at Nottingham and entered in the toll book for the St Matthew's Day fair there.[46]

Horse dealers were not the only ones concerned, of course, and in fact, middlemen in other commodities were earlier and more thoroughly engaged in private dealing.[47] In a collection made by Professor Everitt of some 350 lawsuits heard in the Court of Requests in the sixteenth and early seventeenth centuries, 35 per cent related to private dealings in barley, malt or hops, whereas those involving horses were among a wide variety of items that barely made up 25 per cent of the total.[48] These figures seem to be confirmed by Professor Beresford's work on the common informer. Ingrossing of grain was the most widespread offence, followed by the illegal sale of animals, largely sheep and cattle; that is, if one can extrapolate from Professor Everitt's findings. The composite section – guns, archery and horse – referred to in Professor Beresford's list contains few entries and records infringements of the statute of 4 & 5 Philip and Mary (c. 2) relating to the militia.[49]

After the Restoration, government intervention in the economy became less marked, although the change did not reflect a shift towards a more *laissez-faire* approach. As Professor Coleman has written,

The decay . . . had less to do with any burgeoning concepts of economic liberalism than with the increasing practical difficulties of applying an ancient policy to a changed structure of output – and, moreover, in circumstances in which the urge to reduce costs or to adapt production to new market trends was now far more pressing than the desire to adhere to traditional specifications.[50]

Thus in the corn trade in this period, the slowing down of the rate of population increase eased the pressure upon supplies and led to a more general acceptance of enclosure as well as to the relaxation of the laws concerning grain dealing. Not only were restraints on the export of corn removed but in 1673 bounties were offered to encourage it. The legislation remained on the statute-book until 1772, however, and in years of bad harvests, the old measures were re-enforced again. In the horse trade, restrictions were removed at the same time, and from 1 January 1657 horses could be exported freely upon the payment of a customs duty.[51] In

---

46 J. R. Witty, 'Documents relating to Beverley and District', *Y.A.S.*, 36, i (1944), p. 342; Nottingham tolls.
47 *Infra*, pp. 99–100.
48 Everitt, 'Marketing', p. 544.
49 M. W. Beresford, 'The Common Informer, the Penal Statutes and Economic Regulation', *Econ.H.R.*, 2nd. ser. 10 (1957–8), p. 227.
50 D. C. Coleman, *Economy of England*, p. 179.
51 *Ibid.*, pp. 177–8; *C.S.P.D.*, 1656–7, p. 179.

both cases the measures suggest that the problems of supply of such vital commodities which had concerned Tudor monarchs were no longer so pressing and that the government expected to derive extra income from overseas sales. As Dr Thirsk has observed, the Commonwealth and Protectorate government was anxious to encourage trade and saw in the shipment of horses abroad a means of enriching the country. A few years later, in a discussion of overseas trade, Samuel Fortrey wrote that 'there is not anything of so great profit as the exportation of horses, which of all commodities is of least charge to be raised at home and of greatest value abroad'.[52]

The increase in the business being conducted outside the market place is at times reflected in the pages of the toll books. At Shrewsbury, cattle, and probably horses too, were being sold at inns outside the town in the 1650s, and shortly afterwards the toll books begin to list fewer animals.[53] The entries end completely in 1674 and in the following year the toll keepers were presented by the Grand Jury for failing to maintain a book.[54] At Rothwell the books made at the turn of the seventeenth century record details of transactions entered in them and sums of money due in toll from those which were not. In 1695, 5s. 4d. was received from the sale of 16 horses booked at the Trinity Monday fair (8 June), but 15s. od. more was collected for 42 others. The horses had been sold at Mr Smiths', Fox's and Bodiner's, and included toll on five horses bought by Mr Horton, a notable London dealer and a regular visitor to the fair. Most of the market toll books appear to be partial lists too, recording a handful of transactions a year, and the fuller accounts, those taken at Chester and Oxford, become more perfunctory with the passage of time. At Chester the entries span the years 1658 to 1723 and at Oxford, 1673 to 1745, but numbers dwindle from the mid-1670s and mid-1690s respectively.[55]

Dealers did private business with all sections of the community, but as will be shown in the next chapter, the clearest evidence of their involvement comes from the records of the upper classes. For the others, less information is available; they were less likely to leave any documentation, their resources were in general smaller and the contacts they made were more informal. In 1627 two dealers, while staying at an inn in Potterne (Wilts.) met a man trying to sell a horse. One of them, Robert Bisley of White Cross Street, London, started to bargain with the man but broke off negotiations when he grew suspicious of him.[56]

52 Thirsk, *Horses*, p. 27.
53 P. R. Edwards, 'The Cattle Trade of Shropshire in the late Sixteenth and Seventeenth Centuries', *Midland History*, 6 (1981), p. 84.
54 Bodleian Library, MS Gough Shropshire 12, fo. 76.
55 Rothwell, Chester and Oxford Tolls.   56 Wilts, R.O., Q.S. Hilary Term 1628.

Ordinary people were also engaged in private trading, if in a more casual way than the dealers. The evidence is largely anecdotal, but it does convey the impression of the ease with which horses were bought and sold. Many animals passed between friends and neighbours, a practice which minimised the risks to both parties – the acquisition of an inferior or stolen horse on the one side and the non-receipt of the selling price on the other. Others were bought off strangers, however, and this did increase the chance of deception, especially as there was little consumer protection in early modern England. Abuses certainly did occur and although the sources used tend to be pathological in nature and thus atypical, they indicate at times an almost wilful disregard for safety precautions that much reflect the prevalence of horse trading in the country. In 1609, for instance, George Shepperdson, a Shropshire man, agreed to an exchange of horses without having been party to the original bargain. Edward Footman had seen Nicholas Gough riding Shepperdson's horse and had come to terms with him, affirming falsely that Shepperdson 'should & might freely & w[i]thout trouble vse & imploy him to their best benefitt p[ro]fitt and advantage'.[57]

The nobility and gentry with their deeper pockets and wider contacts had greater flexibility than others in their mode of operation. Thus they used both fairs and private connexions to provide themselves with the sort of stock they required. Richard Blome in his book, *The Gentleman's Recreation*, published in 1686, discussed the breeding of horses for hunting, racing and the road, then advised,

Tis' needless to give directions for Breeding any other sort of Horses; as for the *Coach, Wagon, Cart, Servants*, and all manner of Drudgery, because there is not that Nicety required; and from the Fairs and Horse-Coursers you may be supplied, and save the trouble.[58]

In practice the situation was not so clear-cut; the upper-classes – even the Crown – obtained first-class stock from dealers and from such fairs as Penkridge and disposed of ordinary animals among their friends, relatives and acquaintances. Most of the families whose accounts reveal an interest in the supply of good quality stock seem in general to have made no obvious distinction between institutional and informal channels. The Massingberds of Mumby Hall (Lincs.) regularly used both private and public means to buy and sell, amongst other horses, coach and saddle animals. Between 1658 and 1684 the 26 recorded private transactions have a mean value of £8. 14s. 3d., whereas the 29 deals that took place at

57 P.R.O., REQ 2/411/113, also *vide* STAC 8/225/21 Misc. Jas. I.
58 Blome, *The Gentlemans Recreation*, p. 2.

fairs average out at £8. 0s. 6d. Private business was mainly conducted with friends and relatives, but on one occasion a nag was bought off a Calceby butcher 'Whom I mett withall accidentally at Calceby'. Normally the fairs patronised were local ones at Horncastle, Stainton and Partney, but horses were also sold at Biggleswade and Smithfield. The most valuable animal listed in the accounts, a home bred stallion, was disposed of at Biggleswade, where Mr William Dormer of Rousham Hall (Oxfords.), a breeder of good quality horses, bought it at a cost of £54. 10s. 0d.[59]

As in the case of the Massingberds, agents conducted much of the business for their employers, especially that carried on at fairs, but some gentlemen horse-fanciers took a more personal interest. Diaries and commonplace books, where they exist, often provide insights into the way such people acted.[60] The Clopton diary of 1648–52 records the activities of a small group of friends and relatives who travelled to fairs and private houses in eastern England to obtain or dispose of stock. Among the fairs they visited were Barnwell and Reach in Cambridgeshire, and Cowling and Newmarket in Suffolk, although one of their number, Mr Kemp, also travelled into Lincolnshire and Norfolk to buy horses for Mr Clopton. In a typical run of entries Clopton bought a little grey stoned colt for £3. 10s. 0d. on the morning of 27 April 1649 and a roan stoned nag for £8. 10s. 0d. in the afternoon. Three days later he travelled to Reach Fair and swapped a black mare for a bay stoned colt, receiving £7. 10s. 0d. to boot. On 15 May he went to Newmarket Fair in company with his cousin Brook and Sir Thomas Barnardiston of Ketton Hall and bought a grey gelding for £11. 7s. 0d. Sir Thomas paid out £20. 16s. 6d. for a young chestnut gelding. In the diary that Nicholas Blundell of Little Crosby (Lancs.) wrote in the early eighteenth century, he is shown trading at fairs as far apart as Preston, Ashbourne and Smithfield, conducting business with private individuals. In one exchange he made with Mr Christopher Anderton in 1702 he called the horse 'Swap' in honour of the way he had acquired it.[61] Adam Eyre, the Parliamentary captain of Hazlehead Hall (Lancs.) also kept a diary, and in 1647 recorded in it a number of trips he made around the district to buy horses.

In addition to the business that the upper classes did at markets and fairs, their circle of friends and relatives provided them with a valuable network of private contacts. Numerous references in estate and household

59 Massingberd (M) Colln., MM 6/1/5.
60 This section is based upon Essex R.O., D/DQs 18, Clopton Diary; T. E. Gibson, *Blundell's Diary* (Liverpool, 1895); H. J. Morehouse, 'A Dyurnall or Catalogue of all my Accions and Expence from the 1st January, 1646', *Surtees Society*, 65 (1875).
61 Gibson, *Blundell's Diary*, p. 4.

correspondence illustrate the uses to which these links were put.[62] By dealing with people they knew, individuals might hope to avoid being cheated. This consideration weighed heavily with anyone buying horses; the animals were prone to disease and injury, not always easily detectable, and therefore a personal guarantee was preferable to the risks of the market place. When William Green heard that his cousin, George Warner, wanted a horse, he offered him one of his own. Twice in that month, he said, he had refused £20 for it and hoped that he would agree to that price. 'I hope if hee bee not yet worse ye would not haue mee take lesse then was offerd for if hee had faultes, I would not conceale the[m] fro[m] ye: for I belieue hee is as right a nagge as euer my Father bred'.[63]

Blome, in fact, recommended the practice of doing business with breeders of good quality horses, commenting that 'the surest way of Buying is to be acquainted with good *Breeders*'. This was the course of action which in 1641 William Hawkins intended to carry out in his search for horses for the Earl of Leicester. In a letter to the Earl he wrote, 'I feare they [horses] are hard to be gotten unlease one could meete with some gentlemen that are breeders. I heare that the Lady Lucy hath very good ones that are now to be sold off.'[64] As many of the nobility and gentry were engaged in horse breeding, they not only loaned out their stallions to service the mares of their friends and relatives but also sold one another animals from their stock.[65]

In passing, mention ought to be made of the use of public sales, similar to auctions, as an alternative form of dealing outside markets and fairs. They seem to have grown in popularity during the post-Restoration period and at the beginning of the eighteenth century examples of purchases can be found among the papers of the Massingberds of Gunby (Lincs.) and the Bowes family of Streatlam Castle (Durham).[65] At Beccles (Suffolk) a number of references to sales occur in the corporation records from the late seventeenth century onwards.[67] Where an inventory exists, as in the case of stock sold off the Slyfield House estate in Surrey in 1739, it is also possible to compare the valuations entered in that document with the

62 Salisbury, XX, p. 283; J. W. F. Hill, ed., 'The Letters and Papers of the Banks Family of Revesley Abbey 1704–1760', *Lincs. Record Society*, 45 (1952), p. 43.
63 P.R.O., S.P. 46/83/fo. 91.
64 Blome, *The Gentleman's Recreation*, p. 10; H.M.C., De L'Isle and Dudley MSS, VI, p. 384.
65 *Supra*, pp. 42–6.
66 Massingberd (G) Colln., MG 5/2/7; Durham R.O., Strathmore Colln., Lady Bowes Accounts 1707–13, V609.
67 Beccles Corpn. Records, Rix division IV, Proprietary, IV, Markets and Fairs, (no pagination).

actual prices realised at the sale.[68] The main purpose of such sales often appears to have been the speedy realisation of liquid assets to meet the financial needs of debtors, alive or dead, but this was not always so. Thus, in 1674–5, Sarah Fell of Swarthmoor Hall (Lancs.) used this method to buy and sell a number of horses.[69]

SUMMARY

The development of private marketing in the horse trade did not mean the instant demise of the traditional centres, many of which continued to thrive throughout the eighteenth century. Toll books show that dealers regularly did business at fairs long after the end of the period under review, although inevitably less is known of their private deals. As will be argued in the following chapter, dealers in other commodities were earlier and more thoroughly engaged in private trading.[70]

It is clear however that changes did occur in the horse trade and that they mirrored general developments in the economy. Markets and fairs did come under attack and some fared worse than others. In general the larger centres survived, taking over business from the smaller outlets and acting as entrepôts for horses brought in from a wide area. They strengthened their position too by developing a specialisation in certain types of horses and thus attracting custom from further afield. Of the others, some continued as they had done before, catering for the modest needs of the local population. Many however suffered a decline or failed completely. The agents of change, the middlemen-horse dealers, often chose to work through the regulated outlets, but with their range of contacts they also employed more private means too.

---

68 Surrey R.O., 65/4/22–4.
69 N. Penney, ed., *The Household Account Book of Sarah Fell of Swarthmoor Hall* (Cambridge, 1920), pp. 86, 147, 224, 318.
70 *Infra*, pp. 99–100.

3

HORSE DEALERS

BACKGROUND

In his classic work on middlemen in English business in the period before the Industrial Revolution, R. B. Westerfield emphasises the importance of these people in bringing about the changes that occurred in marketing institutions at the time.[1] In spite of its age, the book remains the best and fullest account of the subject, but unfortunately has surprisingly little to say on the activities of the horse dealers. In a brief survey, Westerfield confines himself to a few random notes on dealers and fairs and gives no indication of the specific functions that such men performed.[2] In fact, whilst the trade exhibited a specific set of characteristics peculiar to itself, it also possessed elements to be found in other trades too. Westerfield writes of the distinction between wholesalers and retailers in internal trade, one set assembling and the other dispersing the wares, and creating patterns of movement towards the merchant and wholesaler on the one hand and towards the consumer on the other.[3] In the internal horse trade there were certainly differences in the scale and scope of the activities of individual dealers but they cannot readily be divided along such lines as they fulfilled the functions of both collectors and distributors. In their dual role, horse dealers were similar to wool staplers in the sense that they sorted out horses into different categories, using quality, function, size, colour and pace as criteria. Of course, the degree of discrimination varied between individuals, the fairs that they attended and the demands of their customers, but this became an increasingly important aspect of the trade as it became more diversified. At the top end of the market those who dealt with the aristocracy had to be particularly discerning. Coach horses, for instance, not only had to be suitable for the job but had to conform to one another in height, shape, colour and pace.

Whereas carriage caused little problem to horse dealers as their stock

---

1 R. B. Westerfield, *Middlemen in English Business* (New Haven, 1915), *passim*.
2 *Ibid.*, p. 202.   3 *Ibid.*, p. 332.

could walk to market on foot, fluctuations in the timing of supply and demand often meant that they had to keep animals on their hands for a while. Warehousing in this case was provided by stable accommodation or grazing grounds, and many of the regular dealers who appear in the toll books (even those living in or near towns) seem to have had access to land, either in the form of agricultural holdings, rights of common or agistments. Urban dealers, especially Londoners, were more likely to keep the horses in stables, but large scale operators such as Harvey Connaway and John Styles of Smithfield possessed both stabling and pasture grounds.[4] With land or accommodation at their disposal dealers could collect horses over a period of time from various sources and dispose of them at will. In years of drought, however, shortage of grass made it more difficult to feed the animals and they had to be sold off, thereby flooding the market.

Inevitably, the closest comparisons can be made with middlemen in other livestock trades who moved stock around the country. There was a similar hierarchy of dealers too, some concentrating on supplying local markets, whilst others operated on a regional or national scale. Fitzherbert, writing in the 1520s, distinguishes between two types of horse dealer, the horse master and the horse courser.

A Horse mayster is, that bieth wylde horses, or coltes, and bredeth theym, and selleth theym agayne wylde, or breaketh parte of them, and maketh theym tame, and then selleth them. A corser is he, that byeth all rydden horses and selleth them agayne.[5]

Coursers therefore fulfilled a similar function in the horse trade as drovers did in the livestock-meat trade. Drovers sold lean stock to graziers or fatstock to butchers but did not improve the commodity whilst in their hands. Horses were not earmarked for human consumption but they nonetheless passed through the hands of specialists who, for instance, broke them in and trained them in the collar before selling them as coach, carriage and cart animals. In the horse trade there was also a tendency, albeit with many exceptions, for coursers to be more concerned with bringing stock into an area rather than taking it away. Thus east Midlands dealers acquired stock bred and perhaps broken-in elsewhere which they then sold locally to horse trainers. Unlike coursers, those horse masters who broke in animals did improve the commodity whilst in their possession, perhaps employing horse riders or breakers, men of more humble means, to do the job for them. Unfortunately, lack of precision in the use of terms and the shortage of information about the activities of the horse masters makes it difficult to draw a clear distinction between them and the

4 *Supra*, p. 19.
5 (John?) Fitzherbert, 'The Boke of Husbandrie', fo. xxxvii.

horse coursers. The toll books provide a single example of a horse master –
William Porter of Arthingworth (Northants.); he was certainly a substantial dealer, regularly buying horses at Worcester in the 1550s and 1560s,
but after initially being listed as a horse master, he was later called a
courser.[6]

Westerfield notes that throughout the sixteenth and seventeenth centuries drovers were both dealers in cattle and drivers of the herds.
However, the emergence of the jobber as a specialist dealer in the
following century was based upon developments which occurred at an
earlier date, Shropshire evidence, for instance, suggesting a division in
function.[7] In the horse trade, dealers were more likely to collect their
animals and drive them away, but occasionally the records reveal the
employment of an agent. These were not factors resident in areas where
the goods were purchased such as those to be found in the corn, wool and
cheese trades but rather servants and employees. These men often lived in
their master's house and, as in the case of Thomas Mason, the servant of
John Styles, travelled to various parts of the country to buy stock.[8]

Later documentation highlights the importance of London dealers, the
counterparts of Westerfield's cattle and sheep jobbers, at those fairs which
they attended in force. When these dealers arrived at particular fairs they
clearly dominated the proceedings, buying up much of the stock on view
and filling the roads back to the capital with their purchases. Like the
jobbers they may also have had 'stock yards' where they could keep a
reserve of animals to use as market conditions dictated. Thus Harvey
Connaway and his partner, John Styles, drew upon each other's pool of
horses whenever necessary. Westerfield suggests that jobbers used their
resources in a positive way to equalise supply and prices but also
negatively to maintain their monopoly of the market.[9] The scale of their
purchases may have enabled the large London horse dealers to exert an
influence upon the conduct of the trade but this cannot be proved.
Elsewhere in the country the dispersal of breeding areas, the complexity in
the pattern of movement of stock across the country and the large number
of dealers involved in the business, made such control more difficult.
Dealers could, and did, involve themselves in the trade at different points
of the chain. Indeed, an analysis of the toll books reveals a far from
random pattern in their location, suggesting that they could be found in
places which offered them the best trading position. Considerations such
as easy access to supplies and to regional fairs, good communications and

6 Worcester tolls.
7 Westerfield, *Middlemen*, p. 189; Edwards, 'Shropshire Cattle Trade', p. 85.
8 Everitt, 'Marketing', p. 554.
9 Westerfield, *Middlemen*, p. 192.

plentiful fodder were obviously important, whilst proximity to centres of population and industry would be advantageous too. Some dealers were located near breeding grounds, collecting stock either privately off the farm or estate or publicly at nearby markets and fairs. Others lived at a distance from the breeding grounds, in felden country or in areas of developing industry, or in or near urban centres. London, of course, was served by numerous dealers living in and around the capital.

CONDUCT OF BUSINESS

Whilst there may have been an obvious market for particular groups to exploit, it is clear from the toll books that dealers commonly visited a number of fairs and traded in a variety of stock. Nowhere can this range of interests be seen more clearly than in the dealings of a group of middlemen living on the Shropshire–Staffordshire border in the seventeenth century, and an analysis of their activities provides an interesting case study. In the area, local gentry families such as the Levesons, Foresters and Charltons began systematically to exploit their mineral resources in this period and thus created a growing demand for pack- and work-horses. At Shrewsbury, some twelve miles away, ideal stock could be bought and a sample survey of buyers at the fairs there between 1600 and 1674 reveals that people from the coal measures' parishes of Lilleshall and Wellington acquired the largest numbers. Richard and Thomas Winsor alone bought a recorded total of 172 horses in the first half of the seventeenth century. Dealers from the area also dealt in good quality saddle animals at Bridgnorth and even better ones at Penkridge. Richard Winsor and his neighbour from Donnington, Lilleshall, Thomas Bradley, travelled together to the fair held at Penkridge on 23 September 1640 where Thomas sold a gelding to a Worcestershire gentleman and Richard bought a mare, two fillies and a colt. At Bridgnorth in the sampled years 1647–9 and 1654–6, known dealers, especially the Bradleys and the Winsors, sold or exchanged 58 nags, 32 mares, eight geldings, four fillies, four colts, one nag colt and an unspecified horse. Many of these mares were the ones which had been bought at fairs in the east and north Midlands and according to the records of Market Bosworth and Derby, members of this group were the persons involved in bringing them into the area.

These horses were sold at local fairs or privately to horse breeders, whose number includes members of the local gentry. In 1678, Robert Sandford esquire bought a mare for £6. 17s. 6d. from William Taylor, the horse courser, who lived at nearby Calverhall, and the following year he obtained two coach mares from him for £20. In 1700 Edward James of Kinvaston, another gentleman, bought a three year old mare from Tealor the jockey for £9. 10s. od., in 1707 a three year old filly for £8. 10s. od., and in 1709 a sucking foal for £3.[10] This dealer was almost certainly John Taylor of Calverhall, and although he was probably a relative of William Taylor's, the registers are silent on this point. William visited Bridgnorth, Shrewsbury and Derby fairs and his career ended around 1680, at the time that John's was just beginning. These dealers also acted as agents for the gentry, selling their animals at such fairs as Bridgnorth and Penkridge or negotiating on their behalf with other gentlemen. In 1655 Thomas Winsor sold a horse off the Leveson family's estate at Trentham (Staffs.), whilst in 1678 Thomas Wickstead, the steward of their Shropshire estate, made two journeys with Thomas Rowley of Preston-upon-the-Wealdmoors to Benthall to look at Mr Benthall's horse, an expensive animal valued at £57.[11] Thomas Rowley was one of the most prominent dealers of the area, regularly visiting Derby, Bridgnorth and Shrewsbury fairs in the second half of the seventeenth century. He also dealt with the gentry, in one transaction in 1686 paying £16 for a horse off the Foresters. By this time he seems to have cut back on his visits to fairs, concentrating upon his farm and upon improving his social standing. He was sometimes described as 'gent' in the records and began to breed horses on his own account. Significantly, an entry in the Forester account for 1688 records a payment made to Thomas's son for bringing a stallion to serve one of the family's mares.[12]

Horse dealers, like their counterparts in other trades, often formed partnerships – Professor Everitt has noted that whilst some dealers traded alone, they were more likely to operate with one or two other men of their acquaintance.[13] Many partnerships were poor, flimsy and, temporary affairs, though the one involving Harvey Connaway and John Styles of the Smithfield was a much larger enterprise.[14] According to Connaway, he and Styles had long been friends and dealers together at fairs throughout the kingdom and elsewhere. The partnership involving William Hill of Cheddar and Thomas Hancock of Wells which lasted some seven years and was broken up at Michaelmas 1630, was far more modest. Both of the men had been dealers in horses before the association and had helped to swell the numbers of colts from the Somerset Levels sold at Winchester in the early 1620s. After they formed their partnership in 1623, however, they disappear from the records, being found neither in the toll books at Winchester nor in those of Taunton. Another partnership concerned

10 Shrops. R.O., Sandford Colln., 2/138; Staffs. R.O., HM 27/2.
11 Sutherland Colln., D593/P/8/2/4, D593/F/2/38.
12 Shrops. R.O., Forester of Dothill Colln., 1224/297.
13 Everitt, 'Marketing', p. 554.
14 *Supra*, p. 19.

William Eaton of Cottesbrook (Northants.), one of the most active dealers in the east Midlands in the first half of the seventeenth century. In 1631 he was involved in a suit concerning the sale of horses at Woodstock (Oxon.) and in it he deposed that he had been in partnership with two other horse dealers, William Smith of Clipston (Northants.) and John Smith of Willoughby (Warwicks.) for two years or more. The latter two may have been related, and another possible member of the family, Edward Smith of Dodford (Northants.) was also involved. At the beginning of the partnership an agreement had to be made about the organization of the business and the money to be ventured by each member. As Edward Smith stated in 1631, he, William Eaton and John Smith, 'doe part stakes and shares as well in proffitte as in the losses of the buyinge and sellinge of all the horses that either of them three shall buy or sell'. Similarly, William Hill deposed that he and Thomas Hancock had employed a joint stock between them to buy horses.[15] Such partnerships, in fact, normally came to light after they had broken up and one party was suing for debts owed by the other.

It is quite likely that the people associated with William Eaton were related, for, as Professor Everitt has emphasised, kin-and-friendship groups were extremely important in the economic organization of the time.[16] In an age of rapid commercial progress, existing marketing and financial institutions proved inadequate and inevitably the conduct of business involved risk. It is hardly surprising, therefore, to find that wherever possible, dealers sought to minimise the danger by using members of the family, together with friends and neighbours. The tremendous amount of immigration into London, for instance, created numerous links with the provinces that could be used to provision the capital. Indeed, Midlands' ironmongers penetrated the metropolitan market in the seventeenth century by making use of 'brothers, cousins-in-law and neighbours to create a network of committed and financially involved partners and agents'.[17] Examples can also be found of such a connexion in the horse trade. In 1614 Miles Partridge of Westminster petitioned in the Court of Requests for the recovery of debts, including £14 for the sale of three horses, due from five people living in Gloucestershire, Herefordshire and Monmouthshire. One of the men, John Partridge of Warmington (Gloucs.), may have been a relative and the grouping of debtors in this area could reflect Miles's personal contact with it.[18] Samuel Dabbs of the Warwickshire horse dealing family was a mealman, living on the Strand

15 P.R.O., C3/405/29. I am grateful to Dr Patricia Croot for this reference; Woodstock Town Hall, Portsmouth Book, 1618–35.
16 Everitt, 'Marketing', pp. 557–8.
17 M. Rowlands, *Masters and Men* (Manchester, 1975), p. 13.
18 P.R.O., REQ 2/397/77.

and apart from serving his own ends, was well placed to organise the London end of his family's business. He evidently associated himself with their activities for he travelled with them to Stratford-upon-Avon in 1646 and to Derby the following year. A family relationship may also have existed between John Spurlock of Somerton (Soms.) and William Spurlock, a butcher from St Giles-in-the-Fields (Middx.), for both attended the fair held at Hatfield Broadoak (Essex) on 26 July 1647 to buy horses.[19]

These ties were strengthened by a family tradition of successive generations being involved in the same occupation. In many local communities, certain crafts were dominated by individual families and in the same way middlemen also remained in the same business for several generations. In the west Midlands' metal industry, Dr Marie Rowlands has identified the Ebb family as braziers in Wolverhampton, Walsall and Uttoxeter in the late seventeenth century and has also noted the continuing involvement of members of the Parkes, Fidoe, Careless, Jevons, Hopkins, Russell and Gibbons families as ironmongers. In addition, Dr Mary Prior has discovered in Oxford in this period dynasties of bargemen such as the Gardners and Tawneys. In north Shropshire, families of country drovers, who included the Dickinses of Ellesmere and Loppington, the Grooms and Tilers of Myddle and Wem and the Moodies of Ellesmere, were instrumental in provisioning local fairs with cattle. At least fifteen members of the Dickins family sold cattle at Shrewsbury between 1600 and 1655 and Quarter Sessions records show that Edward Dickins of Lineal in the parish of Ellesmere, the most prominent individual in the group, was regularly licensed as a drover in the early seventeenth century. In 1625 a note in the list of drovers states that he had given over his trade to his son, John, who continued to sell cattle at Shrewsbury for a number of years.[20]

The advantage of a system based upon the family lay in the degree of flexibility it gave, facilitating the transmission of the trade from one generation to another and enabling its members to act for one another. They could pool their resources, perhaps buying or selling horses for the group at different fairs, or as they gained in experience the younger men could gradually take over more of the responsibilities. In horse dealing, family participation was so common that it was unusual for any of the regular traders to appear as isolated individuals in the toll books. Several members of the Walker family of Newport, Shropshire, traded at Derby, Bridgnorth, Dudley and Kidderminster at the turn of the seventeenth

19 Stratford-upon-Avon, Derby, and Hatfield Broadoak tells.
20 Rowlands, *Masters and Men*, p. 66; M. Prior, *Fisher Row: Fishermen, Bargemen and Canal Boatmen in Oxford 1500–1900* (Oxford, 1982), pp. 139–165; Edwards, 'Shropshire Cattle Trade', pp. 75, 84.

century, whilst later records of Bridgnorth, Banbury and Sutton Coldfield fairs indicate that their involvement continued into the second half of the eighteenth century. The original group consisted of four brothers, Richard, John, James and Gabriel, but as Richard had no sons and John appears to have remained unmarried, the next generation was represented by the sons of James and Gabriel. Thomas, John and Hewitt, the sons of James's son, Richard, and Richard and Robert, the sons of Gabriel's son, Robert, in turn carried on the tradition. Whilst the Walkers stayed in Newport other local families of horse dealers spread out over a number of parishes. The Ingerthorpes of Lilleshall, for instance, had branches at Weston-under-Lizard and Sheriffhales just across the border in Staffordshire and another one a few miles away at Aston Ayre. When John Ingerthorpe of Weston-under-Lizard sold a horse at Bridgnorth on 19 June 1649, the toll keeper recorded that 'he went away in haste before he had tendred his vouchers. But the Seller is known to the toll taker'. The entry continues, 'The seller is well known in this Town his brother Richard Ingerthorp dwelling in Wheaton Aston within 3 miles of this town.'[21] A similar picture can be found in other parts of the country too. In the southwest, one of the leading Somerset families, the Maggs, had branches in Cameley, Shepton Mallet, Hinton Blewett and Marston Biggott, whilst in Devon, William Horwood senior, lived in Barnstaple and his son, William, at nearby Bishop's Tawton. On the northern border, society was based upon surname groups and the ramifications of individual families throughout the area make it a difficult one to deal with. On the northwestern sector, horse dealers from the dominant family of Graham went to Carlisle fair in 1653–4 from seven Cumberland parishes and from one each in Northumberland and Dumfriesshire.

In family dynasties of horse dealers the younger generation normally served an 'apprenticeship' by accompanying their fathers or uncles to fairs where they would gain experience of the business and meet other dealers. There they would watch and learn and perhaps act as voucher. In 1672, John Allen of Peplow in the Shropshire parish of Hodnet, a youth, according to the toll book, stood surety for his father at Bridgnorth's October Fair. In the same manner Robert Stickler, junior, who died in the winter of 1732–3, travelled with his father, Robert senior, in the late seventeenth century to Taunton where he vouched for horses sold there. Occasionally, young men may have been allowed to sell horses under supervision. In 1651 William Skitt, a boy of sixteen at the time, sold a mare at Bridgnorth, and his father, who accompanied him, acted as his guarantor. William senior seems to have given up the trade shortly after this date

21 Bridgnorth tolls.

and by the end of the decade his son was travelling on his own account to the fairs at Derby, Bridgnorth and Shrewsbury. Even after the youngsters had acquired sufficient skill and judgement to trade independently, they often continued to travel to fairs in a family group. Andrew Frizwell of Bedworth, for instance, took his sons, Charles, John and Robert with him to various fairs in the 1680s and 1690s, although they were then mature adults. Charles died in the winter of 1695–6 and Andrew gave up the business at about the same time, his last recorded transaction being an exchange of horses at Bridgnorth on 22 July 1695. He lived until 1711, however, and by then his remaining sons were already training up the next generation. Charles, the son of Charles, was still a minor when Andrew made his will in 1709, but had already been visiting fairs with his uncles for at least a couple of years.[22]

Andrew Frizwell was well into his sixties when he ceased his horse dealing activities and other dealers too pursued careers of remarkable length, considering the arduous nature of the job. Of course, much depended upon personal circumstances such as state of health, outside interests and other ambitions and the availability of younger sons to take over. Richard Winsor of Donnington and Gabriel Walker of Newport must have been sixty before they retired, whilst William Eaton of Cottesbrook was active between the years 1627 and 1661. Andrew Frizwell and Richard Winsor appear to have been reducing their activities in the years before they stopped but other dealers worked almost to the end, and these included several members of the Rocke and Dabbs families (see Appendix 3).

Such family groups often co-ordinated their activities with neighbouring dealers. United by a common purpose, they inevitably became friendly with each other and established kinship links. When Richard Stockton of Bobberhill, Malpas, died in 1583, the appraisers of his goods included John and Owen Griffith whilst his sons-in-law, Randle Stoke and Owen Wickstead, dealers all, acted as executors of his will. Moreover, when John Sainsbury of Devizes drew up his will in 1703, Ambrose, his brother, and Robert Stickler, his cousin, horse coursers, were made his executors, and yet another dealer, Henry Brewer of Barton Regis near Bristol, signed the document as one of the witnesses. A marriage alliance also brought together the Brown and Higginbottom families of Farnsfield (Notts.) whose members were among the most prominent dealers from the mixed-farming area of the county. In Bedworth, Charles Frizwell, senior, married

---

22 For biographical details of the Frizwell family I am very grateful to Mr E. A. Veasey, who kindly gave me a copy of his unpublished manuscript entitled 'The Frizwell Family of Bedworth' (1982).

into another horse dealing family, the Howletts, and in 1701 Mary
Frizwell became the wife of Luke Bradbury.[23]

Travelling from fair to fair, often following a regular annual pattern,
dealers soon established links with others elsewhere in the country too.
They did business together and doubtless spent some time discussing
conditions in the trade and other matters of general interest, perhaps over
a pint in the market tavern. This acquaintanceship can be best seen in the
numerous examples of dealers vouching for one another even though they
lived miles apart. When John Maggs of Marston Biggott (Som.) bought a
horse from Robert Harrington of Whitechapel, London, at Warwick Fair
in 1688, he stated that he accepted the horse 'with this voucher onley
whom he knows'. The voucher, William Harries, came from Old Bedlam,
London, and he must have become acquainted with John Maggs through
meeting him at various fairs around the country.[24] An analysis of the
Taunton toll books of the 1680s and 1690s reveals the difference in the
operation of the voucher system between dealers and non-dealers. Of the
329 entries for which the relevant information exists, 186 (56.5 per cent)
of the vouchers lived either in the same parish as the seller or in an adjacent
one (nineteen examples involved dealers who lived near the seller). Over
two-thirds (68.9 per cent) of the 45 vouchers who came from another
county, however, were dealers. The same pattern can be seen at other fairs
too. At Bridgnorth on 19 June 1700, Gabriel and Robert Walker of
Newport (Shropshire) included John Guy of Castle Cary (Som.), and
Philip Russell of Astley (Worcs.) among their vouchers, whilst John Guy
also stood surety for Richard and Robert Powell of Solihull (Warwicks.)
and Henry Brewer of Barton Regis (Gloucs.). Henry's other voucher was
John Sainsbury of Devizes (Wilts.). Sometimes the record suggests regular
meetings between two sets of dealers over a period of time. The 'Brown'
group of Nottinghamshire often travelled to Bridgnorth in the 1660s and
1670s to dispose of surplus breeding stock and seem to have made
particular use of dealers from the Bromsgrove area such as Nicholas Dunn,
Robert Haynes and Matthew Tolley as their vouchers.

Horse dealers formed a part of the general body of wayfarers which, if
not a new one in Tudor England, only became a recognisable and self-
conscious community at the end of Elizabeth's reign.[25] They met in inns

---

23 Cheshire R.O., Wills and Inventories, Richard Stockton of Malpas, WS 31/27; Wilts.
    R.O., Cons. Sarum, John Saintsbury of Devizes, 10 Nov. 1703; Notts. R.O., PR SW 85/6;
    Veasey, 'Frizwell Family', pp. 4–5.
24 Warwick tolls.
25 A. M. Everitt, 'Change in the Provinces: The Seventeenth Century', *Leicester University
    Dept. of English Local History Occasional Papers*, 2nd ser., no. 1 (Leicester, 1969), pp.
    39–41.

and alehouses, often accompanied each other on the road, and did business in the same places. Travelling around the country, spreading news and perhaps unorthodox views as they went, they were generally looked upon by those in authority as an alien and disruptive influence. Professor Everitt has drawn attention to the prevailing assumption that the wayfaring community spread sedition. In 1574, for instance, the Earl of Huntingdon wrote to Lord Scrope and the Bishop of Carlisle to inform them of the presence in the North of fugitive traitors who had taken part in the recent rebellions. It was suspected, he continued, that letters were being sent through the Western Marches to the Queen of Scots by persons going to York, ostensibly to buy horses. A century later, in May 1689, a warrant was issued to Arthur Clum of the General Letter Office to search for treasonable and seditious printed libels, books and papers about the persons, and in the chambers and warehouses, of all carriers, wagoners, packhorse-men and higglers on the western roads.[26]

STATUS AND SOCIAL CLASS

Socially, horse dealers were not credited with a very high status by contemporaries since in popular opinion they were reputed a deceitful, dishonest, degenerate and seditious group of people. The evidence of the records, on the other hand, suggests that they came from a variety of backgrounds and that many of the prominent dealers who appear in the toll books had some standing in their own communities. One problem is that of identity, for many people bought and sold horses on their own account, especially in carrying and industrial concerns, and they, too, appear in the toll books. Fortunately, the documentation in the end usually singles out the men who were dealers, whilst a comparison of entries at different fairs generally highlights the specialists by the scale and range of their operations, the regularity of their appearances and their association with others of their class. Those dealers who habitually turn up in the pages of the toll books represent the honest, hard-working section of the trade, and were more likely to be men of substance than those accused of deception and fraud who appeared before Courts of Chancery and Requests. In one sense the trade suffered from its growing importance in the economy as it attracted a host of small-time enterpreneurs, often with few scruples and sometimes with openly criminal proclivities. At the lowest level, horses could be bought reasonably cheaply, and the rapidity with which they were sold or exchanged reflected the importance of small profit margins to such men. Among the criminal element supplies were

26 *C.S.P.D.*, Addenda, 1566–79, p. 458; Everitt, 'Change in the Provinces', p. 43.

found free of charge on commons and in fields and stables all over the country. This association of the horse trade with dubious characters on the edge of the business certainly helped to tarnish the reputation of the honest traders and to excite feelings of suspicion and even hostility that surpassed the general condemnation of middlemen.

The top end of the market comprised dealers who regularly turn up in the toll books and who were responsible for moving large numbers of horses around the country. The biggest and most important group came from London. These men were often styled 'Mr' or 'gent', and both in terms of their status and in the scale of their enterprises they should be classed alongside merchants involved in other branches of national, as opposed to purely local, commerce. Horse dealing, in fact, was regularly combined with the prosecution of another occupation, often as a middleman handling another commodity. In his bill of complaint Harvey Connaway called himself citizen and salter of London, and stated that he and John Styles dealt in hay and other commodities as well as in horses. In addition, an analysis of the background of provincial dealers indicates that it was common practice for them to have another trade, especially one that involved the use of horses. Trade *with* horses naturally led to trade *in* horses.[27] A significant proportion of them came from the metal, textile and leather industries, the products of which were normally carried overland on the backs of horses. In the west Midlands such people were the subject of a complaint made by local metal workers to the Staffordshire justices of the peace in 1603. These men, who were 'brought up to these trades have now given over the making of ware; and buying the wares of others that do make them, do sell to other countryes'.[28] Members of this group of middlemen can readily be found in the toll books of Midlands fairs, notably nailers like Richard Harthill of Sedgeley and John Field of West Bromwich and lorimers like William Morley of Wednesbury. In the leather industry a similar complaint was made to the Privy Council in 1619 against artisans turned dealers. The leather sellers were no longer men who 'made drest and sold wares of tanner's leather' but 'men of other trades'. Thomas Rocke, a currier from Stourbridge at the end of the sixteenth century, had standings at Stourbridge and at Wolverhampton markets and was clearly a distributor of ware, but like many others of his family he also carried on a considerable trade in horses.[29]

Middlemen trading in a variety of goods were often described as 'chapmen', a term which contemporaries used in a variety of ways. Dr

27 Chartres, 'Road Carrying', p. 82.
28 J. Thirsk and J. P. Cooper, eds., *Seventeenth Century Economic Documents* (Oxford, 1972), p. 188.
29 Wilson, *England's Apprenticeship*, p. 50; Worcs. R.O., Wills 1593/124.

Margaret Spufford has found that those described as such in their inventories often dealt in an assortment of textiles, haberdashery and some ready-made clothing or accessories. Those who had a small shop also often began to stock more perishable or less transportable goods like tobacco, groceries, 'strong waters' and ironmongery.[30] These are the sort of wares that one would expect to find in a pedlar's pack, and indicate the people to whom the term originally referred. In fact, the word was invariably applied in a general way to anyone who transported goods, especially in a middleman capacity. Of course, horse dealers would come into this category and this is implied by the numerous examples of dealers being termed chapmen in the toll books. This is exactly opposite to the view expressed by Westerfield, who believes that the term had once encompassed all dealers but had by the sixteenth century become restricted to the small pedlar or retail dealer.[31]

Another group who easily developed an interest in horses were innkeepers, and this gives point to their incorporation in London in 1515 of the Company of Horse Coursers. At Northampton there were a number of horse dealers' inns and one, the Blue Boar, was run in Charles II's reign by a courser. At Chester and Oxford during the same period, innkeepers and allied traders were among the most prominent purchasers of horses in the market.[32] Another large body of dealers comprised victuallers and butchers and included members of the Dabbs, Frizwell, Guy, Hunt and Powell families (of the Atherstone district, Bedworth, Castle Cary, Hungerford and Solihull respectively), and individuals such as William Horwood junior of Bishop's Tawton and Humphrey Hanbury of Bedworth (see Appendix 5). Butchers were among the most enterprising of local entrepreneurs, associating themselves with a variety of economic activities. In the early seventeenth century a number of butchers from Newport (Shrops.) acted as wool merchants, collecting parcels of the fine Welsh March wool from local farmers and taking them to wool staplers resident in the district. The Robson and Boycott families, in particular, combined their trade of butchering with that of wool merchants and horse dealers and regularly visited Shrewsbury to buy horses and cattle.[33]

There were also some surprising combinations of jobs. John Thompson, the vicar of Riseley (Beds.), certainly had a respectable calling but

---

30 Private communication from Dr Margaret Spufford; 'The chapman's Stock-in-Trade', in her book, *Petty Chapmen and their wares in the seventeenth-century: the great reclothing of rural England* (1984), pp. 85–105.
31 Westerfield, *Middlemen*, p. 314.
32 Corpn. of London R.O., Journals 11, fo. 236v. I am grateful to Dr G. Ramsay for this reference; A. M. Everitt, *Perspectives in English Urban History* (1973), p. 107; Chester and Oxford tolls.
33 Edwards, 'Midlands Horse Trade', p. 97.

unfortunately he seems to have allowed his horse-dealing activities to interfere with his ministry. According to a petition which the inhabitants of the parish sent to the Bishop of Lincoln in 1603, 'he hath not observed the booke of Comon prayer in doinge divine service on Sondaies and weekdayes but hath followed faires and markets in buying & selling of horses & other merchandize as usuallie as eny man in his parishe contrarie to the lawe in that Case mad & provided . . .'. Plainly secular in temperament he was also accused of not preaching nor making any provision for it, of failing to read the Queen's injunctions or indicating publicly his adherence to the 39 Articles, and of having paid £40 to the previous incumbent to resign the living. He was also castigated as lewd liver.[34]

Many leading craftsmen and tradesmen/dealers had an agricultural holding of some description and their wills suggest that they were active in buying property albeit on a small scale.[35] The size of the holdings the dealers farmed themselves varied, but in general they seem to have been similar to those run by small-scale yeomen or moderate sized husbandmen. Charles Frizwell, a butcher from Bedworth, died in his thirties in the winter of 1695–6, and, as a relatively young man, his inventory may reflect the 'normal' state of affairs. In February 1695/6 the appraisers valued his personal estate at £78. 0s. 5d. and this included farm stock worth £55. 14s. 0d. His holding was basically a mixed one with a small dairy herd and several acres of corn. As he also possessed a waggon worth £5 and three mares with their gearing valued at £8, he probably did some carrying too. His brother, John, who died in 1728, certainly did. Described as a chapman in his inventory taken in August 1728, he left among other things six horses (£30), a waggon and cart (£11) and pack- and hackney saddles. He also possessed a lot of hay (£50), corn (£25) and oats (£21).[36]

Other dealers who came from an agricultural background often seem to have had similar sized holdings. When James Fretwell of Maltby in the early eighteenth century wrote a history of the family and wanted to emphasise the respectability of his uncle, Richard, a horse dealer, he described him as

a sober, good man, and keeps an orderly family, training up his children in the fear of the Lord. He lives upon a small estate of his own there, pleasantly situated; his chief business is buying and selling horses, in which he is very skilful and successful;

34 Lincs. A.O., Lincoln Diocesan Records, Box 58/2/66. I am grateful to Miss Judith Maltby for this reference.
35 L.J.R.O., Probate, Charles Friswell of Bedworth, 23 Apr. 1696; Humphrey Hanbury of Bedworth, 24 Apr. 1722; Luke Satchwell of Bedworth, 11 May 1733, for instance.
36 *Ibid.*, Charles Friswell of Bedworth, 23 Apr. 1696; John Friswell of Bedworth, 25 Oct. 1728.

and which, notwithstanding the general ill-repute that business lies under, he performs with an unblemished character.[37]

In pastoral areas, in particular, dealers could augment the resources of their holdings by grazing their animals on commons and moors. For those living on the Shropshire-Staffordshire border, the Wealdmoors, a low-lying area of fen, or the heaths which lay to the north of it, provided extensive rough grazing. Even if, as elsewhere, these wastes were coming under attack from enclosures, it did mean that there was a greater amount of improved grassland which could be held on short-term leases or hired for agistment, a feature attractive to horse dealers with their fluctuating demands for fodder. Thus Richard Winsor of Donnington leased a small tenement from the Levesons which consisted of a cottage with yard, garden and orchard and five days' math of meadowing. His father had also rented separately a piece of ground calculated at six beasts' gates, but by the time that Richard took over the property, the pasture had been incorporated into the lease.[38] In the South-west many of the Somerset dealers who sold horses at Winchester in the early seventeenth century could use the Levels as grazing lands. John Lion, one of the leading members of the group in the 1620s, had a copyhold messuage of 43 acres and attached to it were rights of grazing on Mark Moor.[39] In the fells and moors of northern England, large areas of common land also underpinned horse breeding and dealing activities. A survey of Haltwhistle, a village on the South Tyne in Northumberland, for instance, reveals that in the mid-seventeenth century there were 2,545 acres of fell and common in the parish and thus the group of local dealers who bought horses at Carlisle at that time would have been well provided for.[40]

Horse dealing was thus often only one element in a complex personal economy and the status accorded to individuals depended upon their position and degree and scale of involvement in these pursuits. Horse dealing by itself conferred little prestige. It could, however, generate additional wealth and help dealers to purchase or lease extra land, thus enabling them to raise their status. In 1605, Thomas Winsor of Donnington was leasing a cottage from the Leveson family and shortly afterwards appears in the records for the first time as a horse dealer. By 1645 he had acquired the lease of Careswell's tenement (50 acres), the Crossfield (18½

37 C. Jackson, ed., 'Yorkshire Diaries and Autobiographies in the Seventeenth and Eighteenth Centuries', II, *Surtees Society*, 77 (1883), p. 171.
38 Shrops. R.O., 38/143–4; Sutherland Colln., D593/G/1/1/13.
39 Corpn. of London R.O., 114 C, Survey of the Manor of Lympsham 1622. I am grateful to Dr Patricia Croot for this reference.
40 Northumb. R.O., NRO 1973, Survey of the Manor of Haltwhistle 1653.

acres) and the Cawderhills (32½ acres). Thomas Rowley of Preston-upon-the-Wealdmoors acted in a similar manner, acquiring leases of land at the height of his involvement in horse dealing in the 1660s and early 1670s.[41] Thereafter, as has already been mentioned, he became more concerned with agriculture and social advancement and settled down to breed horses on his own estate, the White Leasows.

A numbers of horse dealers would have been described by their neighbours as yeomen, although the criteria would have varied from region to region. In pastoral areas such as north Shropshire they were more numerous and less wealthy than their counterparts in mixed-farming regions. Thomas Jones of Kemberton, Shropshire, who died in 1695, leaving a personal estate valued at £105. 6s. 0d., therefore was probably on a par with Thomas Brown of Farnsfield in the mixed-farming region of Nottinghamshire, whose goods were appraised at £197. 16s. 8d. in January 1671/2.[42] Both were described as yeomen by the men who drew up their inventories. On the north-western border with Scotland holdings tended to be smaller even than those in pastoral areas elsewhere in the kingdom, and individuals dealing at Carlisle in the mid-seventeenth century who can be matched up with an inventory seem to have been reasonably prosperous by local standards. Both Adam Pearson of Stone-raise, Westward, and Michael Lightfoot of Kirkland, Wigton, left small but well stocked-farms at the times of their deaths, their personal estates being valued at £67. 9s. 2d. and £54. 2s. 8d. in 1669 and 1670 respectively.[43] As has been shown, the term 'yeoman' was used in a more general way in Tudor and Stuart England and it should also embrace a number of the craftsmen and tradesmen/chapmen who dealt in horses. Below them came a larger group of dealers who were husbandmen or craftsmen and included sons of yeomen and chapmen who would in time take over their fathers' positions. Richard Winsor's holding should put him in this class, although he is variously described in the toll books as 'husbandman', 'yeoman', 'Mr.', 'collier' and 'horse courser'. Nicholas Dunn of Alvechurch (Worcs.), a noted dealer at Midlands fairs in the last quarter of the seventeenth century, possessed a holding of a similar size. He was a copyhold tenant of the Bishop of Worcester and his property consisted of a pasture with his house standing in it, two closes and a meadow. At Bedale (N.R.Y.) John Jackson had a small leasehold estate, consisting in 1618 of a tenement and backside (1 rod 27½ poles), a close of arable in Gill Cross

41 Sutherland Colln., D593/G/1/1/4, D593/G/4/1/1–2, D593/I/1/4; Shrops. R.O., Charlton Colln. 2340, 625/Box 10, 15.
42 L.J.R.O Probate, Thomas Jones of Kemberton 1695; Notts. R.O., PR SW 85/6.
43 Cumbria R.O. (Carlisle), Wills, Adam Pearson of Stoneraise, Westward 1669; Michael Lightfoot of Kirkland, Wigton 1670.

Field (4 acres 1 rod 38½ poles) and a close of meadow on the moor (3 acres 1 rod 8¾ poles). Earlier rentals, however, suggest that like dealers elsewhere, he also acquired pastures on short-term leases.[44]

In the hearth tax returns it appears as though the houses of most of these dealers contained one or two fireplaces, although some of the more prominent ones lived in homes with a greater number than this. This would seem to confirm the general picture that they were men with a reasonable social background and some standing in their own communities. In the North, however, it is difficult to use this source with any precision because of the large number of one-hearth houses. At Scaleby (Cumb.), the home of the largest group of dealers attending Carlisle's horse markets in 1653–4, everyone was assessed on one hearth except Mr Richard Gilpin who was charged on four. A number of dealers appear in the list and, interestingly, they seem to have congregated in certain settlements within the parish, namely at Scaleby village, Scaleby Hill and Barclose.[45] Further south, the greater variation in the standard of housing makes it easier to evaluate their position, though in wood-pasture areas class distinctions were less pronounced than in mixed-farming regions where there often existed greater extremes of wealth. Commenting on the situation in the Forest of Arden, the wood-pasture part of Warwickshire, Dr Skipp placed the occupants of two- and three-hearth houses in the ranks of the substantial or middling peasantry and those with at least four fireplaces among the wealthy. In east Shropshire, roughly half of the dealers recorded in the returns of 1672 lived in houses of two hearths or more. At this date Thomas Rowley still resided in the two-hearth house that belonged to the old family farm, whilst Henry Bradley of Donnington, Lilleshall, continued to occupy the one-hearth cottage that his father, Thomas, had rented from the Levesons, in spite of the fact that he was leasing more land in the parish than most yeomen-farmers.[46] In the mixed-farming area of east-central Nottinghamshire in 1674 most of the dealers were living in houses of two to four hearths, which Professor W. G. Hoskins, writing of the Leicestershire parish of Wigston Magna, judged to be the types of homes occupied by the larger yeomen-farmers of the village. Thomas Brown, one of the leading members of the group and whose status has been discussed above, lived in a four-hearth house. He had been dead for two years at this date, but as he had specifically bequeathed the

---

44 Worcs. R.O., Bishop of Worcester's Colln., B.A. 2636/4(ii) Ref. 009.1; N. Riding R.O., Beresford-Peirse Colln., ZBA 11/8/1/19, 27, 30–3, 49.
45 Cumbria R.O. (Carlisle) photo-copy of Hearth Tax Returns, n.d. (c. 1664).
46 V. H. T. Skipp, *Crisis and Development* (Cambridge, 1978), p. 78; W. Watkins-Pitchford, *The Shropshire Hearth Tax Roll of 1672* (Shrewsbury, 1949), *passim*; Shrops. R.O., 1910/491; Sutherland Colln., D593/G/4/1/6.

copyhold house in which he lived to his son, Edward, his home can be discovered from the latter's entry. Significantly, his cousin, Richard Higginbottom, another well-established dealer, lived in a similar sized house. John, Thomas Brown's eldest son, had moved to a three-hearth house at Edingley and together with his brothers continued the family tradition of horse dealing.[47]

Clearly, horse dealers were not all the disreputable body of men of popular imagination. In the toll books they appear as responsible persons intent upon carrying out their legitimate business. Travelling regularly to various fairs over a number of years, they would soon become known to the officials, especially as they entered their names in the toll book. The records of Bridgnorth fair, which are full of incidental detail, illustrate this relationship quite clearly. When Henry Bradley of Donnington sold a gelding there on 6 February 1673, he only provided a single voucher, yet the toll taker accepted this one and wrote in the book 'the seller well knowne to the toll takers'. Indeed he was. In 29 recorded visits to the fair between 1646 and 1674 he sold 22 mares, 21 nags, 13 geldings, five fillies, four colts and one nag colt, buying three mares and three nags during the same period. At other fairs too, entries in the toll books indicate that many of the dealers were known and trusted. At Barnstaple (Devon) it was common practice for no vouchers to be given whenever a particular seller was known to the buyer or the toll keeper. Thus when William Horwood junior, of Bishop's Tawton, sold a nag on 8 September 1634, the keeper noted 'I knowe the Seller'.

The gentry had a particularly ambivalent attitude towards horse dealers, making use of and complaining about them by turns. As part of their education, many would have learned to appreciate the qualities of a good horse and to know something about its management, but this was often combined with a distaste for the commercial side of the business. As Nicholas, one-time Secretary of State to Charles I, wrote in 1659,

for itt is two professions, a good horse-man and a horse-courser. I pretende to the firste, but knowe nothinge of the seconde, for Ile cosen no bodye. I only take care nott to be cosende, which they finde I can doe reasonable well att thatt.[48]

If the gentry had to do business with dealers it was natural therefore that they should turn to the honest and established men referred to above (see Appendix 5).

In the 1620s, John Styles sold horses to Sir Richard Graham, and

---

47 P.R.O., E179/160/320, E179/254/30; Notts. R.O., PR SW 85/6; W. G. Hoskins, *The Midland Peasant* (1965), p. 195.

48 Sir G. F. Warner, ed., 'The Nicholas Papers, IV, 1657–60', *Camden Society*, 3rd ser., 30 (1921), p. 111.

between 28 March 1625 and 20 April 1626 provided him with nine nags, six geldings and one horse at a total cost of £189. 7s. 4d. At the end of the century, Henry of Nassau also obtained stock off London dealers, two of whom, George Arnold and Edward Horton, were among those who visited Rothwell fair in Northamptonshire. George Arnold also carried out transactions with the Earls of Bristol and Nottingham and with Mr Samuel Tufnell.[49] Provincial dealers were similarly involved. As noted above, gentry from Staffordshire and Shropshire carried on a regular traffic with local dealers and examples can be found elsewhere in the country.[50] Bull of Bedford, allowed credit by John Isham of Lamport, (Northants.) was undoubtedly the same man who made three visits to Worcester Fair at the beginning of Elizabeth's reign, buying five nags and five geldings and selling two geldings.[51] John had made his fortune in London as a merchant adventurer, and had used his wealth to establish himself as a country gentleman. A century later the Ishams were one of the leading families in the county, but although Sir Justinian belonged to a circle of gentlemen-breeders who distributed horses amongst themselves, he still did business with horse dealers such as Hutchinson of Clipston.[52]

To a large extent, the gentry were able to remain aloof from the 'sordid' business of buying and selling horses by employing agents to do the work for them. The Massingberds of Gunby, Lincolnshire, for instance, in the 1700s used Thomas Briggs and William Kirmond in this capacity. Horse dealers, naturally enough, were often employed too. Samuel Pepys made use of a dealer to help him buy horses at Smithfield, as did Edward Wood in 1663. Writing to Mr John Park in London, Wood asked him to send a servant to contact one Frimley, evidently a horse dealer, who could be found at the White Hart or at the Cookshop in Smithfield. Frimley's task was to assist him in buying two good cart mares or geldings for which he was to pay £7 to £10.[53]

Considerable attention has been focused upon this group of dealers because they were the ones who developed inter-regional trade, bought in the greatest number of horses, and provided a range of animals to meet the

49 Norton Conyers Colln.; Herts. R.O., Henry Of Nassau's Accounts D/ENa 07–08; S.H.A.H., *The Diary of John Hervey First Earl of Bristol* (Wells, 1894), pp. 121, 123; Notts. R.O., Finch Colln. DG 7/1/19b; Essex R.O., Langley's (Great Waltham) Estate, D/DTu 276.

50 *Supra*, pp. 80–1

51 G. R. Ramsay, ed., 'John Isham, Mercer and Merchant Adventurer', *Northants. Record Society*, 21 (1962), pp. 71, 127–8.

52 N. Marlow, ed., *The Diary of Thomas Isham of Lamport* (Farnborough, 1971), pp. 155, 161, 209.

53 Massingberd (G) Colln., MG 5/2/7; H. B. Wheatley, ed., *The Diary of Samuel Pepys* (1905), pp. 162, 168; Middlesex R.O., Wood Papers ACC 262/43/29.

needs of an increasingly varied and discriminating market. Thus they had
an importance out of all proportion to their numbers, for they formed only
one part of the business which was filled out by a mass of lesser men. The
latter tended to be poorer and more mobile and although not necessarily
less honest, were more likely to have been responsible for the abuses so
loudly complained about by contemporaries. Without the same social
background or economic resources they were more dependent upon what
they could sell, perhaps combining horse trading with small-scale dealing
in whatever else they could turn to a profit. They therefore had to live by
their wits and it is not surprising to find them accused of sharp practice.
Unfortunately for the legitimate dealers, the trade had a long tail, at the
end of which were to be found some very dubious characters. It included,
for instance, dealers accused of doing business with two horse thieves in
Staffordshire in the winter of 1608–9.[54] The thieves had sold horses in
pastures and fields, and not openly in markets and fairs, and 'have had
divers chapmen secretly to receive them at their hands, who almost are as
ill as the horse stealers themselves'.

Lesser horse dealers remain shadowy figures who undoubtedly appear
in the toll books, but are difficult to distinguish from non-specialists who
bought one or two horses. As a more transient element, moreover, they
have left little trace in other records. One inventory of a horse courser,
described as such, has been found and perhaps he might be taken as a
representative of this class. The goods of Thomas Witty of Surfleet (Lincs.)
were appraised in 1694 and his entire personal estate consisted of four
horses worth £20, a reasonable price, especially at the normally low
inventory valuations (see Appendix 6).[55] It is clear however, that such men
had a fairly humble background and were consigned in popular estimation
to the sub-group of rogues and vagabonds in which a sixteenth-century
surgeon, writing in another context, included 'tinkers, tooth-drawers,
pedlars, ostlers, carters, porters, horse-gelders and horse-leeches, idiots,
applesquires, broom-men, bawds, witches, conjurors, soothsayers,
rogues, rat-catchers, runagates and proctors of spittle houses'.[56] The
records of markets and fairs reveal that a wide range of people of modest
means who were in some way associated with the general business of
keeping horses, also dealt in them. Just as motor mechanics today tend to
have one or two second-hand cars on display, so blacksmiths, farriers,
ostlers, horse breakers, horse leeches and hackneymen dabbled in horse
dealing too. Blacksmiths and farriers were the most stable element in this

54 Thirsk and Cooper, *Seventeenth Century . . . Documents*, p. 331.
55 Lincs. A.O., Inventory 191/218.
56 Quoted in P. Williams, *Life in Tudor England* (New York, 1964), p. 108.

group, as the need of a smithy tied them to one place. Individuals such as George Rowley of Watling Street in the Shropshire parish of Wellington, or members of the Waring family of Stratford-upon-Avon, Shipston-upon-Stour and Warwick, in fact, were among the regular dealers at a number of Midlands fairs. Horse breakers and horse leeches, on the other hand, were far more mobile and, to contemporaries, much less respectable. Thus, when in 1626 Edward Gorges recommended a horse breaker to Sir Hugh Smyth, he stressed that he was 'very carefull and diligent, and (as farr as I can perceave) no gadder abroad, or haunter to ale howses. And for that he is so ragged a poore fellow, the lesse money will satisffie him'.[57] Literary evidence for this attitude can be seen in Ben Jonson's play, *Bartholomew Fair*, in the comic character of Knockem who, although called a horse courser, was in fact a horse leech.[58] These people occasionally turn up in the records of various markets and fairs dealing in horses in a small way.

Hackneymen, too, as could be expected, dealt in horses. According to the waterman in Henry Peacham's book, *Coach and Sedan*, hackneymen away from their job, were

good for nothing except to marry some old Ale-wife, and bid his old acquaintance welcome, to turne horse-courser, become a Gentlemans baylie or butler in the Countrie, or by meanes of some great man, get a place in a hospitall.[59]

However, hackneymen, like victuallers, who also tended to be associated with the hiring of horses, came from a variety of backgrounds. At the bottom were many people such as Richard Veredy, a labourer of Sedgeley (Staffs.), who owned a single horse, but there were others – Hobson of Cambridge, for instance – who operated on a much bigger scale.[60] Of course, the larger enterprises had a much greater turnover of stock; as hackney horses did not last many years, hackneymen thereby gained an unsavoury reputation that was partly due to the belief that they dealt in broken-down nags ruined by countless careless riders. The horses that Hanibal Castleton of Islington possessed seem to have been reasonably inexpensive saddle mounts, if the prices he paid at Market Bosworth in 1613 can be used as a yardstick, although one grey racking mare he purchased there for £6. 7s. 0d. was clearly of a better quality.

Petty chapmen also come into the general category of lesser dealers. Richard Preece of Bridgnorth bought and sold one or two horses in the town in the third quarter of the seventeenth century but is not recorded at

57 Bristol R.O., AC/C46/9.
58 Ben Jonson, *Bartholomew Fair* (1614), *passim*.
59 Peacham, fo. C 3.
60 P.R.O., C3/185/47; Crofts, *Packhorse, Waggon and Post*, p. 23.

any other fairs of the area and only traded on a small scale. More is known about Charles Moon who, like many others in his position, seems to have had no fixed place of abode. He sold horses at Oxford market in 1682 and 1683 and gave as his residence Deddington in Oxfordshire. In 1685 he was arrested at Shrewsbury on suspicion of stealing horses and stated in his examination that he 'hath no habitation' but lodged with John Wicketts who kept the Bell at Deddington. Although a case was never brought against him, witnesses spoke of sharp practice engaged in by Moon and his partner, John Taylor. Moon languished in gaol until the following year when he petitioned the local Justices for his release and although his fate is not certainly known, he appears to have been freed.[61] At Taunton Fair, held on 17 June 1691, a man with the same name claimed to be a chapman from Foxham in the Wiltshire parish of Bremhill, and stood voucher for William Brewer, a horse dealer from that place.

These small-scale dealers haunted fairs all over the country but they could be found in the greatest numbers at Smithfield, where the size and variety of the market offered opportunities for traders at all levels. The large working population of London, augmented by others constantly moving in and out of the capital, required considerable numbers of cheap horses which these men could provide. At the beginning of the seventeenth century Thomas Dekker, an entertaining if extravagant commentator on the low life of the time, wrote of them (see Appendix 7)

you shall finde euery Horse courser for the most part to bee in quality a coozener, by proffession a knaue, by his cunning a Varlet, in fayres a Hagling Chapman, in the Citty a Cogging dissembler, and in Smith-field a common forsworne Vilaine.[62]

Smithfield had a particularly bad reputation, and whilst there must have been many satisfied customers, those who complained about their treatment at the hands of the dealers were the ones who had their transactions recorded. The size and anonymity of the market there certainly attracted shady characters from all over the country, intent on selling stolen animals or palming off worn-out jades at inflated prices.[63] Although the most prominent men in the trade were based there, the reputation and social background of many of the other Smithfield dealers probably accounts for the low position they held among London companies at the end of the Middle Ages. Two late fifteenth-century lists places them 72nd and 78th out of 73 and 81 crafts respectively, and although their incorporation into the Company of Innholders in 1515 resulted in an improvement in their

61 Shrops, R.O., Shrewsbury Corpn. Records 2270.
62 Thomas Dekker, *Lanthorne and Candle-light* (1608), fo. H 3v.
63 *Infra.*, p. 114.

ranking order, this was due to the status of the craft they joined. In a case heard in the Court of Requests in 1593, Hugh Barbone accused William Pascall, whom he had met at Smithfield and whom he called a horse courser, of sharp practice. Pascall, of course, protested his innocence, strenuously denying that he was a horse dealer as is 'most slaunderouslie and malitiouslie alleidged'. Perhaps he felt to admit it would prejudice his case.[64]

ATTITUDES TOWARDS HORSE DEALERS

Unhappy experiences at the hands of some helped to give all horse dealers a poor reputation and this multiplied the effect of the general hostility felt towards all middlemen by many contemporaries. For much of the period under discussion the whole class was viewed with suspicion and their operations hampered by restrictive legislation. The needs of an expanding population may well have necessitated new and more flexible methods to deal with the increasing problems of supply, but people felt concern about the opportunities for abuse that they presented. During the course of the Tudor and Stuart period the government came to a grudging acceptance of the need for middlemen, but in a series of legislative measures sought to control their actions, forcing them wherever possible to go through the regulated market. Horse dealers were subject to many of the same regulations as other groups of middlemen. They were certainly involved in private dealing, and a careful analysis of toll books reveals cases of other marketing offences, especially regrating.

Horse dealers, however, were by no means the only culprits. Charles Whitney a wool merchant from Dursley (Gloucs.), put forward his belief in free enterprise in the strongest possible terms when at Shrewsbury in 1698. According to a witness, when the bellmen of the corporation proclaimed that all wool should be sold in the market, Whitney replied that 'he would lay out Money where he pleased and that Mr Mayour might kiss his Arss'.[65] Nor were horse dealers the biggest culprits either. They were not averse to profiting from the situation if market conditions were in their favour but opportunities came less frequently and less dramatically than they did in the corn and grain trade, for example. In times of dearth there must have been a great temptation for dealers in these commodities to corner the market and hoard supplies until the price rose. In a letter written to the Queen's officers in Cheshire in 1596 or 1597, the Privy Council informed them that they had heard of a 'great quantity of mault

---

64 Corpn. of London R.O., Journal 9 fo. 81b, Journal 10 fo. 374; P.R.O., REQ 2/176/11. I am grateful to Prof. Jack Fisher for this reference.
65 Shrops. R.O., Shrewsbury Corpn. Records 2285.

and other graine brought to ... Nampwiche which is bought up and ingrossed by the richer sorte and after sold againe at higher rates, to the oppression of the poorer sorte'.[66] Brewers and maltsters, in fact, were notorious offenders. Brewers were among the biggest buyers on the corn markets and having often contracted for their supplies months in advance, were well placed to profit from the distress of others. Maltsters too dealt in large consignments. The Enfield maltmen, in particular, acquired something of an evil reputation, a witness in 1583 complaining that they forestalled the market by buying directly off the farmers, and caused the price of grain in the market to rise. Moreover, they ignored London's markets and dealt directly with the bakers and brewers, some of whom became so involved that they were ruined.[67]

Other groups of middlemen therefore found themselves more sorely tempted to ignore official markets and regulations than the horse dealers, and it is undoubtedly true that the most hysterical reactions were reserved for such people as the maltsters and brewers. Nonetheless, in day-to-day business the horse dealers appear to have had a particularly poor reputation and this is borne out by an examination of contemporary records and literature. Some seventy years before Dekker was to make his comment, Fitzherbert pursued an identical theme. Writing on the difference between a horse master, a horse dealer and a horse leech, he continued his discussion by noting that 'if ye hadde a potycarye to make a fourthe, ye myghte haue suche foure, that it were harde to truste the best of them'. As Fitzherbert implies, belief in the essential dishonesty and deceitfulness of horse dealers as a group, formed the basis of contemporary attitudes towards them and influenced the judgement of those with whom they came into contact. William Harrison later in the century was emphatic in his condemnation when he stated that 'there is no greater deceit used anywhere than among our horsekeepers, horsecorsers, and hostelers'. In this context it is interesting to note that one dealer who was present at Kidderminster Fair on 7 June 1705 called himself 'honest' John Cleminge, a clear indication of and response to popular opinion.[68]

These descriptions have a remarkable similarity to current views on an equally maligned section of society, the second-hand car dealer. I have written elsewhere of horses as the internal combustion engine of pre-mechanized England and, as has already been shown, they played as vital a role in the economy of the time. Moreover, suspicion of both sets of dealers stemmed from the same causes, the size of the demand for their wares and

66 *A.P.C.*, N.S., 26, 1596–7, p. 399.
67 Everitt, 'Marketing', pp. 575–6, 583–4; Pam, *Tudor Enfield*, p. 5.
68 Fitzherbert, *Boke of Husbandrie*, fo. xxxvii; *Harrison's Description*, ii, Third book, pp. 4–5; Kidderminster tolls.

the possibilities of deception. Horses in early modern England, as vehicles today, were required in large and ever-increasing numbers and were also bought by people who may not necessarily have known the points to look for in an animal. Vehicles are complicated pieces of machinery, requiring a certain level of competence to discern their road-worthiness, but at an earlier date the appropriate skills were no less a factor in the judgement of horseflesh. Age and condition were obvious criteria but because of the susceptibility of horses to injury and disease, a fact reflected in the wealth of literature on the subject at the time, there were plenty of pitfalls for the untutored and unwary. In the diary which Oliver Heywood, a Yorkshire clergyman, kept in the late seventeenth century, he ruefully recorded an occasion when he was thus taken in. In February 1689 he exchanged his saddle-horse for a mare belonging to a carrier who had come to the house. It was 'a louely mare to look on, and ride on, he had given 11[li] to Mr. Langley for her, I gaue 5[li] 5[sh] to boot, she was a very likely beast, but proved moon-blind thus I was cheated, much perplexed, prayed to God about it, they told me she would goe stone blind.'[69]

Naturally, people thus duped suspected dealers of deliberate dishonesty. Thomas Dekker noted

And whereas in buying all other commodities, men striue to haue the best, how great so euer the price be, onely the Horse courser is of a baser minde, for the worst horse-flesh (so it be cheape) does best goe downe with him. He cares for nothing but a fayre outside, and a handsome shape (like these that hyre whores though there be a hundred diseases within), he (as the other) ventures vpon them all.

Dealers, he said, sought out horses that looked 'fatt, fayre and well fauor'd to the eye and especially those in the popular colours, the milk white, the grey, the dapple grey, the coal-black with its proper mark (white star, white heel etc.) and the bright bay'. Moreover, as they were skilled in finding out defects themselves, they could acquire horses cheaply, which, especially if young and outwardly unblemished, could be easily disposed of.[70]

Horse dealers often guaranteed the soundness of their animals and these statements were occasionally recorded in the toll books of markets and fairs. When William Brewer of Foxham (Wilts.) exchanged a brown mare at a fair held at Taunton at the end of the seventeenth century, he warranted it sound 'every where'. Some dealers were more generous and included a money-back guarantee if the horse did not live up to expectations. The dark-brown seven-year-old mare that Richard Clark of Old Stratford sold at Warwick on 7 January 1687/8 was 'warrented in fole if

69 J. H. Turner, ed., *The Reverend Oliver Heywood B.A.*, IV (Bingley, 1885), p. 134.
70 Dekker, *Lanthorne and Candle-light*, fos. H 3–4.

she proues otherwise before the first day of May 20 shillings to be returned
back to ye buyer'. Most people, nonetheless, safeguarded themselves by
inserting let-out clauses into their statements. Thus, when John Welch of
Morton (Notts.) sold three colts at Nottingham fair on 21 September
1650, the toll keeper wrote that 'the vendor will warrant them now to bee
sound for ought hee knowes'.

Dekker undoubtedly overstated his case on the disreputable character of
horse dealers, but examples of dishonesty can certainly be found among
the records (see Appendix 9). In the case heard in the Court of Requests in
1593, referred to above, Hugh Barbone, the petitioner, claimed he had met
William Pascall at Smithfield, but as he had not wanted to buy anything
there, Pascall persuaded him to come to Uxbridge Fair four or five days
later, where he knew someone who was bringing a nag for sale. There, they
met one Pennington, a common horse courser, whose horse Barbone
eventually agreed to buy for £4. He had been influenced in his decision by
Pascall who told him that at the price the horse was 'a very good
pennyworth for that he knowes the same to be a very perfecte good nagge'.
However, he had travelled no more than twelve miles on the animal when
it became so lame that it would go no further. Men 'skilful in horses'
subsequently told him that the horse had been lame for some time and he
accused Pascall of knowing this, especially as he suspected that it was
Pascall's own animal. Pascall, of course, denied the allegation.[71]

Inevitably the trade contained many unscrupulous individuals but, as
has been suggested, there were honest dealers, and moreover it would be
unfair and misleading to assume that dealers had the monopoly of
deception. If an intimate knowledge of the business gave them an advantage and presented them with more opportunities, others were as suscep-
tible to the same temptations. Anyone left in possession of a suspect horse
would have wanted to dispose of it quickly, even if on occasion it meant
the suppression of certain facts about it. The looseness of occupational
labels in this period and the wide range of trades involved in ancillary
horse dealing unfortunately make it difficult to apportion guilt between
specialist and non-specialist sellers, but contemporary documentation
suggests that a wide cross-section of society was involved.

Even gentry were not immune. Among the hundreds of horses listed in
their account books, a number of old, defective or diseased animals are to
be found, which may or may not have been so described to the prospective
buyer. As Dekker warned, particular care had to be taken when buying
horses with fashionable colours, since they mostly belonged to members of
the gentry and were 'seldome or never solde away, but vpon some fowle

71 P.R.O., REQ 2/176/11.

quality, or some incurable disease, which the Beast is falne'. Some gentry seem to have been experts in the deceits of horse trading. In a letter that Mr Bitterfield wrote from Claydon to Edmund Verney in 1662, he commented upon an exchange of horses that Edmund's brother, Henry, had made with John Risley. 'Had you seen or heard how Mr. H V and Mr. Jo. Risley cheated one the other in the exchange of two admirable jades, with what craft & confidence it was carryed, twould make you intermit a little of your serious thoughts to take a laugh.'[72]

This catalogue of abuses reinforces the earlier suggestion that lack of knowledge lay at the heart of the problem, creating opportunities for deception and making people wary of doing business with horse dealers, the obvious scapegoats. Anxiety over the possibility of being cheated is apparent in a letter which Sir Ralph Verney received from his aunt Sherard in 1655. She had bought him a mare and was pleased that he found the gift acceptable. 'I am most harteyli glad as the maier pleseth you. I tooke it uppon trust, for I have noe scill in horsis my selfe'. Many others, for the same reason, must have shared the view of William Hawkins, expressed in a letter that he wrote to the Earl of Leicester in 1641, that he was 'much afraid of dealing with horse-coursers'.[73]

SUMMARY

It is clear that when doing business with horse dealers one had to be prepared for hard bargaining, and the very nature of the trade led to a certain amount of sharp practice. Undoubtedly, there were many rogues in the trade and the various forms of deception so graphically described by Thomas Dekker did occur. Just as many people today can be taken in by the outward appearance of a second-hand car, so there were gullible customers for horses in the Tudor and Stuart period. However, many others, then as now, failed to tell the truth about the product they were trying to sell. Even more than today, with our tighter controls over unfair trading and misrepresentation, the buyer had to take care over the product he was purchasing. It would be wrong, however, to brand the whole class of horse dealers as a deceitful and dishonest group of people. One may gain an impression of bad faith and even outright criminal behaviour if one is analysing the records of the personal courts of the Crown or those of Quarter Sessions and Assize. Records of markets and fairs, together with personal details gathered from other sources, nonetheless, act as a correc-

---

72 M. M. Verney, ed., *Memoirs of the Verney Family from the Restoration to the Revolution 1660 to 1696* (1899), p. 85.
73 M. M. Verney, ed., *memoirs of the Verney Family during the Commonwealth 1650 to 1660* (1894), p. 256; De L'Isle and Dudley MSS, VI, p. 384.

tive to this prejudiced view. From these it can be seen that an important section of the trade was managed by people well-integrated into the local community and no worse in their conduct than those around them. Indeed, it paid them to act honestly and openly, as disreputable ones were eventually found out and ostracised.

4

———— ◯◯◯ ————

HORSE STEALING

Horse stealers were called 'priggers of prancers' and were well-established figures in the Tudor and Stuart underworld. According to Thomas Harman, writing in 1567, these men travelled the country dressed in jerkins of leather or white frieze, holding a little white wand in their hand. They lurked near pasture grounds looking for suitable horses and, if challenged, pretended to be lost.[1] If this sounds as likely as robbers wearing masks and striped jerseys and carrying bags marked 'swag', the sources reveal that some thieves did fit this description. In 1647 a man seen walking near the place where a horse had been stolen at Beverley carried a whitish coloured staff, whilst another suspect in Shropshire in 1703 was dressed in a white close-bodied coat, a white waistcoat trimmed with black and a pair of buckskin breeches with silver buttons. In 1647 Edward Dowson, a soldier stationed at Kirk Stanley (W.R.Y.), stated that he had had a sorrel gelding stolen from the churchyard there and suspected Robert Ashworth of Rossendale (Lancs.) of the crime. He had been observed wandering about the town asking the way to Arkendale, Dowson averred, although he knew that he had not gone there. In 1700 a servant of Evan Gerard of Haighton (Lancs.) noticed two strangers lurking near his master's stable one evening and going up to them, was asked the way to Preston. When he went to the stable early the next morning, he found that two geldings were missing.[2]

A thief on horseback was called a 'lanceman' and on foot a 'trailer'. The trailers had saddle, bridle, stirrups and spurs with them which could be folded up and carried in a bag, ready for use when required. In a deposition heard at Shrewsbury in November 1690, Margaret Hoult of Grinshill (Shrops.) spoke of the occasion the previous year when she had met the suspect at her house. Her neighbour, Mr William Heath, had lost a mare

---

1 Thomas Harman, *A Caveat for Commen Cursitors* (1567), fo. C iiiiv.
2 Shrewsbury Corpn. Records, 2291; P.R.O., ASSI 45/2/1/8, P(alatine of) L(ancaster) 27/2 part 1.

that night and she remembered that the man calling himself Henry Flint carried behind him a bundle folded in a coat which looked like a saddle.[3]

THE SOURCE MATERIAL

The material that forms the basis of this chapter is to be found in the records of the Quarter Sessions and the Assizes. Assize indictment files for the Tudor and Stuart period exist for the special jurisdictions of the Palatinates of Chester, Durham and Lancaster and for four out of the six circuits, namely, the Oxford, Norfolk, Northern and Home Circuits. Of the latter, however, only the Home Circuit provides sufficient information to be used effectively, and I have therefore made a special survey of the records of this court. The region, because of its proximity to London, can hardly be taken as typical of the whole country, but nonetheless the individual counties do offer a meaningful contrast.[4]

Extensive use has also been made of the depositions of witnesses and suspects taken by the Justices of the Peace as part of their statutory obligations. As they were not, legally speaking, documents of record, depositions did not have to be kept and therefore their preservation around the country has been a matter of chance.[5] Among the Assize records of the period, those for the Northern Circuit exist in the greatest number and, apart from a few early examples, begin in 1640. Depositions also survive for the Oxford Circuit from the 1680s. Of the Palatine jurisdictions, the documentation for Chester which starts in 1530 is the fullest, but some of the bundles are in a poor condition and as a I write, have been withdrawn for repair. The Duchy of Lancaster's records commence in 1663 and for Durham there is extant material from the end of Elizabeth's reign, although of a fragmentary nature until the eighteenth century.[6] A considerable number of depositions can be found among the Quarter Sessions records too. Some general collections are in print and occasionally, as for Bristol and Southampton, the depositions have been extracted and published by themselves. Unfortunately, the bulk of the documentation still remains in manuscript form alone and its use is

---

3 F. Aydelotte, *Elizabethan Rogues and Vagabonds* (Oxford, 1913); Shrewsbury Corpn. Records, 2276.
4 J. S. Cockburn, ed., *Calendar of Assize Records: Essex Indictments Elizabeth I* (1978); *Hertfordshire Indictments Elizabeth I* (1975); *Kent Indictments Elizabeth I* (1979); *Surrey Indictments Elizabeth I* (1980); *Sussex Indictments Elizabeth I* (1975).
5 J. S. Cockburn, 'Early-Modern Assize Records as Historical Evidence', *Journal of the Society of Archivists*, 5(1974–5), p. 216.
6 These records are to be found in the P.R.O. (Chancery Lane) and the class numbers are as follows: Northern Circuit depositions ASSI 45; Oxford Circuit ASSI 5; Palatine of Chester CHES 38; Palatine of Lancaster P.L. 27; Palatine of Durham DURH 17.

hindered by its sheer volume, range of subject matter and physical condition. These sources have to be used with extreme care for many pitfalls await the rash and unwary. As Dr Sharpe commented in his study of crime and delinquency in an Essex parish in the early seventh century, 'Only the most insensitive student of Assize and Quarter Sessions documents can fail to realize their limitations, and only the most unimaginative can fail to ponder upon the prospects of going beyond them'.[7]

The jurisdiction of the Quarter Sessions and the Assizes continued to overlap during the period under discussion in spite of the convention that capital felonies, including horse stealing, should be heard at the latter. In the comparatively highly populated South-east and in urban centres elsewhere in the country, overcrowded gaols were often delivered by local magistrates. Other cases went straight to the Court of King's Bench or were removed there.[8] Apart from the *lacunae* in the documentation, it is virtually impossible for other reasons to arrive at an accurate figure for the incidence of a particular crime. Many went undetected or were never brought to court. Edward Hext, a Somerset magistrate and a clerk in Star Chamber, thought in 1596 that 80 per cent of all criminals evaded trial.[9] Some bills were returned *ignoramus* by the grand juries (about one in eight in the eighteenth century according to Professor Cockburn) but as there was no need to preserve them, they often failed to be recorded. Even if cases were prosecuted, the verdict and the punishment could be influenced by such factors as social status and the connexion of the accused with the place where the offence took place.[10]

The problem of defining generalized social status terms such as 'yeoman', 'husbandman' and 'labourer' has already been discussed in connexion with dealers, but it is clearly relevant here too.[11] Dual occupations and abrupt changes in jobs tend to make precise categorisation difficult as well. In 1674, one suspected horse stealer said that he had given up his trade as a miller three years earlier because he had had no mill, and since then he had been engaged in buying and selling fish, glass bottles and pots 'by any of which he could gett the best profitt'.[12] Professor Cockburn too has noted the looseness of status terms and the effect in indictments of the legal ruling that suspects could not be attributed with an illegal occupation such as vagrancy. 'Exactly how many notional occupations and domiciles

7 J. A. Sharpe, 'Crime and Delinquency in an Essex Parish 1600–1640', in J. S. Cockburn, *Crime in England 1550–1800* (1977), p. 90.
8 See J. S. Cockburn, *A History of English Assizes 1558–1714* (1972), pp. 86–97, for a fuller account.
9 B. L. Lansd. MS 81, fo. 161. Quoted in Cockburn, *Crime*, p. 50.
10 Cockburn, *Crime*, pp. 19–20; Cockburn, *Assizes*, p. 127.
11 *Supra*, pp. 87–94.
12 P.R.O., ASSI 45/11/3/119.

lie behind the bland facade of single, unassociated indictments', he observed, 'will never be known.'[13]

It is encouraging therefore to discover that the figures drawn from this source are very similar to those obtained from an analysis of the depositions of the Northern Circuit for the years 1640–99. Professor Cockburn believed this source to be superior to that of indictments in such matters, since the legal ruling did not apply. R. A. Houston, in a study of literacy rates in the North in the period 1640 to 1750, based his work on the depositions, observing that they had 'escaped the sweeping criticism levelled against the accuracy of assize indictments', although he sensibly advocated care in their use.[14] My own impression is that the depositions are more accurate, especially as the accounts given often make it possible to evaluate the information presented on occupations and residences. It is true that some of the details may be fictitious, and that it was in the interests of the prosecutors and the accused respectively to underplay or exaggerate the social/occupational state of the accused, respectability and social status being crucial in decision-making at all levels of the machinery of criminal justice. Nonetheless, the stories can often be corroborated by reference to associated depositions of victims and witnesses and this makes it easier to evaluate the accuracy of the statements.

HORSE STEALING: PRACTICE AND PREVENTION

The records do show, when due allowance has been made for their inadequacies, that horse stealing was quite widespread in Tudor and Stuart England and contemporary concern over this is reflected in the series of measures carried out by the government in the second half of the sixteenth century. One Act of 1547 sought to increase the deterrent effect of the law by making the crime a felony without benefit of clergy.[15] The two Acts of 1555 and 1589 which aimed at tightening up control of the trade by regulating the sale of horses more strictly had, as their avowed objective, the aim of making it more difficult for stolen horses to be disposed of.[16] According to the Act of 1555, stolen horses had hitherto been sold secretly outside the market place and this had hindered the attempts of owners to find their animals. In this respect however the measures were not entirely successful, for as the government admitted in the preamble to the 1589 Act, they 'have not wrought soe good effecte for

---

13 Cockburn, *Crime*, p. 63; Cockburn, 'Assize Records', p. 225.
14 Cockburn, 'Assize Records', p. 216; R. A. Houston, 'The Development of Literacy: Northern England, 1640–1750', *Ec.H.R.*, 2nd ser., 35 (1982), pp. 202–3.
15 1 Edward VI c. 12.
16 *Supra*, pp. 55–60.

the repressinge or avoydinge of Horsestealinge as was expected'. Indeed, the suggestion was that the situation had deterioratd since 'through most Counties of this Realme Horstealinge is growen so common as neither in Pastures or Closes nor hardlie in Stables the same are to be in safety from stealinge'. Apart from the need for vouchers who should 'trulie knowe' the seller, the Act provided that accessories were to become liable to the full rigours of the law by being deprived of all rights of clergy.

Professor Cockburn has used the indictment files of the Home Circuit to pinpoint three surges in property offences during the reign of Elizabeth, one of which occurred in the years 1585–7, and this may account for the timing of the Act.[17] Moreover, 1588 was the year of the Armada and naturally the government would have been worried about any increase in horse stealing, particularly in the South-east. In Essex, Kent and Surrey, the counties with the best documentation, the number of cases certainly rose in 1586, especially in Surrey, although the general trend becomes clearer the following year. 1588 was an even worse year in Kent, the most sensitive area, and allowing for looseness in the dating of offences noted by Professor Cockburn, and the more general limitations of the source, there were probably more thefts in the county that year than in any other one in the period.[18] It was also a poor year in Essex but only a slightly inferior one in Surrey.

The effectiveness of the Act is more difficult to assess, especially as the results can be read both ways. A decline in the number of prosecutions from 1589 onwards could indicate its deterrent effect, whereas a larger number of cases could also suggest the greater ease with which horse thieves were discovered. In Essex the number of indictments rose sharply, although they fell off the following year and fluctuated at a lower level until 1596. In Kent the information obtained from the one surviving file implies a continuation of the trend from the previous year. Only in Surrey did the figures fall and here too there was a marked increase in 1590.

Whatever the intentions of the Act, in practice its terms must have been difficult to administer. It was almost impossible to restrict sales to known persons or to those with 'respectable' vouchers, however assessed, and officials inevitably had to rely upon trust. These were shortcomings which could be exploited by horse stealers. In a case involving a gang of thieves who wanted to dispose of some stolen horses at Aylesbury and Leighton Buzzard fairs in 1683, John Holtham in his examination stated that the reason he sometimes went by the name of Cooke was due to the fact that his mother had married again to a man of that name. His accomplice, Thomas Randall of Braughing (Herts.), had entered his name as James

17 Cockburn, *Crime*, pp. 67–9.   18 Cockburn, 'Assize Records', pp. 225–6.

Ward when he stood as voucher for Holtham at Leighton Buzzard Fair, but confessed that he could give no reason for having done so.[19] Vouchers were found by chance too, and if this did not matter to people trying to sell a stolen horse, it was worrying for potential buyers of it. When Thomas Crumock of Fewston in the Forest of Knaresborough sold a mare at New Malton in 1652, he induced Richard Calvert of Shipton to be his guarantor, having by chance met him at the market. Calvert then persuaded Henry Hodgson of Cornbrough, a stranger to both himself and Crumock, to be the other voucher.[20]

It would be wrong however to assume that the measures had no effect, for the records of Quarter Sessions and Assizes are full of cases of horse stealers caught by their inability to find vouchers. Whether the Act had a deterrect effect one will never know, although on one occasion at least it clearly influenced a thief's actions. In 1598 Richard Brinley of Leekfrith (Staffs.) confessed that he had stolen a horse which he had then ridden to Market Drayton (Shrops.) to sell. On being told that he could not sell it without a voucher, he turned round with the intention of returning the animal. Unfortunately, he succumbed to temptation on the way and tried to sell it at Almington where he was arrested.[21]

In toll books unguaranteed transactions, if recorded, can be seen in cancelled entries and an occasional explanatory note. When John New the younger of Worfield (Shrops.) sold a filly at Bridgnorth in 1655, the sale was made void when he did not produce any vouchers. At the same fair in 1692, an exchange of horses was held up until one of the parties brought good vouchers. The casualness with which some vouchers were found at markets and fairs makes it unwise to assume that all such sellers were thieves, but it did make people wary of dealing with them and inevitably aroused suspicion. In 1675 at Bury St Edmunds, John Brand, a labourer, tried to sell a mare to Thomas Smith, a brewer in the town. Smith refused and the animal was then offered to Thomas Norman, in whose house the negotiations were taking place. Norman said that 'if he ded cum honestly by hir he would swap with him' but although Brand promised to get someone to vouch for him, he did not return. Suspicion often led to arrest. At Thirsk in 1649 Richard Thwaites was approached in the market place by a butcher from York who asked his opinion of a man who had offered him a horse without a voucher. After being shown the man and the horse, Thwaites arrested him and set out for York Castle with him.[22]

19 Beds. R.O., HSA 1684 W82–6.
20 ASSI 45/4/2/6–8.
21 S. A. H. Burne, ed., 'Staffordshire Q.S. Rolls, IV, 1598–1602', *Staff(ord)s(shire) Hist(orical) Coll(ectio)ns* (1935), p. 148.
22 West Suffolk R.O., Bury St Emunds Borough Records, D8/1/1; ASSI 45/3/1/6.

The toll book and voucher system also provided a record of transactions against which the statements of suspects could be checked. In 1700 Thomas Collins of Dinchope (Shrops.) stated that he had bought a certain mare off William Shipman at Bridgnorth Fair on 22 July 1699. A search of the toll books of all the fairs held there in 1699 and early 1700 however fails to reveal the name of either Collins or his mistress, on behalf of whom he said he had bought the animal. The seller, on the other hand, was a real person who lived at Bridgnorth and who sold two horses there during this period. This is the only example I have been able to check in the records but it was a procedure that was regularly carried out. In 1664, for instance, James Langram of Cowbrow (Westmorland) was arrested whilst riding a horse that had been stolen from James Simpson of Ripley (W.R.Y.). Langram claimed to have bought it at Northallerton Fair, but when Simpson looked at the toll book, he found that nothing resembling it had been tolled for.[23]

Entries in the toll books detailing age, colour, pace and distinguishing marks made it easier for owners to locate their stolen horses. In 1678 William Nunnes of Street Houses came to Malton to see if two little grey nags he had lost had been entered in the book. Finding the description of one of them there, he managed to locate it in the hands of Thomas Hobson of Cropton.[24] Whilst travelling around looking for evidence of their stolen horses, owners also had the theft publicly announced ('cried') at various markets and fairs in the vicinity, together with a description of animals taken. This procedure did work too. On 7 December 1677 George Stockdale of Weston had a mare stolen and hearing no news from his neighbours, had it cried at Beverly, Weeton, Pocklington and other market towns in the area. Eventually, on 25 January 1678, Thomas Halliday of Warter came to him, saying that he had seen such a horse. Having been given the details, Stockdale went along to look at it and recognised it as his own. On one occasion a thief was caught trying to sell a horse that had already been cried at the fair. In March 1669 William Cornforth, a carrier, brought a note to the toll booth on the Tyne bridge at Newcastle, describing a horse that had been stolen from Mr Ralph Crathorne of Crathorne (N.R.Y.). A short time afterwards John Best brought it to be entered in the toll book, having exchanged it for another horse. As it appeared to be the one stolen, he was arrested and put in prison.[25]

In the late seventeenth century, details of stolen horses also began to appear in newspapers such as the *London Gazette*, although the coverage given was a restricted one both in terms of the parts of the country from

23 ASSI 45/7/1/134.   24 ASSI 45/12/2/124.
25 ASSI 45/12/3/27; ASSI 45/9/2/11.

which they were stolen and in the social classes of the people who placed the advertisements. In 1685, 133 horses were listed in the *Gazette*, and of the 131 usable entries two-thirds had been taken from London and the south-eastern counties. Less is known of the social/occupational status of the 108 individuals who had lost the animals, but significantly in the 39 instances where it was given, 36 belonged to the upper classes. Only three tradesmen – a tanner, butcher and horse courser – were included and of these the tanner was also called 'Mr'. Most of the horses were either geldings (64) or mares (40) and seem in general to have been saddle mounts, although references to coach and cart-horses, to Punches and to strong horses indicate the inclusion of draught animals. Over one-half of the horses (55.6 per cent) were between fourteen and fifteen hands in height and of the others those of at least fifteen hands were slightly more numerous (23.4 per cent) than those under fourteen hands. Details of the horses were given in the advertisements and rewards, normally at least £1, were offered as an added inducement for the return of the animal.[26]

Thieves tried to get round the problem of identification by changing the features of the horses, cutting manes and tails, obliterating or painting on blazes and stockings or altering the ear marks. In 1696 a Bristol woman, arrested in Gloucestershire, deposed that she had been urged on by William Lynch who had promised to teach her how to obliterate and change marks on horses. Such practices were commonplace. Valentine Harrison, a dishonest alehouse keeper from Lower Bentley (Worcs.), was arrested in the summer of 1605 whilst 'trimming' and 'marking' a horse in the forest. In 1647, when Richard Dorrey of Buckfastleigh (Devon) went one morning to fetch his nag out of the close where it had been grazing, he found nothing more than parts of its ears, mane and tail lying in a pool of blood on the ground.[27]

To avoid detection it was also common practice for thieves to dispose of horses at a distance. Indeed, to overcome this abuse was one of the aims of the 1589 Act. Horse stealing had become widespread, the preamble stated, because of 'the redye buyinge of the same by Horscorsers and others in some open Fayres or Markettes farr distant from the Owner, and with suche speede as the Owner cannot by pursuyte possible helpe the same'. The Act did not eliminate it however, and in a general survey of the depositions of the Northern Circuit and the Palatine jurisdictions of Lancaster and Chester from 1640 to 1699, nearly one-half of the horses had either been sold or taken in the custody of the suspect at places over 25

26 *London Gazette* 1685.
27 J. A. Sharpe, *Crime in Early Modern England 1550–1750* (1984), p. 106; P. F. W. Large, 'Economic and social Change in North Worcestershire', unpublished Oxford University DPhil Thesis (1980), p. 97; East Devon R.O., QSB/Box 55, Epiphany 1647/8.

miles away from the scene of the crime. Only one horse in eight was found within six miles of the theft. In a case heard in the Palatine court of Lancaster in 1696, William Dawson, a nailor from Overhilton (Ches.) deposed that he had been offered a horse at a cheap rate if he would 'Engage to take the . . . Nagg farre Enough of their Habitacions and Sell him'. Later, when he had bought it, he was pressed 'not to offer to Sell the . . . Nagg at any place neare home'. Dawson left the same evening and travelling north, passed through Preston and Lancaster before stopping the night at Kirkby Lonsdale. The following day at a place beyond Kendal he met a man he said was a distant relative of his, although he did not know his name, and sold him the nag for 45s.[28]

Almost two-thirds of the horses were taken to another county or riding. In Yorkshire, horses from the West Riding were more likely to cross the Pennines, although some came from further afield. In general, however, a north–south flow of traffic can be discerned with horses from the North Riding, for instance, being driven southwards over the wolds or northwards into Durham or Northumberland. Elsewhere in the region a similar pattern persisted, except in Lancashire where a significant number of horses were disposed of in the West Riding. In the far north, horses crossed the Scottish Border too. In 1691 George Hayrop of Newcastle-upon-Tyne was accused of stealing a mare near the town of Martinmas and of going straight up to Scotland with it.[29] Thieves thus tended to operate along the main lines of communication, reflecting, on the one hand, the desire to move booty from one area to another as quickly as possible, and on the other the involvement of travellers passing through, whose thefts were often of an opportunistic nature.[30] The flow of horses across the Pennines appears in part to have been due to the volume of traffic moving between Lancashire and the West Riding, especially to the respective textile areas. Others were brought over by 'professional' groups of thieves like the one operating in the Bewcastle area (Cumb.) who in the early eighteenth century were stealing horses in Yorkshire and Durham as well as in Westmorland. After being collected together at Bewcastle horses were taken up to Scotland for disposal.[31]

Thieves mingled with reputable dealers at many markets and fairs around the country. In Yorkshire the depositions record the use of over 30 centres spread throughout the three ridings and the choice of a particular outlet was clearly influenced in some instances by the availability of the fair. On 15 May 1676 Chris Wilson of Etton (E.R.Y.) found that one of his

28 P.L., 27/2 part 1.
29 ASSI 45/4/3/62.
30 *Infra*, pp. 119,131.
31 North Yorks R.O., DC/RMB, 3/3–4.

mares had been stolen during the night. As he knew of a fair being held at York, some 28 miles away that day, he travelled to the city and discovered that his horse had been sold there an hour earlier.[32] Even fairs selling high quality stock such as those at Ripon and Malton in Yorkshire or those at Penkridge and Ashbourne elsewhere in the country had a certain amount of illicit traffic too.[33] There, honest traders were joined by a more undesirable element, attracted by the large gathering of people and the prospect of easy pickings. At Malton, the uncertainty of the date of its celebrated September Fair meant that all through the month many vagrants, travellers and foreigners arrived in the area and menaced the lives of the local inhabitants. In 1661 the local magistrates attempted to alleviate the problem by setting severe penalties on those who came to town or who entertained horse sellers before 20 September.[34]

London was a favourite outlet, attracting thieves because of its size and anonymity. The scale and variety of the capital's demands brought in traders from all over the country and a strange face was, as a result, less noteworthy. Some of the thieves had travelled a considerable distance. In 1606 two men from the Welsh Border took a gelding and a mare down to the Smithfield to be sold, standing voucher for one another there, and giving false names and addresses. In 1684 two others who had stolen a couple of mares in Lancashire, were arrested in Liverpool as they were about to embark on a boat for Ireland. Confessing to the crime, one of the men, Anthony Whitfield, stated that the horses had been ridden straight down to London and sold at the Smithfield.[35] Horse stealers from Surrey and other neighbouring counties disposed of stock in the capital too but some, perhaps mindful of the need to put distance between them and the scene of their crime, moved horses the other way. The Welsh Border–West Midlands region seems to have been a popular destination, possibly because of its communications' links with the South-east and because of the number of horse fairs held there. In 1536 one Fuller of the Bell at Croydon was said to be a receiver of stolen horses which he took up to Bewdley (Worcs.) to be sold. Similarly, John Donne (alias Appowell) and his 'fellow', Walter, accused of stealing five geldings from Otford Park (Kent) were on their way to Wales with them when they were arrested at Dudley (Worcs.).[36] Donne was possibly of Welsh extraction and this

32 ASSI 45/11/3/112.
33 ASSI 45/4/1/66; ASSI 45/4/2/8; ASSI 45/6/3/113; ASSI 45/10/1/108–111; ASSI 45/12/2/123; ASSI 45/17/4/37; Staffs. R.O., 1287/10/2, fos. 184, 188, 192a–b, 196, 200.
34 C. Atkinson, ed., 'Quarter Sessions Records', *North Riding Record Society*, 6 (1888), p. 35.
35 Shrewsbury Corpn. Records, 2214; P.L., 27/1.
36 J. M. Beattie, *Crime and the Courts in England 1660–1800* (Oxford, 1986), p. 169; L. & P. Henry VIII, Addenda, I, i, p. 401.

suggests one factor determining the direction in which thieves took their booty. In 1680 Timothy Sweeting of Spalding (Lincs.) was suspected of having stolen a horse belonging to John Burton, who lived in the same parish. Hearing that Sweeting had been born near Thirsk (N.R.Y.), Burton had a hue and cry sent there and before long was informed that he had been arrested in the town.[37]

One or two fairs, apart from Smithfield, had a certain notoriety and therefore attracted thieves. The Cold Fair held at Newport (Beds.) was well known as a centre for horse dealing and horse stealing, and at the Holyrood Fair at Durrest near Tewkesbury a thieves' market was organised every night at which anything could be bought, from a stallion to a pair of shoes. At dawn the stolen goods disappeared and more honest business was conducted. At Adwalton near Bradford the fortnightly markets were informal and unlicensed until 1577 when John Brooke, on whose land they took place, was granted a charter. As has already been shown, it attracted people from a wide area and without regulation it was difficult to control.

But by reason that hitherto these markets and fairs had been there held without right and that goods and chattels are sold and bought without knowledge and goods and chattels dishonestly acquired were brought on the several days to ... Adwalton and thieves and robbers thereof escaped in safety to the great loss of our subjects' goods and not a little to the injury of the State ...

At Carlisle in the early seventeenth century an irregular gathering took place on Kingmoor, to the north of the regulated fair on Carlisle Sands, but in 1625 the authorities, worried by the opportunities for abuse which the fair offered, closed it down and ordered the dealers to trade on the Sands.[38]

By travelling some distance the thief might hope to break through the circle of fairs at which the theft was proclaimed and also make it more difficult for the owner to locate the sale in a toll book. A more pressing reason however was to try to shake off his pursuers. In 1584 two geldings were stolen from a stable in Shrewsbury and within two hours parties were riding off in a number of directions, unfortunately without success.[39] Owners with their servants and friends often went to great pains to regain their horses, an indication of the value and the importance placed upon the animal. In 1695 John Crowfoot, an innkeeper at Blyford (Suffolk), had two mares stolen from his stable and 'rode Severall Hundred Miles in

37 ASSI 45/12/4/123.
38 G. Salgado, *The Elizabethan Underworld* (New Jersey, 1977), p. 67; W. Robertshaw, 'Notes on Adwalton Fair', *Bradford Antiquary*, N.S., 5 (1927), p. 53; R. S. Ferguson and W. Nanson, eds., 'Some Municipal Records of the City of Carlisle', *C.W.A.A.S.*, extra ser., 4 (1887), p. 281.
39 W. A. Leighton, 'Early Chronicles of Shrewsbury', *T.S.A.S.*, 3 (1880), p. 300.

Search of them'. They were eventually found at Ludlow in Shropshire.[40] Sometimes the depositions give details of the chase. In 1690 Robert Mallaber of Thorngrafton (Northumb.) had a horse taken from his stable and followed the suspect, William Middleton, from Hexham, through Richmond, Grinton in Swaledale and Middleton in Teesdale before finding him on the moors at Allenheads (Northumb.). After taking him to the house of John Whitesmith of Coalclengh, he asked after the horse and located it in the hands of William Nicholson who lived near Eastgate in Weardale. Mallaber thus made a round journey of over one hundred miles to catch the thief and recover the horse. Ironically it may have been easier to follow thieves in such wild and desolated areas because of the limited options open to them and because a stranger passing through would have been all the more remarkable. Similarly in marsh and fen-country where the routeways converged on ferries, thieves could be pursued more effectively. In 1641 Robert Whittingham of Stainton (Lincs.) lost a grey mare from his grounds and sent his servant, John Farmery, to look for it, telling him to keep special watch on the ferries. At Kinnold ferry over the Trent he was informed that a man riding on a grey nag and leading a mare such as the one he was seeking, had crossed over. At Sandtoft he picked up the trail again but then heard no more of him until he came to Rawcliffe ferry. Learning there that the suspect had led the mare over, he pursued him to Langrick ferry where a number of people, including the ferryman, told him that the man had passed that way. Farmery went over and rode to Barmby on the Marsh where he left a description of the man and the horses. He continued on to Howden but in the meantime the inhabitants of Barmby had arrested a person they believed to be the one sought. They sent word to Farmery at Howden who returned and recognised his master's horse in the hands of the suspect.[41]

Away from the area of the theft the crime may have been unknown but thieves still faced checks on their activities, both institutional and of a more informal kind. Strangers were bound to be treated with more suspicion and therefore had to give a better account of themselves by providing proper vouchers and firmer evidence of their ownership. In 1667 at Leathley near Otley (W.R.Y.), two strangers were arrested as suspicious persons and 'finding the . . . persons in seuerall tales' they were thought to have stolen the horses they rode upon. In 1677 a Hertfordshire man and his wife, obliged to answer charges of stealing three horses and quantities of cloth, gave themselves away by their contradictory and unlikely stories.[42] Back at home suspicion fell upon those persons who had

40 West Suffolk R.O., P516, transcript made by Peter Christie of P.R.O., ASSI 15/59/6. I am grateful to Peter Christie for this reference.
41 ASSI 45/15/4/73; ASSI 45/7/2/131.   42 ASSI 45/8/2/63; ASSI 45/12/1/28.

disappeared shortly after a theft had taken place. In 1626 John Keate, the constable of Ramsbury (Wilts.), had a black mare stolen from his stable and suspected Robert Fisher, a local butcher, of the offence, as he had been away for a few days. In 1649 Christopher Stephenson of Rossington (W.R.Y.) was accused of stealing nine mares, colts and foals belonging to John Gresham off Hesley Common (Notts.). The reason for his suspicion, Gresham said, was the fact that Stephenson had been seen among the horses two days before the theft and had not been heard of since.[43]

There were other signs which aroused people's suspicions too. Many horses seem to have been 'windfall acquisitions' and were thus offered at bargain prices. A Star Chamber case in the reign of Elizabeth reveals that Davie Cadwallader the elder was tried for stealing a bay filly worth £4 from Cletterwood (Montgs.) which he sold shortly afterwards at Dudley for £1. 10s. 'muche vnder the price she was worthe'. In 1627 Robert Bisley, a horse courser from White Cross Street, London, refused to do business with a man whom he met at an inn in Potterne (Wilts.) when he found that he could not obtain any vouchers and moreover did not care what he had for the horse 'soe he might Finger some money'. Later that year in a case heard in the East Riding, James Greenleaf, gent., deposed that as constable he had been told by some of his neighbours that Adam Mellor had offered to sell a mare 'at so lowe a price as did giue great Suspition that the Mayre was stolne'.[44] An associated factor was the quality of the animal. When in 1664 Tristram Taylor of Austwick was approached by a stranger, he wondered how he had come by such a good horse 'beeinge Stoned could bee noe lesse worth then tenn pounds'. He did not believe the story told him, adding that the man had put up his horse at outhouses and had avoided towns. In 1685 two Cheddar men, Thomas and Valentine Kerton, came under suspicion of stealing a horse 14½ hands high and worth between £8 and £10. One of the brothers had been seen riding the animal over the Mendips and the witness remarked that as neither of them could have been the owner of so good a horse, it must have been stolen.[45]

'Professional' thieves on foot may have taken riding tack around with them to use if the opportunity presented itself, but lack of such foresight caught others out. In 1595 Richard White of Prescott (Lancs.) was taken, riding a horse without a saddle or shoes. A century later, in 1686, a young man at an alehouse in Ribchester (Lancs.) aroused suspicion when he arrived on a gelding without a saddle but with a very new bridle. When John Jones stopped at Overton (Ches.) in 1680 he had a saddle on his horse but it had been tied on with rope. In 1663 the saddle of William Baker of

43 Wilts. R.O., Q.S. Mich. 1626; ASSI 45/3/1/191.
44 P.R.O., STAC 5/C54/17; Wilts. R.O., Q.S. Hil. 1628; ASSI 45/11/2168.
45 ASSI 45/7/1/147; Somerset R.O., Q/SR 1685 163/1.

Holbeck (Lincs.) was 'only a wispte of straw', whilst that of Thomas Lyley, a clothier from Liversedge (W.R.Y.), consisted of bracken taken out of the forest.[46]

When confronted, some thieves refused to offer an explanation or tried to bluster their way out of trouble. In 1647 John Ingleby (alias Howe) stated that he had not attempted to clear himself as he had bought the horse he was accused of stealing and did not therefore have to account for it.[47] Normally however an explanation of sorts was given and examination after examination reveals variations on a few basic themes. The most popular excuse was the one made by John Owen of Myddle (Shrops.) and which was reported by Richard Gough in his history of the parish. Owen, he wrote, 'confessed that the horse was his, and made that idle excuse which every silly theife will doe, that he bought him of a stranger upon the roade'. Numerous examples appear in the records. In 1579 Richard Blakeway of Cronkhill (Shrops.) had to account for six horses that had at one time or another passed through his hands. Three of them, he said, had been acquired off strangers, two of whom he had met on the road, and none of them had been tolled or vouched for. In 1647 Samuel Shaw of Brampton Bierlow (W.R.Y.), asked for details of a mouse-coloured mare, replied that he had bought it in Barnsley at an unknown house, off a stranger whose name and address he did not know. The following day he sold the animal to a man he met on the road about four miles beyond Brampton but once again did not know his name or where he lived.[48]

Explanations which even sounded unlikely were put forward. Horses, for instance, regularly 'adopted' people. In 1689 John West of Birstall insisted that after he had bought a stallion at Everingham

Hee was followed by a Mare, which Hee Endeavoured to beat back from Him, but could by noe Means doe it, nor could Hee ryde from Her, shee still following, in soe much that at last the Mare was the occasion that the Horse threw Him . . . vpon the Ground, rann from Him soe that Hee lost the . . . Hors.

John Taylor of St Botolph's, Aldersgate, stretched credulity even further with the story he told at the Bedfordshire Assize in summer 1678. He had been in Smithfield, he said, negotiating the purchase of a mare off Humphrey Blackwall but they had not been able to come to terms. Finally Taylor agreed to pay £3. 2s. 6d. if he could have a ride to see if he liked it. Leaving 6d. as an earnest, he rode the mare one-half mile out of town to show it to a friend but when he returned Blackwall had disappeared. He therefore rode the horse to Dunstable where he sold it in the fair for £2.

46 CHES 38/43; P.L. P.L. 27/1; CHES 38/41 part 2; ASSI 45/6/3/1; ASSI 45/11/3/33.
47 ASSI 45/2/1/147.
48 Gough, Parish of Myddle, p. 92; Shrewsbury Corpn. Records, 2207; ASSI 45/11/1/140.

Even if involvement were admitted, the suspect often claimed that the horse had only been borrowed or that the instigator was someone else. One case heard at Appleby in 1660 not only neatly combined the two but brought in the supernatural as well. Needing to be at market early in the morning, Miles Atkinson took a mare out of a close at Gathorne, 'mou'd by the instigation of the Divell,' as he said. He took it, he asserted, 'not in any felonious intent but to restore her againe within a weeke'.[49]

SCALE OF OPERATIONS

Involvement in horse stealing, as in property crime in general, varied in scale and intensity from individual to individual. Many instances came into the category of impulsive, unpremeditated crime carried out because the opportunity presented itself. Numerous unattended horses were taken off commons or out of fields and closes by people passing through. Some riders with tired nags or people without a mount of their own utilised whatever they could find to help them on their way. On occasions there may have been no intention to steal the animal but apart from the risk of arrest before it was returned, many were abandoned either through fear of discovery or through laziness. In 1632 two teenagers from Brixham (Devon), ordered by their master to fetch the bullocks from the moor, took a mare they found on the highway 'the way beinge farr and foule and they weary, itt being also a rainy day'. They rode it some distance then left it on the road, not intending, as they said, to steal it.[50] Other horses, similarly found, were clearly taken to be sold. In 1681 William Wigham confessed that he had taken a bay galloway off the common near Newbrough and then, as a result of the theft, had stolen a saddle from an outhouse near Grindon Rigg between Newbrough and Carlisle. Later he exchanged the horse with the servant of Mr Bowie, the minister of Crosby, receiving 14s. to boot.[51]

Many individuals of course were on the look-out for horses to steal. As Harrison noted of serving men (although the practice was more widespread) they 'walke vp and downe in gentlemens and rich farmers pastures, there to see and view which horsses feed best, whereby they manie times get something, although with hard aduenture'. There were those, he wrote, who had confessed on the gallows to have had 40, 50 or 60 stolen horses hidden away in various parts of the country. Francis Hetherington, for instance, was a notorious outlaw and just before his

49 ASSI 45/15/3/121; Beds. R.O. HSA 1678 S74; ASSI 45/5/7/4–5.
50 East Devon R.O., Q/SB Box 42, Mich. 1632.
51 ASSI 45/13/1/139.

execution at the Assize held at York in 1617 acknowledged the theft of over 100 horses.[52] Such wide claims, which may have been magnified by bravado, rumour or malicious intent, are difficult to verify, although on the other hand, as the evidence heard at criminal trials was concerned solely with the offence or offences at issue and not with the accused's criminal history, the picture given is often a partial one.

This problem also makes it difficult to find out precise details about gangs involved in horse stealing, since apart from the lack of information on accomplices only one or two members may have been involved in the particular incident. Nonetheless, some idea of their composition can be pieced together using such documents as the depositions. Some of the gangs may have been ephemeral groupings, perhaps brought together for a single enterprise. Even the more 'permanent' gangs tended to be fluid in their composition, often loosely organised around a nucleus of central figures. Personnel were drawn in as the need arose or according to the particular crime being contemplated and at times links were established with other criminal groups. Also associated with the gang were a number of accessories – people who kept safe houses or who acted as messengers, informers or receivers – and their support was vital to the principals. In 1618 Lord William Howard described John Armstrong (alias Gowdie) of Bewcastle (Cumb.) as 'a notorious theefe and a great receitor of theeves, which is more pernitious to the countrey then to be a theefe'.[53] Alan MacFarlane has identified fourteen main characters who were involved with the Smorthwait gang of Westmorland in one capacity or another, but in the text he refers to others too. Only a handful ever went out on an operation however, and the participants varied according to the particular crime. The burglary of Robert Robinson's house at Old Hutton in 1680 was carried out by six men, including William and Henry Smorthwait, William Manning and Edward Bainbridge. When in 1684 William Beeby, a drover, was robbed on the highway by Whinfell Park Side three men were in the party, Edward Bradrick, Richard Hugginson and William Smorthwait. Edward Bradrick was far more active as a highwayman than the Westmorland gang and from his house in Leeds, his exploits took him all over the North. Apart from his implication with others of the Smorthwait gang in at least three of the four instances of horse stealing, he also acquired other horses on his own account. On one occasion, on 4 November 1682, he, together with William Crossland and Robert Taylor, took out of a close a gelding belonging to Richard Lumley of Leeds. Later

---

52 *Harrison's Description*, II, p. 230; G. Ornsby, 'Household Books of Lord William Howard of Naworth Castle', *Surtees Society*, 68 (1878), p. 444.
53 Ornsby, 'Lord William Howard', p. 439.

in the same night they stole from another close near Leeds a gelding belonging to Joseph Sykes and a mare of Robert Gowlands. The clipping and counterfeiting activities of William Smorthwait brought him into contact with another criminal group and one moreover whose network covered the North and even extended down to London.[54] Another group in the 1690s, who appear to have been more closely involved in horse stealing, were based in Yorkshire but carried out thefts in Nottinghamshire and Lincolnshire as well. They disposed of some stock at Ripon and Knaresborough but took others up to Scotland, on one trip north returning home via Lancashire and Craven. According to the information contained in the various depositions, about a dozen men belonged to the gang and this figure is confirmed by the statement of Edward Sheepshanks who tried to turn King's evidence after the ring had been broken up in the winter of 1698–9. Members of the group went out in twos and threes to steal horses, bringing them back to John Hutton who appears to have been the leader.[55]

John Hutton was a blind man, living at Stoney Houghton (Derbys.), and apart from organising the gang's activities, was responsible for disposing of the booty. One victim, perhaps with a certain amount of malicious exaggeration, deposed that he had heard that Hutton 'had sold one Hundred Horses at least in his time and none of them his owne'. Edward Sheepshanks stated that on one occasion Thomas Armstrong and Peter and Joseph Hardcastle had brought him two mares and a gelding that they had stolen. These horses were taken to Ripon Fair to be sold and it was there that Hutton was arrested. For the Smorthwaits a number of people helped them to dispose of their goods, including alehouse keepers such as Brian Thompson of Kirkby Lonsdale and Isabel Taylor of Clapham. Bradrick deposed that 'Isabel Taylor of Eldroth Lane near Clapham in Yorkshire mother of John and William Taylor, keeping a tippling or alehouse hath several times resetted goods and other things which she hath known to be stolen'. Associated with the Bewcastle group were John Story of Bewcastle, John Armstrong of Woodhead and Edward Noble of Crew who acted as their receivers, sheltering the thieves and the stolen goods, and sharing in the proceeds.[56]

The activities of a gang of horse thieves working between Shrewsbury and Warrington is known in some detail because of an examination taken of John Norman, aged nineteen, who acted as a spy (see Appendix 9).

54 A. Macfarlane, *The Justice and the Mare's Ale* (Oxford, 1981), pp. xi–xii, 48–60, 137–140, 147–8.
55 ASSI 45/17/2/51; ASSI 45/17/4/6.
56 ASSI 45/17/4/3; ASSI 45/17/4/37; Macfarlane, *The Justice . . .*, p. 154; North Yorks. R.O., DC/RMB 3/3–4.

When the ringleaders, the Harrisons, met him he had been sleeping in the barn of an alehouse at Acton Bridge near Weaverham (Ches.). They found out that he begged for a living but commented that 'if he would goe with them hee should never need to begge again'. A week later, having established him at Richard Baker's inn at Weaverham, they persuaded him 'to take notice as hee went about the Contrey where likly horses were that they would come and steale them'. Norman appears to have moved between a number of safe houses. Apart from Richard Baker's he stayed at widow Fletcher's; an alehouse in Cuddington in Weaverham; the Red Lion at Over; Thomas Fluitt's house in Warrington; an alehouse in Bickerton; High Wickstead's house in Bell o'the Hill, Malpas; and an alehouse in Whitchurch (see Map 5). Some of the occupants of these places, at least, seem to have known what was going on:

... hee [Norman] verrily beleeves that Hugh Wixtid & his wife & Children doe verry well Know & perfectly understand the sayd Thomas Harrison & Richard Harrison what & whence they are & have been long privy & had Knowledge of their wayes & courses in Horse stealing ... and ... Thomas Harrison haveing declared to this Examinant great confidence which hee put in Hugh Wixtid.

The gang had been operating in Lancashire and the Welsh Border for six years, moving between Warrington and Shrewsbury, selling at each town horses stolen in the area around the other. At the Warrington end of the business, Thomas Fluitt the elder acted as 'receivour and disposer of all such Horses as sayd Harrisons or his marrowes did bring to him'. Thomas Fluitt's son, Thomas junior, lived at the Black Dragon in Shrewsbury and he 'did use to receive all such horses as the sayd Harrisons or his Marrowes had stolen in the Contreys about Warrington'.[57]

It is interesting to note the role that alehouse keepers played in criminal activity, especially as accessories and receivers. As Dr Clark has noted, 'there was a broad consensus of opinion among the middling and (to some extent) the upper ranks of society in Tudor and early Stuart England that alehouses were a new and increasingly dangerous force in popular society'. At the bottom of the victualling hierarchy, they provided a range of services for the poor and it is hardly surprising that contemporaries viewed their proliferation with alarm. Apart from their regular local clientele of small craftsmen, journeymen, husbandmen and labourers, they also attracted poor and rootless migrants, 'men of questionable status, at best tolerated, quite often disliked by local residents'.[58] This attitude is reflected in the volume of petitions to Justices of the Peace to reduce them in

57 CHES 38/41 part 2.
58 P. Clark, 'The Alehouse and the Alternative Society', in D. Pennington and K. Thomas, eds., *Puritans and Revolutionaries* (Oxford, 1978), pp. 48, 68.

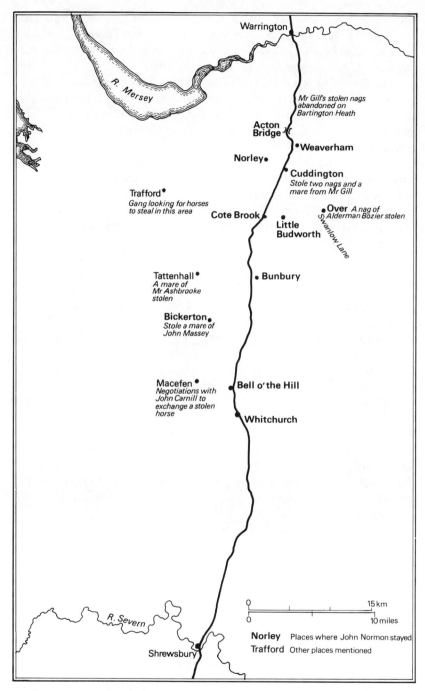

5 Places associated with the activities of the Harrison Gang and their relationship with the main road between Shrewsbury and Warrington

number or to suppress particularly notorious establishments. In 1691, for instance, the Justices at Shrewsbury were told by Thomas Dawes, a minister, that he had received many complaints about one of his parishioners, Eleanor Hanton, who kept a disorderly alehouse. She seldom came to church, he reported, and on Sundays as he walked past her house, he had often seen 'many idle People a tipling' there. Her malicious gossiping moreover caused continual disturbance among her neighbours and like her husband, 'a Man of no very good Character', she was clearly unfit to carry on her trade.[59]

Even allowing for the natural tendency towards exaggeration, numerous suspect alehouses undoubtedly existed. The proprietors tended to come from the same social classes as their customers and, subject to identical social and economic pressures, were often drawn into some form of illicit activity. Many were located in the suburbs of towns or in the new and expanding squatter settlements in forests and heaths, where the absence of close supervision and the preponderance of poor people caused particular concern. The waste of Slimbridge in 1639 was said to have attracted many poor people from outside and thus overburdened the township with 'beggarly cottages ... and alehouses and idle persons'. In the Forest of Feckenham, hamlets grew up on Webheath and Bentley Common in a remote corner of Tardebigg parish, consisting of people with no rights of common but who looked to the forest for a living. Here at Lower Bentley, Thomas and Valentine Harrison kept a 'peltering' alehouse where they maintained 'many disorderly persons' and were themselves engaged in deer poaching and horse stealing. In Somerset, in a case heard in 1607, William Norman of the Exmoor parish of Winsford deposed that he had seen Christopher Norman at James Pearce's house deep in conversation with three suspicious strangers immediately before he had stolen a horse from the vicar of Bishop's Monkton. According to the witness, Pearce, a man of very evil behaviour, kept a suspicious and dangerous tippling house in the parish and had entertained rogues, runnagates and thieves there for thirty years.[60]

Detailed studies of parishes as diverse as Myddle (Shrops.) and Terling (Essex) have shown how widespread was the problem of drunkenness in the early modern period, and only a proportion of people who frequented alehouses would have been involved in criminal activity.[61] Nonetheless,

59 Shrewsbury Corpn. Records, 2271.
60 Everitt, *Farm Labourers*, pp. 409–12; C. Hill, *The World turned upside down* (Harmondsworth, 1975), pp. 125–6; P. F. W. Large, 'North Worcestershire', p. 97; Somerset R.O., Q/SR 1607 2/13.
61 Hey, *Myddle*, esp. pp. 227–8; K. Wrightson and D. Levine, *Poverty and Piety in an English Village: Terling 1525–1700* (New York, 1979), pp. 134–5.

rogues and vagabonds of all kinds, including horse thieves, would inevitably have gravitated there to meet one another, to plan their operations or to dispose of their goods or merely idly to pass the time. In 1650 when John Dunn, a draper from Howden, East Riding, accused John Foster, a local labourer, of stealing a grey mare of his, he gave as his reasons

John Foster is knowne and obserued to be a Man of an Idle life, and although he hath a wife and children having little, or no meanes, (knowne to his neighbours) wherein to maintayne them, yet seldome or never setteth himself to any labour at all, but spendeth much in ale (as is reported) both at Alehouses and at his owne house.

Moreover, like many other thieves, he had an alias, and this fact clinched the matter.[62]

It is Dr Clark's conclusion that much of what did take place in alehouses was 'amateur, small-scale and sporadic'.[63] Many dubious characters did pass through, but it does not follow that their nefarious activities were connived at by the proprietors. In 1596 one of the Essex justices, Sir Thomas Lucas, even wrote to the court to testify to the good character of an alehouse keeper at Ford Street in Aldham, suspected of having dealings with a notorious horse thief. The latter implicated the alehouse keeper but this evidence, Sir Thomas urged, should be rejected as worthless. Alehouse keepers moreover were well placed to notice suspicious persons and to have them arrested. In 1686 James Halsall of Ribchester (Lancs.) called for the constable when a suspicious young man arrived at his establishment. The following year Thomas Wilson of The Griffin at Nantwich, suspecting that a traveller was riding a stolen horse, questioned him and obtained a confession. He too sent for the constable. Actions like these helped to sway influential local opinion, so necessary if alehouse keepers were to retain their licences, or to avoid suppression if they had not received one, an increasingly important consideration as the seventeenth century progressed.[64]

THE SOCIAL BACKGROUND OF HORSE STEALERS

Evidently, people viewed the activities of the members of the criminal fraternity with a mixture of concern and distaste. Suspects were often characterised as lewd and idle people, with no visible means of support, and occasionally immoral too. David Lloyd ap Owen, a Montgomeryshire

---

62 ASSI 45/3/2/62.
63 Clark, 'The Alehouse', p. 57.
64 F. G. Emmison, *Elizabethan Life and Disorder* (Chelmsford, 1970), p. 291; P.L. 27/1, CHES 38/43; Clark, 'The Alehouse', pp. 70–1.

man, in 1609 was 'a great ayder maynteyner and abbetter of fellons and hath him selfe bene once or oftener Indicted of felonye'. His confederate, Richard Keffin (alias Lloyd) of Twyford (Shrops.), moreover, was 'a man notoriously knowen in the Country where he dwelleth to be of most wicked Lewde and Infamous life and to haue liued in Adultery with seuerall women in the life of there owne husbands'. One suspect in Devon in 1628 was 'an idle and suspicious person', as was another from Pontefract in 1680. Daniel Arnold, accused of stealing a horse out of a close at Cawood (W.R.Y.) in 1656, was 'a lude person' who lived 'in a dissolute highway' and although he had no obvious source of income, rode about with pistols and kept high company. Two men aroused the suspicion of an informant in the case of a theft of a mare from Thornton fields (E.R.Y.) in 1662, 'neither of them haveinge whereon to live nor applying themselues to any labour nor are to bee seene in the day where they are knowne'.[65] In spite of a certain amount of exaggeration, designed to blacken the character of the suspect, such comments undoubtedly reflect contemporary attitudes towards those thought to be a disruptive element in local society. It is interesting therefore to examine the backgrounds of these people to see how closely they were identified with the places they committed their crimes and to consider moreover if social and economic pressures had any bearing upon their actions.

An analysis of the indictments of the Elizabethan Home Circuit quickly reveals the problems highlighted by Professor Cockburn. 'Yeomen' were also described as tailors, clothworkers, butchers, husbandmen and labourers in Essex; as labourers in Hertfordshire; as carpenters, husbandmen and labourers in Kent; and as fishmongers, ostlers and labourers in Surrey. In such instances the individuals concerned have been placed in the more precise occupational category or in the lower social one. The evidence provided by these records should not be strained too far, but it does correlate quite closely with data collected from depositions heard in the Northern Circuit from 1640 to 1699. Almost one-half of the people indicted in the South-east in Elizabeth's reign were said to be labourers (47.3 per cent), the figure, incidentally, that M. J. Ingram found for all thieves in early Stuart Wiltshire (47 per cent).[66] In the Northern depositions of the second half of the seventeenth century, labourers, servants and known vagrants accounted for 43.1 per cent of the total, by far the largest group of suspects. In a general but rather fragmentary survey of Quarter Sessions depositions for the country as a whole in the Tudor and Stuart

65 P.R.O., STAC 8/225/21 Misc. James I; East Devon R.O., Q/SB Box 37 Mich 1628; ASSI 45/12/4/52; ASSI 45/5/3/1; ASSI 45/6/3/67.
66 M. J. Ingram, 'Communities and Courts: Law and Disorder in Early-Seventeenth Century Wiltshire', in Cockburn, *Crime*, p. 130.

period, some 119 entries can be used and of these nearly two out of every five people were classed as labourers (37.8 per cent).

The next largest category comprised craftsmen and tradesmen, although in practice, in crafts which required little skill or capital, or in trades such as alehouse keeping which served the poor, there was little to distinguish them from the labourers. In the South-east in the late sixteenth century, under one-quarter of the people indicted were craftsmen or tradesmen (22.6 per cent) with county variations ranging from 14.1 per cent in Hertfordshire to 33.1 per cent in Sussex. A large number of occupations are represented, with butchers, shoemakers and tailors heading the list. The latter two crafts tended to be filled with men of comparatively humble means who may have succumbed to temptation in a crisis, but butchers could be quite wealthy men. It is possible that as many horse thieves also stole other animals, some of the 'butchers' had merely given this as their occupation in order to account for their movement of stock around the country. Conversely, as the Assize clerks occasionally seem to have confused accessories with the principals, such people may have been merely receivers of stolen goods, either wittingly or not.[67] In the Northern depositions a century later, craftsmen and tradesmen also occupied second place with almost one-third of the recorded entries. Many of the occupations represented are the ones most commonly to be found in town and country, with blacksmiths and tailors in the first two places. Some indication of the importance of the textile industry is given in the number of clothiers and weavers mentioned, together with a scattering of associated workers – dyers, fullers, fellmongers and shearmen. In the Civil War period, soldiers or men masquerading as such formed another significant group. One or two innkeepers, alehouse keepers and tapsters are mentioned in both sets of documents but hardly in the number which would lend substance to a belief in the infamy of their calling.

In the indictments a number of people in these two categories were undoubtedly vagrants, their true status being protected by the legal ruling that they could not be assigned a proscribed occupation. Depositions often imply and, on occasions, specifically state that this was the case. In the South-west one such person, John Christophers, arrested on suspicion of stealing a horse, was asked in June 1606 to give an account of his movements. A Wiltshire man, he said that he had come back from London at Michaelmas and had wandered around the country ever since. He described himself as a painter, although he had kept a barber-surgeon's shop in Smithfield, and was travelling about to find work. On May Day he had been at Wells, staying there three or four days before moving on to Sir

---

67 Cockburn, 'Assize Records', p. 222.

Thomas Thynne's house near Warminster (Longleat), where he had remained a week. After that he had spent two nights at Westbury, going on from there to Sir William Paulet's house at Edington for a fortnight's stay. In the adjoining county, the Somerset magistrates in September 1675 heard the story of William Harvey who had been a servant of the governor of the house of correction at Taunton. Since leaving his master, Harvey stated, he had not been settled in any place but had sometimes been in Wiltshire, sometimes in Somerset and sometimes at Sparkford. In Yorkshire, in a case heard at Hovingham in January 1647, the accused, John Dobson, confessed that 'he hath wandored in the moores without anie certen Cohabitation nether hath bene reteyned into anie mans service and hath soe lived a yeare and moore but ... hath often gott work in the moores at severall places'. Another suspect, William Daltry, when examined by the West Riding Justices in 1663, was described as 'a wanderinge person [who] wandereth vp and downe ye Cuntry'. In evidence given against James Hodgson in 1668, John Webster of Borrowby (N.R.Y.) spoke of him as a labourer of Borrowby but added that he was 'a person of euill fame and of no certane abode or settlement'. In 1685 when John Emott of Gisburn (W.R.Y.) had a horse stolen, he blamed the theft upon Hugh Hudson of Sutton, 'a wandering & vagrant person'. Further north, in Cumberland, John Urwin of Kingfield, examined in June 1674 about the theft of a horse, confessed that since March 'he did nothing but Run vp and downe a begging beyond Carlisle and on this side'.[68]

Of the other groups mentioned in indictments and depositions, 'yeomen' were the most numerous. It is impossible to gauge how many actually farmed land as opposed to those for whom the style was a status term, and this makes it difficult to evaluate the background of such people. However they must have been of a superior status to the labourers and to most of the craftsmen and tradesmen. In Essex in the period 1620–80, one in ten of those accused of horse stealing were styled as 'yeomen' or 'gentlemen', although in general the latter class do not appear very frequently. If they were involved, it was often in cases of highway robbery, a criminal activity which seemed to attract young gentlemen in search of an easy living. In Essex four of seven gentlemen indicted for horse stealing in Elizabeth's reign were accused of this offence and in Surrey the proportion was six out of nine. In the Smorthwait gang of the Lake District, William Smorthwait aspired to the minor gentry and had served (badly) as High Constable for the Lonsdale ward of Westmorland in 1677–8. Edward Bradrick, the Leeds highwayman, was also described in

---

68 Wilts. R.O., QS Trinity 1606; Somerset R.O., Q/SR 1675 125/22; ASSI 45/2/1/66; ASSI 45/6/3/34–6; ASSI 45 9/1/39; ASSI 45/14/2/65; ASSI 45/11/1/167.

various documents as a gentleman. A number of the other members of the group moreover were classed as yeomen. An example of someone of even higher social status is to be found in the Quarter Sessions records of the North Riding in 1675; Sir William Blakeston appeared there, charged with three others with assaulting Ralph Halliday on the highway at Black Hambleton and stealing a sorrel gelding valued at £3 from him. Significantly he possessed an alias and the addition of the charge included three different addresses in Durham, north Yorkshire and Cambridgeshire.[69]

Surprisingly, there is little evidence in the Elizabethan indictments of the Home Circuit of the involvement of workers from the local textile and iron industries in horse stealing. Of course, in the periods of crisis noted by Professor Cockburn they may have concentrated their efforts upon the theft of more immediately useful goods – meat animals, corn and other foodstuffs and clothing. This is perhaps all that one can expect when examining one aspect of a problem and it could account for the inconclusiveness of the evidence. In the first surge, that of 1572–4, horse stealing incidents increased in Essex and Surrey but not in Kent, where numbers fell far short of the cases recorded in the opening years of the reign, a troubled period in all three counties. Horse thefts rose again in the mid-1580s (1585–7), the time of the second surge, but it is difficult to disentangle this period completely from the surrounding years. The situation eased in the early 1590s (though there was some local variation) and only in 1596, with the onset of the third surge, did the figures become uniformly bad. The increase in activity at the time was clearly connected with the dreadful conditions then prevailing: the harvests of 1594–7 were terrible and, occurring one after the other, caused widespread distress. Desperate men turned to crime, and horses were obvious targets, readily available and, in spite of official action, easily disposed of.

An analysis of the Essex Quarter Sessions' and Assizes' records in the period 1620–80 indicates that the incidence of horse stealing continued to fluctuate. The greatest number of recorded cases were brought to trial in the quinquennium 1645–9 and this reflects the continuing shortage of horses caused by the Civil War.[70] Market prices were particularly high in these years and thus provided an incentive to steal. Evidence from around the country reveals that the thieves included soldiers and ex-soldiers, who may have resorted more readily to crime because of the brutalising effect of army life. Many were troops from the defeated royalist armies, young men free from the restraining influence of their home environment, with no skill

69 Macfarlane, *The Justice* . . ., pp. xi–xii; J. A. Sharpe, *Crime in Seventeenth-Century England, a County Study* (Cambridge, 1983), p. 98; C. Atkinson, 'Quarter Sessions Records', p. 25.
70 Sharpe, *Crime in Essex*, p. 93.

in any trade and with less inclination to follow one, but who were well versed in the arts of coercion and who had acquired a taste for adventure.[71]

The tendency of the Assize clerks to write down the place where the offence was committed as the residence of the suspect precludes a comparison of local with long-distance crime. Only historians with local knowledge can interpret the names on the files and make a reasoned assessment of the relationship of particular individuals with specific communities. As Dr Sharpe has noted of Kelvedon Easterford, Essex, 'perhaps all those alleged thieves who cannot be connected to the parish by any evidence other than their indictments, were drawn from the ambulatory population of vagrants, semi-vagrant migrant workers and servants in search of employment'.[72] In the North where parishes were often larger, especially on the bleak moorlands, an analysis of the more accurate depositions indicates that in the late seventeenth century one suspect in four resided in the parish in which the horse was stolen. As in the South – in Wiltshire in the early seventeenth century and in the Essex parishes of Terling (1560–1699) and Kelvedon Easterford (1600–40) – their status was low and they tended to occupy a marginal position in local society.[73] Mostly servants or labourers and often employed in a community on a casual basis for a short length of time, their situation combined maximum opportunities for theft with the minimum degree of social responsibility. Suspicion naturally fell upon them therefore, at times with good reason. In 1662 when John Piggott, a yeoman from Bolton-on-Dearne (W.R.Y.), lost a horse, he accused his servant, Anthony Sherwood, of the theft. Sherwood had left without permission on the night that the animal had been stolen and had to be brought back from Melton-on-the-Hill, over forty miles away. Sent to have the theft cried, he had run away once more and had eventually been arrested at Pontefract.[74]

Other thieves, if not resident in the parish, came from the locality and therefore would have known of any likely targets. M. J. Ingram, in his study of crime in early seventeenth century Wiltshire, has used a six mile radius as the criterion for 'neighbourliness' in this sense and this is the distance I have adopted.[75] In the North the depositions indicate that

71 C. V. Wedgwood, *The King's War 1641–1647* (1958), pp. 532–3; H. G. Tibbutt, ed., *The Letter Books of Sir Samuel Luke* (1963), pp. 317, 355, 366, 565; Bristol R.O., 04438, Deposition Book, 31 Oct. 1646; E. Devon R.O. Q/SB Box 53, Easter 1644; ASSI 45/3/1/40, 55, 166.
72 Sharpe, 'Crime and Delinquency', p. 101.
73 Ingram, 'Communities and Courts', p. 130; Wrightson and Levine, *Poverty and Piety*, p. 120; Sharpe, 'Crime and Delinquency', p. 101.
74 ASSI 45/6/2/92.
75 Ingram, 'Communities and Courts', pp. 129–30.

almost one suspect in five came from within six miles of the theft. For such thieves it was a simple matter to find suitable stock on the extensive commons of the region or to discover unattended animals in pastures and fields, especially if they were on the look-out for them. In 1650 a Morley man with some others took a horse off Batley Common (W.R.Y.) and when arrested was forty miles away in Chesterfield. Similarly, a horse stealer from Fewston in the Forest of Knaresborough had the whole of the forest to draw on for his supplies.[76] The depositions also indicate hidden connexions with particular areas. The links in a chain involving a horse taken from Thorpe in the West Riding parish of Burnsall, for instance, can be put together from the detail given of the suspect, Edward Howson, 'a person of loose carriage'. The horse was eventually found in the stable of Jacob Farrar of Warley near Halifax, the town where Howson had lived since his marriage to a local girl. Farrar had previously acquired the animal off a person who had bought it from Howson's father at Cracoe where he lived. This township, where Howson was born and where he still had family connexions, lay a mere three miles from Thorpe.[77]

There still remains a considerable number of people who were a long way from their recorded homes when they stole horses. In the North the majority of the suspects came from outside the locality (55.6 per cent) and of these almost one-half had journeyed more than 25 miles (47.1 per cent). Some, like Edward Howson, had connexions with the district in which the crime took place, but in general they must have been strangers. Many were merely passing through and comprised an assorted group of travellers – vagrants, migratory workers, soldiers and sailors, craftsmen and traders pursuing their callings, servants employed on their masters' affairs and a host of others engaged in a wide range of public and private business.[78] In 1663 John Smith, a webster from Midgley (W.R.Y.), took a horse out of a close at Hambleton over thirty miles away and rode it to Rossington Bridge. Others were travelling on personal matters, perhaps on foot or on a tired nag, and stole a horse they happened to see on the way. One such person was David Montgomery, who in 1675 confessed to stealing a horse belonging to Alderman William James of Carlisle. He had disembarked, he said, at Newcastle-upon-Tyne and had been making his way to Whitehaven to catch a ship home to Ireland when he had come across the horse.[79] Many 'professional' thieves also stole horses at a distance. London was a major attraction, offering, as it did, both anonymity and opportunity and this may account for some of the large numbers of thefts in Southwark. The busy roads leading to London would

---

76 ASSI 45/3/2/46; ASSI 45/4/2/6, 8.   77 ASSI 45/11/2/84–5.

78 *Supra*, p. 119.   79 ASSI 45/6/3/142–3; ASSI 45/11/2/182.

have stimulated horse keeping in the vicinity and this is the reason why in 1585–6 Chris Phillips stole 23 horses at Harpenden (Herts.), for although it lay some fifty miles away from his recorded residence at Hockley, Essex, it was situated near the Watling Street.[80] Gangs elsewhere in the country also travelled around looking for stock, often selected for them by a system of spies and local accomplices.

In the enquiry after a theft, suspicion naturally fell on strangers seen in the area. In 1642, when John Robinson of Norton, County Durham, had two nags and a mare stolen, he suspected William Scott (alias Armstrong) of Coddell in the parish of Guisborough together with three others, of the crime. Scott had not only been seen in company with the men who had sold three horses to John Cole of Guisborough, but had also been noticed sitting under the hedge near the ground where the horses had been stolen. In 1693 John Bostock lost a horse from his pasture at Gamston and believed it had been taken by two suspicious-looking persons seen near the close where he had put it. As today, those with 'form' often found themselves accused of any offence that had taken place. On 9 March 1672 Stephen Shepherd of Long Preston (W.R.Y.) had a horse stolen from his grounds and believed Edmund Brockden, a tailor from Slaidburn, had committed the crime. That night, it was said, some of Shepherd's neighbours coming over the moors had seen Brockden and had told others to 'looke to their horses that night for Brockden was on the Moores'. In 1695 Henry Bradley of Chipping (Lancs.) lost a mare from a close and he and his friends went to look for it, enquiring after any suspicious people in the area. After a fortnight one of his neighbours, Richard Sudell of Thornley, found out that George Simpson, 'an idle person', had been living in the area for some time.[81]

Inevitably some of the suspects were said to be horse dealers. John Edwards, who confessed at the Kent Assizes in 1590 to ten of the twelve indictments laid against him, was clearly a 'professional', but no more examples appear in the calendars of the Home circuit during Elizabeth's reign. Under James I, moreover, John Wells, a horse courser, indicted for highway robbery in Hertfordshire, remains the sole representative of the trade.[82] Admittedly, Wells was also classified as a labourer, and it is possible that others are hiding behind this generalised term. There certainly were dishonest dealers and of course their trade did give them an excellent cover for theft or receiving. In 1609 one Dorset thief claimed he had been encouraged in the crime by his accomplice, William Bartlett.

80 *Supra*, p. 36.
81 ASSI 45/1/4/47; ASSI 45/16/3/64; ASSI 45/10/1/21–2; P.L. 27/2 part 1.
82 Cockburn, *Kent Indictments*, p. 307; J. S. Cockburn, ed., *Calendar of Assize Records: Hertfordshire Indictments, James I* (1975), p. 46.

Bartlett, he maintained, had told him that as he did a considerable amount of horse dealing in the North with his father, he could sell the horse they had stolen there. In Northumberland, Christopher Bell of the Peth was accused by Lord William Howard in 1618 of being a common horse coper and a great conveyer of stolen horses.[83] In the same way, thieves called themselves dealers in order to account for the horses in their possession and for their movement around the country. In 1583 Richard Evans, suspected of stealing a horse at Warwick, offered as a defence a tale of trading activity all over the Midlands. In 1608–9 two men travelled from Derbyshire into the neighbouring county of Stafford 'vnder the name and colour of horsequorsers', but as they had 'an ill name' in Derbyshire, they were suspected to be horse stealers. The furtiveness of their actions – selling horses in fields and avoiding towns – also gave rise to suspicion. Involvement in legitimate trade appears to have been part of the defence of Thomas Harrison of Tildesley (Lancs.), accused in 1699 of stealing a bay gelding and a dun mare then in the possession of Richard Marshall. He and Marshall, he stated, were 'partners in buying and selling Horses' and had bought the animal off Francis and Joseph Midsley near Harewood Bridge (W.R.Y.) on 13 May between two and three o'clock in the morning.[84]

Only one or two of the dealers who appear in the toll books are known to have been accused of horse stealing and in each case were either found not guilty or demonstrably did not suffer the prescribed punishment of hanging. In 1613 Haniball Castleton of Islington was indicted for stealing a horse belonging to Ellis Hatch of Bobbing (Kent). The verdict is not known but four years later he lost a horse of his own, and in 1626 'one Honnyball' of Islington was cited as the seller of a horse to a suspect picked up in Reading.[85] In 1631 William Eaton of Cottesbrook (Northants.), already referred to as a noted dealer, fell foul of the voucher system when trying to sell some horses at Woodstock Fair on 22 September. He had brought Edward Smith of Dodford (Northants.) with him to act as his voucher, but as Smith had openly declared himself to be his partner, his testimony was disallowed. Smith therefore tried to persuade another man to vouch for Eaton but in front of the toll man the stranger thus co-opted said that he did not know him and refused to co-operate. Eaton was then arrested and in his examination denied that Smith was his partner, although admitting that he did work with John Smith of Willoughby who

83 Somerset R.O., Q/SR 1609 8/53; Ornsby, 'Lord William Howard', p. 445.
84 Sharpe, *Crime in Early Modern England*, pp. 116–17; D. H. G. Salt, ed., 'Staffordshire Quarter Sessions Rolls, Easter 1608 to Trinity 1609', *Staffs. Hist. Collns* (1948–9), pp. 27–9; ASSI 45/17/4/28.
85 W. le Hardy, ed., 'Middlesex Sessions Records, 1612–4', *Middlesex County Records*, N.S., 1 (1935), p. 284; W. le Hardy, ed., 'Middlesex Sessions Records, 1616–18', *Middlesex County Records*, N.S., 4 (1941), pp. 323–4.

was his (Eaton's) colleague.[86] The argument looks specious, but I find it difficult to believe that Eaton, who regularly tolled for his horses at Market Bosworth and Derby, should have been engaged in illicit activity. Moreover he continued openly and honestly to buy horses at Derby until 1661. Another dealer, Charles Moon of Deddington (Oxon.), was arrested at Shrewsbury in 1685 and, in spite of no charge being made against him at the following Assize, he was still a prisoner in 1686. In his petition he pointed out that although the horses he was said to have stolen had been advertised in gazettes and elsewhere, no-one had come to claim them and that in the meantime he had received nothing and was likely to perish through want.[87]

Whether or not they were guilty will probably never be known, for felons regularly escaped the penalty in a number of ways. Juries could either return the bill *ignoramus* or, if it went to court, bring in a verdict of not guilty.[88] In the Home Circuit during Elizabeth's reign at least one-quarter of the people indicted as principals or accessories were found not guilty. In such cases the possibility of acquittal was aided by the activities of such men as Richard Keffin of Twyford (Shrops.), who in 1609 was said to be 'a Corrupte dealer in Causes betwene partye and partye and one that hath sollicyted Jurors and witnesses to saue seuerall murderers and theves and other felons from the penalty of the Lawe'.[89] Thefts could also be classed as petty larceny if the jury stated that the value of the goods stolen were worth less than 1s. od. It was difficult to reduce the value of horses to this level however, for even dead animals were worth a few shillings more for their hide and as dog meat. Nonetheless Joan Lutes (alias Hatch) of Dagenham (Essex) in 1591 was found guilty of petty larceny to the value of 10½d. in spite of being indicted for the theft of a bay mare (£1. 10s.), a rein (6d.) and saddle (8d.), four ells of russett cloth (£1. 4s. 8d.) and several pieces of linen (£1).[90] Legally, all principals found guilty of horse stealing during the Elizabethan period, and after 1589 all accessories too, could expect only the death sentence and because of the seriousness with which the offence was viewed, were more likely to suffer the full rigours of the law.[91] In practice, however, a considerable number avoided this fate. According to Professor Cockburn, many judges ignored the distinction between clergyable and non-clergyable felonies and in the Home Circuit in

86 Woodstock Portsmouth Book 1618–35.
87 Shrewsbury Corpn. Records, 2270.
88 Cockburn, *Assizes*, p. 128.
89 P.R.O., STAC 8/255/21 Misc. James I.
90 Cockburn, *Assizes*, p. 214.
91 Beattie, *Crime*, pp. 167–70; Sharpe, *Crime in Essex*, p. 97; Sharpe, *Crime in Early Modern England*, p. 69.

the years 1558–1603 twelve people, including three accessories, escaped in this way.[92] Others were reprieved and in the Home Circuit, pardons, especially the general one of 1581, accounted for 27 (4.8 per cent) of those found guilty and for whom the verdict is known. Such acts of clemency were not entirely altruistic and young able-bodied men so saved were often drafted into the forces. In 1581 one of those pardoned, William Morgan, a Sussex man, then at large, was to be recruited into the navy. In 1620 the Privy Council, on being informed of a suitable young man by the recorder of Norwich, issued a warrant to reprieve him and to order him to be delivered to Sir Thomas Smyth, the governor of the East India Company, in London. Two others were similarly reprieved by warrant during the following years. In Essex in the period 1620–80 of the 59 horse thieves indicted, just over one-fifth of the suspects were hanged, whilst fourteen were reprieved and a further five were transported.[93]

CONDITIONS ON THE NORTHERN BORDER

The account of horse stealing given so far has indicated the general pattern to be found in most parts of the country, reflecting a situation where such activities clearly placed the perpetrators beyond the pale of ordered and settled society. Conditions on the northern border, especially before the Union of the Crowns in 1603 however, were much different. In the Debateable Lands, Nichol Forest or Bewcastle in Cumberland or in Tynedale or Redesdale in Northumberland, lawlessness was virtually a way of life, a situation which was exacerbated by the social and economic pressures of the period from the middle of the sixteenth century.[94] Other parts of the country faced similar problems but distance from the central government, a hostile border and a peculiar form of social organisation based upon surname groups, all added to the general confusion. In 1541 it was reported that both Tynedale and Redesdale were 'overcharged with an excessive number of inhabitants more by many than the profits of the same country may sustain' and so 'the young and active people for lack of living be constrained to steal or spoil continually either in England or Scotland'. In Cumberland

Of by-employments there is no evidence, other than the habitual border industries of blackmail [that is, protection money] and reiving which supplemented the

92 Cockburn, *Assizes*, p. 128.
93 *Ibid.*, pp. 129–30; Cockburn, *Sussex Indictments*, p. 150; *East Anglian Miscellany* Jan.–March 1909, p. 11; *A.P.C.*, 1621–3 (1932), p. 356; Sharpe, *Crime in Seventeenth-Century England*, pp. 97–8.
94 J. S. Cockburn, 'The Northern Assize Circuit', *Northern History*, 3 (1968), p. 122.

inadequate pastoral farming of these north Cumbrian borderers and, likewise, the large number of needy Scots of Liddesdale and Eskdale.[95]

In North Tynedale and Redesdale the Halls, Charltons, Robsons and Milburns presented intractable problems to the Tudor administrators, whilst in north Cumberland the Grahams ruled supreme. In 1592 it was said that the Grahams could raise a mounted force of 500 men, ideal troops for defending the border but as reivers a source of continuous danger to their neighbours.[96] In these circumstances horse stealing was often on a grand scale and more akin to the plundering of armies than to the actions of small groups of criminals standing apart from society, as characterised the rest of the country. Typically, in 1513 more horses were lost at Flodden through the activities of the men from Tynedale and Teviotdale after the battle than during the engagement itself. In 1584 the inhabitants of Elsdon, the largest village in Redesdale, informed the commissioners that 600 Liddesdalers had burned down their homes, murdered fourteen men, taken and held for ransom 44 prisoners, driven away 400 kine and oxen and 400 horses and had taken household goods worth £500. Although the figures were probably inflated, the enterprise must have been a large one. Of the 200 incidents recorded in the *Calendar of Border Papers* between January 1587 and May 1590, some were of minor horse thefts of the kind to be found elsewhere in England but others related to raids involving up to 400 or 500 men. Losses amounting to 4,863 cattle, 3,550 sheep, 340 horses and 157 prisoners were reported.[97] In Cumberland the difference in attitude which characterised the Border area is perhaps illustrated by the successful raid which Walter Scott, the Keeper of Liddesdale, made in 1596 on Carlisle Castle to rescue the notorious thief and horse stealer, Kinmont Willie. Some weeks later John Carey, acting as governor of Berwick, retaliated by sending 50 horsemen into Scotland to hunt down a horse thief called John Douglas who was cut to pieces when he was found. On the western border, operations culminated in the 'ill-week' which followed the death of Elizabeth on 24 March 1603. Led by the Grahams, large numbers of Scots and English clansmen raided as far south as Penrith, reputedly killing six men and taking for ransom fourteen others. Over 5,000 cattle, sheep, goats and horses were said to have been driven away and £6,750 worth of damage inflicted on property.[98]

95 R. Newton, 'The Decay of the Borders: Tudor Northumberland in Transition', in Chalklin and Havinden, *Rural Change*, p. 10; R. T. Spence, 'The Pacification of the Cumberland Border, 1593–1628', *Northern History*, 13 (1977), p. 63.

96 Newton, 'Decay of the Borders', p. 7; Spence, 'Pacification', p. 61.

97 Machin Goodall, *Foals*, p. 135; Watts, *Northumberland*, pp. 28–9; Newton, 'Decay of the Borders', p. 21.

98 Watts, *Northumberland*, p. 117; Spence, 'Pacification', pp. 91–2.

As a result of this action the Grahams lost much of their local support and thus the authorities were able to move against them to curb their power.[99] Although this was accomplished, conditions on the Border did not change overnight. In 1605 James I published a proclamation in both kingdoms, exhorting the inhabitants on both sides of the border to put down their arms and forbidding them from owning a horse over the value of 50s. sterling. In 1617 however the Privy Council felt it necessary to re-affirm the order, threatening one month's imprisonment for offenders.[100] In 1611 a border commission was issued, specifically designed to reduce the level of horse stealing in the region. So many people, it stated, went about on foot searching for unattended horses that henceforward all travellers were forbidden to walk about the countryside unless they possessed a licence given to them by a Justice of the Peace. Magistrates were to chase away all prosperous looking vagabonds and unemployed persons with no visible means of support on the assumption that they were thieves.[101] Nonetheless in the list of murderers and felons in Cumberland which Lord William Howard prepared for the Privy Council in 1618 a number of 'notorious' horse stealers were included, of whom Patrick Story of Peel of the Hill was particularly noteworthy 'for stealing, receiting and owt putting, surpassing all the theeves of Bewcastle'. In Northumberland in the years 1627–9, suspected horse thieves formed the largest group indicted at the Assizes. John Charleton of the Bower, for instance, was said to be 'a fugitive and notorious theife' when he was indicted for the theft of cattle, sheep and horses in 1629.[102]

One of the problems which concerned Lord William Howard was the continuing protection afforded to thieves either through the intimidation of witnesses or through the intercession of powerful or well-placed friends. Patrick Story, he observed, was not brought to trial for acting as an accessory in a crime in which he was clearly implicated,

which kind of dealinge causeth poore true men to be silent when they have just cause to complaine, and inbouldneth prowde theeves to persever in their villanie, well knowing their owne securitie through either the oversight or negligence or corruption of officers.

At Solport, John Martinson of the Hirst, 'a common noted theefe, and a receitor of theeves', had long practised that trade 'under the countenance of a knowne officer', enjoying an immunity which not only made him more

99 Spence, 'Pacification', pp. 97–128.
100 Machin Goodall, *Foals*, p. 150; H.M.C., 12th. Report, Appendix, part vii, Lord Muncaster of Muncaster Castle MSS, p. 229; A.P.C., 1616–17, p. 381.
101 Watts, *Northumberland*, pp. 181–2, quoting P.R.O., S.P. 14/65/17
102 Ornsby, 'Lord William Howard', p. 440; J. Hodgson, ed., 'Calendars of . . . Prisoners . . . in the High Castle and in Newcastle-upon-Tyne and the Assizes for Northumberland in the Years 1628 and 1629', *Archaeologia Aeliana*, i, part ii (1822), pp. 149–70.

audacious but which also made other people afraid to complain. One of
the thieves enjoyed the protection of Sir William Hutton, a Justice of the
Peace, and in his letter to him Lord William wrote of his own attitude
towards such offenders: 'Forasmuch as there is nothing more expedient
for the reduceinge of those parts to be civilitie and obeydience then a strict
and constaunt course of justice.' Accusations of corruption still continued
however. At the Quarter Sessions held at Hexham in July 1707 the grand
jury presented William Lowes, the County Keeper, to be a person that

protects rogues and theives and that it is A Comon practice of those very persons
employed under him to take Away the Inhabitants Horses of this County and Ride
them for A Quarter of a Year or more & soe turn them of Soe Abused that the . . .
Horses is Good for nothing Soe that this County by such practices is become A very
burthen to the Inhabitants of the Same & A publick Scandale to our Neighbouring
Countyes.

They therefore asked the Bench either to set aside the system of county
keeping or else appoint an honest man to the post.[103]
    Among the County Keeper's duties was the supervision of the booker
system which originated in the peculiar and unsettled conditions on the
Border and which enabled the owners of stolen horses and cattle to obtain
some compensation for their loss. A victim had 48 hours to report such
thefts to the 'booker' at the nearest market town, who would record the
incident and give him a certificate.[104] If the animal had not been recovered
by the time of the next Quarter Sessions, he could petition the magistrates
for a sum equal to its value. From one point of view this should be a good
source of information, since it clearly was in the interest of the victims to
have their stolen animals recorded. Many of the Quarter Sessions rolls are
missing however and there is a strong suspicion of under-registration.
How many people, for instance, suffered the fate of Lancelot Simpson of
Armathwaite? On Easter Monday 1693, having had a black gelding stolen
the previous Saturday, he went to Carlisle to have it booked, but
unfortunately, the booker was out, as was the one at Kirkoswald where he
went next. By this time it was too late to have the theft recorded. Figures
survive for the years 1686–1712, and they do show considerable fluctuations in the incidence of horse stealing.[105] 1691 appears, in spite of the
vagueness of the material, to have been a critical year. At the Midsummer
Sessions the parishioners of Alston Moor petitioned the magistrates to act

103 Ornsby, 'Lord William Howard', pp. 440, 442, 476; Northumberland R.O., QSB Vol.
    26 Mids. 1707.
104 J. L. Kirby, 'Border Service 1662–1757', *T.C.W.A.A.S.*, N.S., 48 (1949), p. 128.
105 Cumbria R.O. (Carlisle), Calendar of Cumberland Q.S. Petitions Mich. 1686–Easter
    1762, Original MSS Class 2/11.

against the thieves who were plaguing the area. They had lost eight valuable horses since 14 May, they said, and had been put to a great deal of trouble watching over or housing their horses at night. Similarly the tenants of Lord Carlisle and Lord Preston in Eskdale Ward asked the Justices of the Peace to suppress the moss-troopers and thieves who had stolen many horses and cattle from them in the previous three months.[106]

SUMMARY

Except on the Scottish border before 1603, where horse stealing appears to have been part of an accepted way of life, traffickers in stolen horses occupied one end of a continuum in the trade, at the other end of which were placed the legitimate dealers discussed at length in Chapter 3. In between there was a considerable overlap; horse dealers were not exempt from human weaknesses and no doubt were often guilty of sharp practice if the opportunity presented itself. Many, moreover, may have mixed legitimate business with illegal activities, and receiving, as in the case of the Staffordshire dealers in 1608–9, seems to have been the most common offence. Nonetheless, horse thieves can clearly be distinguished from the reputable dealers who did so much to develop the trade during the course of the Tudor and Stuart period. Of necessity thieves had to be more secretive in their dealings and even when obliged to go through the proper channels were likely to give false names and addresses. They came from lower social classes than the legitimate dealers, too, and tended to move on the fringes of the communities in which they lived, if indeed, they could call any place their home. Many were only temporary residents, working for a few weeks or months in one place before moving on elsewhere, whilst others were permanent vagrants. In every way less responsible members of society than their respectable counterparts, they helped to give the trade its bad name. At markets and fairs, for instance, they mingled with honest dealers and apart from trying to dispose of stolen horses, were readily involved in violent and anti-social behaviour. The restrictions imposed upon horse dealers at Malton in 1661 were specifically aimed at the unruly and dishonest element amongst them but unfortunately the honest dealer suffered too.

106 *Ibid.*, Mids. 1691–7, Mich. 1691–25, Mich. 1702/17, 19, 21, 24, 26, 28, 30, 32, 34, 36, 39, 41, 43, 45, 47, 51, 53.

CONCLUSION

Because of the vital role that horses played in the social and economic life of Tudor and Stuart England, the means whereby the animals were produced and distributed to those who needed them were matters of great concern to contemporaries. The expansion of trade and industry and the growing efficiency of farming, for instance, were developments which depended to a considerable extent upon the ability of breeders to increase supplies and on the efforts of dealers to improve the efficiency of the market. The growth in demand for saddle horses of all types also had to be catered for. Fortunately, productivity and efficiency did improve and by the end of the period not only did more people possess horses but they could also choose one bred to perform specific tasks. As a result, horse keeping in the widest sense provided an income for thousands of people working either directly or indirectly in the trade, and therefore did much to increase the wealth of the community.

Horses had a social as well as an economic value, since at all levels of society, they were regarded as status symbols. At the top end of the market the upper classes could display their wealth by the purchase of costly horses at prices which owed as much to the dictates of fashion as to the functional capabilities of the animals. At a lower level too, the purchase of a horse raised the owner's standing in his community. Apart from the economic advantages it gave, possession of a horse made the owner more independent, allowing him to travel further and more quickly and to enlarge his social horizons. Thus in many villages the division between horse owners and the others must have represented a real social distinction. Ownership was a form of conspicuous consumption and therefore particularly sensitive to fluctuations in the economy. In good times a larger proportion of the population may have felt they could afford to buy one and thus improve the quality of their lives. At Yetminster (Dorset) the proportion of householders with horses rose three-fold in the period 1590–9 to 1660–9, prompting Dr Thirsk to observe that 'we are driven to conclude that some of the peasants' additional wealth was being spent on

horses to enable them to ride instead of walking to market'.[1] In unfavour-
able times, on the other hand, horses may have been among the first items
to be sold – they cost a lot to feed and maintain, depreciated rapidly in
value after a few years, were prone to injury and disease and perhaps were
not fully used. Even among the upper classes economies occasionally had
to be made; on the Thorndon estate of the Petre family at the beginning of
the eighteenth century, it was felt that a major saving could be made by the
sale of useless horses, the disposal of the hounds and the dismissal of
superfluous servants such as huntsmen.[2]

Given the importance of horses in the economy and the general
interventionist policy of the government, it is not surprising to note that
various regulations were made to control the trade. Initially, action was
motivated by military and strategic considerations – Henry VIII's wars
had shown up the deficiency of the native stock – and measures were
undertaken to increase the supply of good-quality saddle mounts and
draught horses. The production of bigger and better stock was enhanced
by the import of animals from abroad, whilst at the same time attempts
were made to limit the breeding of small horses at home, especially by
preventing the haphazard coupling of undersized stock on the commons
and wastes. The export of horses valued at a certain level was banned,
although there were exceptions and licences could be obtained. In the
domestic trade the government acted in accordance with its overall policy
of supporting the traditional marketing institutions, the markets and fairs,
by legislating against middlemen and trying to stem the tide of private
marketing. Illicit traffic was controlled by action against horse stealers.

Not all of the government's measures were successful or even well-
directed but undoubtedly the trade did flourish and improvements in both
quality and quantity were made. With regard to raising breeding
standards, the Crown took the lead, importing stock from abroad and
maintaining a number of studs around the country. The upper classes were
expected to participate too, being encouraged to do so partly by legislative
action and partly by persuasion. Of course, individuals responded in
different ways, but because of the status which the possession of a fine
string of horses conferred on the owner, many were attracted to the
business. Indeed, a number became enthusiasts. They may in many
instances have been primarily concerned with outward show, becoming
especially interested in producing horses for such leisure pursuits as racing
and hunting and for pulling their coaches, but their activities did have
more general effects. In particular, they made a valuable contribution
towards the raising of standards; they spent time and money in choosing

---

1 Thirsk, *Horses*, p. 6.   2 Essex R.O., Petre Colln., D/DP/Z 37/16.

and keeping suitable stock and helped to promote good breeding practices. Gentlemen who were involved in horse breeding could be found in many parts of the country, since much depended upon individual initiative and interest. In general, they were less cost-conscious than farmers and there must have been a number of individuals like Sir Richard Cholmondeley of Whitby and Sir George Reresby of Thrybergh Hall who chose to breed horses rather than pursue some more profitable enterprise.[3] Significantly, however, the most active horse breeders could be found among the gentry of leading breeding areas such as Yorkshire and Durham and this suggests a degree of integration with the local economy.

The influence of the upper classes was also felt in a more indirect manner. Their interest in horse racing, for instance, gave prominence to centres like Newmarket and brought in revenue to towns where meetings were held. The involvement of the gentry was crucial to the success of meetings since they provided much of the prize money and most of the horses. In 1665, as a result of a dispute over the entry of horses at Chester, the gentry boycotted the race there for a time and if they had not relented, the meeting would have been placed in jeopardy.[4] The growing fashion of riding in coaches also stimulated the development of a number of towns, especially that of London; the practice made it easier for the gentry to take their families there and encouraged the development of urban social life.[5]

Among the rest of the population, small-scale horse breeding continued to be widely practised but certain areas stand out as centres of production. The availability of grass was the dominant factor and thus breeding tended to be located in pastoral regions, although farmers in mixed-farming districts which possessed adequate grazing land were also involved. Increasingly, however, the latter areas came to specialise in rearing animals bred elsewhere, training them up in the collar and feeding them on locally grown fodder crops. This division in function was a beneficial one since it meant that farmers in particular areas could devote their time to those aspects of the business best suited to local conditions. In breeding areas young stock were sold off the farm after two or three years, releasing grazing land for brood mares and their foals and thereby making effective use of the facilities. In rearing districts, on the other hand, farmers did not have to divert valuable resources to breeding animals and could stock up their holdings with work horses and colts in training.

By the early seventeenth century there existed in England a large and

---

3 *Supra*, pp. 43–4.
4 Longrigg, *The English Squire and his Sport* (1977), p. 85.
5 L. Stone, 'The Residential Development of the West End of London in the Seventeenth Century', in B. C. Malament, ed., *After the Reformation: Essays in Honour of J. H. Hexter* (Univ. of Pennsylvania, 1980), pp. 177–9.

varied stock of horses from which people could draw animals for use in a number of specific tasks. The country was no longer dependent upon imports from abroad and this self-sufficiency in such a vital commodity fitted in well with general economic theories of the time. In fact a former trend was reversed, for English horses, once deemed to be among the worst in Europe, began to find favour abroad. Until the mid-seventeenth century, stocks were protected by the ban on exports, even if the fiscal needs of the Crown prompted it to allow animals to leave the country under licence. Many others were exported by illicit means, dissipating the nation's resources without providing any compensatory income, and in spite of the government's best endeavours, the traffic was never brought under control. By the 1650s, however, attitudes were changing and in 1656 it was decided to throw open the trade. Developments had proved so successful that, the Civil War notwithstanding, there was a surplus stock of horses at home and exports could therefore be contemplated without compromising national security. At the same time, by charging a duty on every sale a valuable source of revenue would be generated, and by helping to meet the demand from abroad, the incidence of smuggling would be reduced.

Production was raised and diversified, as indicated above, by the activities of the upper classes and by the emergence of specialised breeding and rearing areas. In consequence, the trade in horses between various parts of the country increased. Pack-horses from the moors of the North and West, for instance, were taken to centres of industry, whilst larger draught horses, bred in the vales, were raised in rearing districts and then sent to towns to serve as cart and carriage animals. The widening of the market in horses, as in other commodities, required changes in the organisation of the trade, since existing facilities were inadequate to meet the increased scale of business. From this point of view the government's policy of control and regulation was often counter-productive because it hampered the development of new and more flexible means of marketing, essential if the country were to be effectively provisioned. Fortunately, in the pursuit of its aims the government proved rather ineffectual and its intervention had less adverse effect than might otherwise have been the case. Like many of its attempts at social and economic control, measures taken to regulate the horse trade were introduced at times of difficulty and pursued energetically for a number of years. Thereafter, however, enforcement tended to slacken off and become crisis-sensitive.

The government was particularly concerned to stop the spread of private marketing, a development which made economic activity more difficult to control. People involved in the horse trade were certainly subject to the same marketing regulations as those engaged in other branches of commerce, but they were further limited by specific measures aimed against them. Early examples of private dealing can be readily found, but it seems as though the problems of supply experienced during the course of the Civil War acted as a major factor in its growth. Although markets and fairs continued to be held, the sudden and unprecedented increase in the demand for horses of all types had an undoubted effect upon the way in which they operated. The scale of the armies' requirements and their ability to exert pressure upon the means of supply, for instance, made it easier for them to reorganise the market in such a way as to facilitate the acquisition of stock. Horses were a vital commodity and to secure an adequate flow of animals it seemed unwise to rely upon chance purchases at the normal outlets. The number of horses at particular centres may have been insufficient and moreover there was inherent danger in a system which concentrated their sale at venues subject to interference by the enemy. In effect therefore, markets and fairs were forestalled and even in the South and the East, areas firmly under the control of Parliament, private means of obtaining horses were adopted.[6]

Nonetheless, fairs remained important outlets for the sale of horses throughout the whole period, as they did for livestock in general, as the basic development, the emergence of specialist centres, was compatible with their continued existence. These centres came to dominate the trade because of certain geographical advantages – access to breeding or rearing stock or location at nodal points of the trade – and they therefore drew in more business to themselves. This made the trade more efficient since as the distances travelled increased, it was important to concentrate resources and to establish where horses of a particular kind could be readily bought or sold. As a hierarchy of fairs developed, some places suffered, yet many smaller outlets continued to exist as feeders for the more prominent centres or, as they had always done, as markets for the local population.

The agents of change, the horse dealers, like other groups of middlemen, were much maligned by contemporaries, although they performed a vital service in organising the trade. With the growth of regional specialisation, the widening of the market, and the development of specialist centres, a more professional approach was needed. Not only did it require a greater amount of expertise to understand the operation of the market, but it also took more time to move stock over long distances. By their actions, dealers integrated the resources of the country more effectively, reducing the incidence of local shortages and stabilising prices.

Much of the distrust of horse dealers stemmed from the fact that horses

6 For instance see P.R.O., S.P. 28/130 part 3, S.P. 28/128(8); A. M. Everitt, 'Suffolk and the Great Rebellion', *Suffolk Record Society*, 3 (1960), pp. 89–92.

were such an essential item and that many of the people who bought them did not know how to distinguish between good and bad ones. Some individuals were remarkably gullible too. In 1612 Francis Williamson esquire of Lincoln's Inn petitioned the Court of Requests about a horse he had obtained from John Graves, a Smithfield horse dealer. The latter, he said, had recommended a gelding which was 'absolute sounde and perfect' and, despite a discharge from the nostrils, free from 'the mourning of the chint' and all other diseases. Williamson, rather foolishly in the circumstances, bought the animal and five days later rode it away on a journey. Before long however, the horse started to labour and it died at Abingdon in spite of the attention of the best farrier in the area.[7]

Whilst the horse dealers who regularly appear in the pages of toll books were reputable men with some standing in their communities, there were unscrupulous individuals who operated at the edges of legality. They were particularly active among the lower levels of society, offering broken-down animals to poor people who could barely raise the asking price or deceiving others into thinking that they were giving them a bargain. Among these dubious characters, sharp practice easily merged with openly criminal behaviour.

The movement of stolen horses around the country seems to have mirrored the flow of legitimate traffic – in northern England, many moorland ponies found their way to developing industrial centres whilst in the South, London provided a large and anonymous market for the disposal of stock. In this respect thieves used the normal avenues of trade as cover for their activities and this suggests that the buoyant demand for horses provided a major incentive to steal.

Horse dealers were human and prone to weakness but in this they should not be singled out for special attention. Those who knew little about horses, however, were well advised when buying one to take along someone with greater expertise. Failure to do so was the mistake made by Francis Williamson in his dealings with John Graves in Smithfield, an error that was compounded by his willingness upon the word of the seller to overlook evident signs of disease. Gentry families regularly made use of dealers as their agents and their expert knowledge would have been very welcome in appraising the value of a potential purchase. This was the advice given by Richard Blome, who recommended that the prospective buyer should take along 'some able and trusty *Farrier*' with him ' to make enquiry into those hidden Maladies, which might escape . . . [his] own or anothers search' and thereby avoid being cheated.[8]

7 P.R.O., REQ 2/396/80.
8 Blome, *The Gentleman's Recreation*, p. 10.

Government legislation did not eliminate horse stealing but neither did it stifle the development of the legitimate trade. In some respects it encouraged growth by stimulating better breeding practices and where the measures could have been harmful, they were not consistently applied. From the middle of the seventeenth century moreover, a change of emphasis is discernible: the old regulations were not abolished but merely held in reserve and not enforced to the same extent. In practice, there was less need to enforce the rules. Developments in breeding had increased the number and range of available horses and with the improvement in real wages, they were being distributed among a wider section of the population. More people rode horses, and large draught horses started to appear on the farms, at first in the South but eventually throughout the whole country. If the process had not been completed by the end of the Stuart age, the trends were clear and progress continued to be made in the subsequent period.

APPENDIX I

STABLE EXPENSES OF LORD PAGET OF BEAUDESERT, STAFFS., 1579

(Staffs. R. O. Paget Colln. D(W)1734/3/3/276)

March	3	Imp' paid Mr Fulgame for his sumpters Geldinge bowght of him the iiith daye of marche 1578 the some of six pounds	£6
April	1	Item paid for xx tie strickes of Ottes bowght in Darbie the Fyrst daye of Apprill 1579 of Burtonn messure	14s. 0d.
	2	Item paid for ii quarters iii strickes of Ottes bowght in Burtonn	12s. 3d.
	17	Item paid for one Quarter of Ottes bowght at newe Castell Vnderlynne	7s.
	17	Item paid Simsonn the Saddeller of Burtonn for thinges necessarie for the Stable betwixt november 1578 and the xxvii daye of Apprill 1579	£1 6s. 1d.
Maye	3	Item paid for iii loade of haye bowght agaynst your Lo: commynge to horecross of Banckes and of Gregorie Winkelcott	£1 10s. 0d.
August	6	Item paid for xxii strickes of Ottes bowght of Mr Patt of Westonn	12s. 10d.
	25	Item paid for ix Strickes of ottes bowght at Mr Bayllyffes of Burton of one Nycholas wryght of Moddersawll	6s. 9d.
	29	Items paid Simsonn Saddler vpponn his bill the xxixth of Auguste 1579 for necessaries for the Stable the Some	£1 2s. 7d.
Sept.	21	Item paid Jhonn Fearnne vpponn his bill the xxith of September 1579 for necessaries for the Stable	6s. 6d.
Oct.	1	Item paid for iii strickes of Ottes bowght the firste of October per Vinsannt	2s. 10d.
	7	Item paid Bulleker for keeppinge of horses in the Stable the viith of October 1579 one weeke	1s. 0d.
	7	Item paid Banckes of Bromeley for Ryeddinnge of iii coults of my lordes the vii of October 1579	10s. 0d.
Novbr.	14	Item paid George Middeltounn horseryeder for Breackinge of iii of my Lordes coultes and for goewinge to Lenntton faire for his paynes the xiiiith of November 1579	£1 8s. 4d.
	15	Item paid Bulleker for helpinge for to dresse horses in the Stable tow weeckes the xvth of November 1579	2s. 0d.

OTHER REFERENCES

July 1 (1581)	Item paid for shoewinge of the Great horse xxd . . . and pd. for lettinge of the Baie nage Bloud and givinge him a drincke xiid wch beforesaid nage ys Called Baie Welder	(2s. 8d.)
Sept. 25 (1581)	Item paid for a Saddell the xxvth of Sept. 1581 bowght at pencaridge Faire and for the furnature for yt	12s. 8d.
Feb. 25 (1581/2)	Item paid for shoewinge of the graye coulte wt ys called my young master Hobye and viii removes to Middelton the xxvth of Feb	1s. 10d.
May 4 (1582)	Item paid for a Saddell for Mr. Ward when he wente vppe to London to carye monie on the iiiith. of Maii 1582	5s. 2d.

—— OOO ——

THE ACCOUNTS OF SIR RICHARD NEWDIGATE, A HORSE ENTHUSIAST

(Warwickshire R. O. Newdigate of Arbury Collection, CR136/V/142)

1691 3 Aug. Least my Wife Son or Relations should think I overprize my Horses, I will here set down the Names & Prizes of Captain Wilkinsons Mares as I had them from his own Mouth, & because I would not go to his prize I lost my labor, only bought one little Mare & Foal the very worst he had which cost me 20 Guineas but the mare had 2 great bone spavins yet I sold the Colt to his son for £60 at four year old & I would fain have had one of his mares of his own breed for forty pounds (which that I bought was not) & of forty mares which he had (& owned that he had too many) he would not take under fifty pounds for any one

Age	Names	Price	Color
14	Old Turk	£200	bright bay
16	Old Wilks	150	Chesnut bal faced 2 white legs
10	Young Turk much foundred	100	bright bay
6	Strawberry	100	sandy Grey
5	Smithson	100	bright bay
9	Laiton which I bought	110	black
	Cheater	60	
	Barb Mare	60	
	Blackburn	60	
18	Coal	60	Grey Flea bitten
	Foenick	60	sorrell bal faced near leg behind white
	Sudell treads very low (-) pasterns	60	sorrel
	Pudsey		
	Young Wilks		
	Heber		
	Tempest 2 bone spavins		bloud bay
	Bierly		
	Y(oung) Cheater		
	Sandy Grey		two white legs
	Babington or Nipping Nell		

these 8 & 12 more whose names I had not time to take, are fifty pounds apeece And
Mr Darcy & others that breed ask greater rates for far worse horses then mine
Make much therefore of your own breed My Son

For the Horses which I had in the year 1690 Aug. 5 See pages 160 & 161 of my
Book of Corn & Cattle Whereby it appeares that I had then 59
viz. For the Saddle Young & Old   33
    For the Coach   12
    For the Cart   14
              Total   59

Of which There Died 3 viz Roantail and Tempest of the 33 & Fleckno of the 12
Were Sold 3 viz White Horse & Omphale of the 33   Norbury of the 12
But then I bought Turk, Chestnut, Laiton, Arabian Mare which continue the 33
& 1 little black Mare which I sold 2 year ago, came again of her self
and of the Residue of the 12 I put 4 to Cart So the Account stands thus in 1691

33   for Bread & Saddle
& 1   or for Saddle   6 Geldings
                            8 Stoned
      for Saddle & Bread   16 Mares
&   more vide infra p. 2   4 more
 6   for Coach
 3   bought at Hinkly   9 Coach
18   For the Cart   18
            Total   61 Horses

1691 3 Aug. I will keep this Book only for Horses

Age	Names	Color	Kind or Sex	Price	Number
18	Eidalme	A White	Mare	£50	1
6	Posthuma	Bright bay with a blaze	Mare	50	2
6	Foenick	Dapple Grey	Mare	60	3
9	Laiton	Black large with white feet	Mare	110	4
6	Arabian	Grey partly strawberry with black Mane & Tail	Mare	50	5
3	Young Omphale	A fine Grey inclining to Strawberry	Filly	30	6
3	Neopolitan	A Dapple Grey	Filly	20	7
9	Hollow back	Grey little	Mare	15	8
8	Dusty	Grey stout	Mare	12	9

All these but Laiton & Arab are of my own Breed & those I bought of Captain
Wilkinson for the prizes set against them

Number	Age	Names	Color	Sex	Marks	Price/by whom bred
1	11	Dorin	bright bay	Mare		£20 Sir Charles Skrymsher
2	9	Richmond or Wilks	Chestnut	Mare		12 Mr Wilks of Tonsall

Number	Age	Names	Color	Sex	Marks	Price/by whom bred
3	6	Troop	Grey	Mare	Very large but foul shapd	12 Dick Bryan

For 12 Mares of which 10 fine ones all but Dusty & Troop

Galloway's or small Mares

1	11	Dun or ThiefA black Dun		trots & walks & gallops extra-ordinary well	04
2	9	Trub	bright bay with Star & Snip	paces well & gallopes rarely	10
3	11	Heriot	Sorrell with a blaze	trots well but gallops rarely	04
4	5	Shelly	bright bay no white but a black seam down her back	paces very well	08

the 2 Middlemost are excellent Hunters as Hollow back Dorin & Richmond

Total		16 Mares		Prices	£367
	of these	7 are fine Mares for Breed			
		2 Dusty & Troop for War or Winter riding			
		2 for Summer Pads Dun & Shelly			
		5 rare Hunters			

1691 3 Aug.   Stoned Horse

Number	Age	Names		Marks	Price	Breed
1	15	Dervise	Brown bay		£60	A naturall Turk
2	12	Almus	Brown bay	with a Star	30	Foenick
3	4	Young Eugent	black Grey	with a blaze	50	Neopolitan
4	5	Grele	light Grey		40	Foenick
5	4	Wilkinson	Chestnut	with a Star & 2 white feet	60	Captain Wilkinson of Laiton got by the Turk
6	2	Tempest	Grey		20	Wilkinson & Eugent
7	1	Eidalmes Colt	Grey		20	Foenick hors
8	1	Omphales	Grey		20	Neopolitan

Total   8 Stones horses of which 6 fine 2 Plain Price 300

of which 1 Stallion Dervise
1 Hunter Grele
2 Warriers Almus & Eugent
4 Colts unbackt

Geldings

1	4	Snead	Sandy Grey large Foenick Gelding	20.00.00	Eugent & old Sorrell Mare
2	6	Pad	Brown bay with a blaze	20.00.00	
3	8	Polipheme	Bloud bay	10.00.00	

Galloways

4	5	Wrexham	Grey	4.00.00
5	11	Dun Nag	Dun	2.10.00
6	7	Stray	bay	2.00.00

Total 6 Geldings of which
    2 Hunters Polipheme & Stray
    3 Pads
    1 Colt unbackt Snead I after cald him the Foenick Gelding

6 Coach Mares ⎫ bought at Hinkly	£80
1 young one ⎭	
2 Coach horses 3 year old apeice next grasse	30
18 Cart horses (for 14 of which see Corn a Cattle book)	80
6 Geldings for the Saddle	58
8 Stone horses for the Saddle	300
16 Mares for the Saddle & Breed	367

Total 60 Horses   whose Value is   £915

57	besides one Gelt Colt came of Omphale comes 2 year old	£15
4	& one bay Filly of Dusty Grey	10
Total 61	& one little black stray Mare	0.10.0

I think these are all
no there is one more grey Colt came of Eidalme comes 2

3 Aug. 91   Mem This Year I have no Foales because I bought not Eugent of
               J. Merry till late last year & designed to go to Ireland & take him,
               so I thought giving him Mares would make him unlucky.

               Mares put to horse this Year
               Dorin ⎫ to Eugent
               Wilks ⎭
               Laiton to the Turk

Mem   Scatter Stones on Horse rail Griff hill & Beristead & Middle Holly
               Kidding before winter

               Quickest the Horse railes

               Put Eidalme Posthuma Foenick & Arab to horse next January
               according to De Gray

               Put Laiton & Y. Omphale & any of these that fail & Dorin &
               Wilks 8 mares to horse to Dervize next Spring

               Splay all Mare foales that are not very fine

Sell   ⎫ Posthuma, Neopolitan, Hollow back, Dusty Grey,
8 mares ⎭ Dun, Heriot, Shelly, little black Mares
2 Stoned horses Almus, Grele
6 Geldings Snead, Pad, Polipheme, Wrexham, Dun Nag, Stray
2 Coach Mares Goodwin & Archpole
4 Cart horses Mops Tilly Brock & 2 of Kinders

Rules

Take Care not to be overstockt with horses

Breed few but Choice

The Reason I design to put 8 mares to the Turk next year is because he growes old & will not serve long & will crosse strain admirably

Rather give away some horses then sell underfoot

Sell the worst Cart Jades for any thing, & turn off some yearly to Cart, even of the best breed

Keep few Idle horses I have now

10	for Coach	3 too many
18	for Cart at least	
8	for Hunting	few enough
4	for War	too few
5	Pads	enough
1	Stallion for breed	
6	Mares	
8	Colts & Fillys unbackt	
1	black Tit	

61

Be Sure Put no Coach or Cart Mares thô they do seem fine to a right bred Horse. Beware a bastard breed.

Value not Selling   Wee breed to save Buying

─── ○○○ ───

EXTRACTS FROM THE PROBATE WILLS OF THE ROCK FAMILY OF THE STOURBRIDGE AREA

(H.W.R.O. BA 3585 Class 008. 7/1593/124. Thomas Rock of Stourbridge, Worcs. yeoman 18 July 1593)

Item my will is that my horses and coltes shalbe sold by my...wife & the money...accrewing...shalbe diuided equally between her & my...thre yongest children...

(H.W.R.O. BA 3585 Class 008. 7/1609/87) John Rocke of the parish of Rowley, Staffs., chapman, 3 September 1609)

...also I giue vnto him [Roger Rocke, eldest son] all my furniture belonge to my horesses with towe of the beste horsses or mares that he Cane Chuse amongeste my horessces within one weeke after my decease with sufficiente haye to winter them & also all the Deates I haue owinge vnto me in whose handes soeuer thay be...

(H.W.R.O. BA 3585 Class 008. 7/1609/152) Roger Rocke of Rowley, Staffs, 11 (-) 1609)

...to my brother Thomas Rocke the worst of my two horses which my father gave me...

APPENDIX 4

———— ○○○ ————

A LEADING HORSE DEALER: HUMPHREY HANBURY OF BEDWORTH, WARWICKS.

(Probate inventory and will at Lichfield Joint R.O. Probate 1696 + name + parish)

An Inventory of the Goods & Chattells of Humphrey Hanbury of Bedworth in the County of Warwick who Departed this life Sept 5th 1721

Imprimis his purse and apparell	40	0	0
In the Kitchin			
5 Chairs		3	6
2 fire shovells & 5 pair tongs		2	6
2 pair of pothooks & spitts & a little back & a grate		12	0
2 skreens & a Coffer		8	6
2 tables 1 dozen of trenchers		6	0
1 dozen & ½ of plates		15	0
29 pewter Dishes	4	0	0
6 Candlesticks & a pewter one and a Chamber pot		4	0
6 wooden dishes 6 spoons & a ladle			11
a driping pan 3s. 2 brass potts 30s.	1	13	0
2 Iron potts 2s. a brass Kettle 21s.	1	3	0
a Brass pot 15s.		15	0
1 warming pan		2	6
1 pair of bellows & sawcepan		1	6
2 Brass Kettles		6	0
1 grate & a Bacon Cratch		16	0
	11	8	11
In the parlour			
20 books		10	0
9 pair of sheets & other linen	2	10	0
2 Oval Tables		15	0
1 Hanging press		10	0
14 Chaires		12	0
	4	17	0

In the Dairy

20 strike of Malt	4	0	0
1 sadle & horse Coller a pair of Hames		4	0
3 dozen & ½ bottles 1 pauchim & Cream-pot		4	0
1 Chair & 2 formes		1	0
	4	9	0

In the Chamber over the parlour

a Cheese rack & boards		10	0
1 bed stead & set of Curtains		14	6
1 feather bed 2 1i.10s.	2	10	0
1 blanket & a pair of sheets		5	0
2 bolsters 2s.6d. a trunk 2s.		4	6
	4	4	0

In the Chamber over the House

2 bedsteed		14	0
2 feather beds	6	0	0
4 blanketts 20s. 2 pair of sheets 16s.	1	16	0
2 pillows & 2 bolsters		16	0
2 sets of Curtains 2 1i. 19 cheses 25s.	3	5	0
9 Chaires 12s. 2 tables 3s.		15	0
1 Chaffe bed & 1 flock bed		5	0
2 pictures in frames		1	6
1 twigen Basket			4
1 Clock	2	5	0
	15	17	10

In the little parlour

1 siluer Tankard	9	0	0
2 bed steads		4	0
1 feather bed	1	10	0
1 wool bed		5	0
1 blanket & a pair of sheets		10	0
1 bolster 3s. 1 wooden Chair 6d.		3	6
	11	2	6

In the Brewhouse

8 Brewing tubbs	2	0	0
2 Churmes 5s. 5 pails 2s.		7	0
1 Cheese press 8s. 3 bucketts 2s.		10	0
a Cheese fat a suter & wooden platter		3	0
a pair of pot Hooks & Cullender			8
1 farnis	2	0	0
a steane pot and a Milke pan			6
a wooden hipper & a flasket		2	0

a pewter dish & a pewter pint		2	6
a frying pan			6
spun Jersey		18	0
		6	4	2

In the Hutching orchard
6 Heifors & a Calfe — 13 0 0

In the Home Grounds
2 Cows & 6 sheep — 6 0 0

In the meadow
4 Cows — 8 0 0

In the Common feild
14 sheep — 2 10 0

In Chrachley Ground
4 horses — 15 0 0

In the Hog Sty
2 sows & piggs — 5 0 0
2 Store piggs — 1 6 0

In the Rick yard
5 Ricks of Hay — 40 0 0

In the Barne
Corne — 20 0 0
a parcell of oats — 10 0 0

In the Yard
a waggon — 1 10 0
a Cart — 1 5 0
a Harrow & plow — 12 0

123 13 0

─── ⭕⭕⭕ ───

WARWICK CASTLE ESTATE: ACCOUNTS FOR THE YEAR ENDING MICHAELMAS 1656: TRAVELLING AND STABLE EXPENSES

(Warwicks. R.O. Warwick Castle Collection, CR 1886/411)

To Mr Taylor for a horse for my Lord 21 Mar	012 00 00
To a browne guelding for his Lordshipp by Jonas 29 Mar	014 05 00
To Cluff the Horscourser for a browne bay nagg for his Lordshipp per acquets per Ralph Woodward 16 April	012 00 00
For a black guelding for Mr Robert which Mr Chernock bought for him in Bedfordshire per Ralph Woodward	010 00 00
To Gray the Horscoursers man by him	000 05 00
To Davis the Bitmakers bill for the Coachhorses 5 Maii	000 12 00
To Oxley the Horscourser for a horse for my Lord by Ra:Woodward per acqets 2 Maii	014 00 00
To Slater the Harnesmakers bill 30 Maii	021 05 00
To Mr Baraclough by bill for grass for the saddle horses 31 Maii	003 08 00
To bennet the Smiths bill for the Coach horses 12 Junii	002 04 06
To Higgs the sadlers bill for my Lord 13 Junii	004 15 06
To him by bill for Mr Robert 13 Junii	003 04 06
To Bennet the Smiths bill for my Lords horses 13 Junii	002 16 06
To Clough the Horsecourser for a guelding for his Lordshipp 13 Junii	023 00 00
To a bay mare which his Lordshipp bought of Mr Smith 25 Junii	014 00 00
To a Bay Stone horse which his Lordshipp bought of one Mr Maynard per Clement Banwell 5 Julii	030 00 00
To a bill for mowing and making hay 16 Junii per J: Atton	023 04 03
To the exchange of a horse by Clem Banwell	001 10 00
Expended at Frinckford	000 05 06
To Mr Algernon in part for a nagg bought of him for Mr Fowk	000 15 00
To Barnard Chalkely for a loade of straw	000 18 00
To Slater the Harnesmakers bill 5 Sept	002 00 00
To Chevall the Sadlers bill for my Lord 13 Sept	007 00 00
To Bennet the smiths bill for his Lordshipps horses 22 Sept	003 10 00
To him by bill for the Coach horses 27 Sept	000 13 00
To Shuttleworth the Coachmakers bill 2 Oct	009 10 00
To Mr Alernoon in further part for Mr Fowkes horse	000 05 00
	255 12 09

——— ◯◯◯ ———

THOMAS WITTY OF SURFLEET, LINCS., HORSECOURSER. GOODS APPRAISED 30 MAY 1694

(Lincs. A.O. INV 191/218)

May the 30th 1694

An Apraisment then Taken of the Goods of Thomas Witty of Surfleet A Horsecorcer

 for one white horse
 one putack Colored horse
 one Bay horse
 one Browne bald horse

which were praised the same day and month before mentined by us hoes names are here vnder subscribed at the rate of Twentie pounds whereof wee haue sett to our hands

John Sharper
George Metcalfe
Robert Obrey

——— ◯◯◯ ———

THOMAS DEKKER, LANTHORNE AND CANDLE-LIGHT OR THE BELL-MANS SECOND NIGHTS WALKE (1608)

OF GINGLERS OR THE KNAUERY OF HORSE COURSERS IN SMITH-FIELD DISCOUERED

At the end of fierce battailes, the onely Rendeuouz for lame souldiers to retire vnto, is an Hospitall: and at the end of a long Progresse, the onely ground for a tyred Jade to runne in, is some blind country faire, where he may be sure to be sold. To those Markets of vnwholesome Horse-flesh, (like so many Kites to feede vpon Carion) doe all the Horse-coursers (that roost about the Citty) flie one after another. And whereas in buying all other commodities, men striue to haue the best, how great so euer the price be, onely the Horse courser is of a baser minde, for the worst horse-flesh (so it be cheape) does best goe downe with him. He cares for nothing but a fayre outside, and a handsome shape (like these that hyre whores though there be a hundred diseases within); he (as the other) ventures vpon them all.

The first lesson therefore that a Horse-courser takes out, when he comes to one of these Markets, is to make choyse of such Nags, Geldings, or Mares, especially, as are fatt, fayre, and well-fauor'd to the eye; and because men delight to behold beautifull coullors, and that some coulours are more delicate (euen in beasts) than others are, he will so neere as hee can, bargaine for those horses that haue the daintiest complexion; as the Milke-white, the Gray, the Dapple-Gray, the Cole-black with his proper markes (as the white starre in the forehead, the white heele, &c) or the bright Bay, with the like proper markes also. And the goodlier proportion ye beast carries or the fayrer markes or coulour that hee beares, are or ought to bee watch-words as it were to him that afterwards buyes him of the horse-courser, that he bee not coozend with an ouer-price for a bad peny-worth, because such Horses (belonging for the most part to Gentlemen) are seldome or neuer solde away, but vpon some fowle quality, or some incurable disease, which the Beast is falne into. The best coulours are therefore the best Cloakes to hide those faults that most disfigure a Horse: and next vnto coulour, his Pace doth often-times deceiue and goe beyond a very quick Judgement.

Some of these Horse-hunters, are as nimble knaues in finding out the infirmities of a Jade, as a Barber is in drawing of teeth; and albeit (without casting his water) hee does more radily reckon vp all the Aches, Crampes, Crickes, and whatsoeuer disease else lyes in his bones: and for those diseases seemes vtterly to disslike him, yet if by looking vpon the Dyall within his mouth, he finde that his yeares haue struck but fiue, sixe, or seauen, and that he prooues but young, or that his diseases are but newly growing vpon him, if they be outward, or haue but hayre and skin to hide them, if they bee inward, let him sweare neuer so damnably, that it is but a Jade, yet he will be sure to fasten vpon him.

So then, a Horse-courser to the Merchant, (that out of his sound judgement buyes the fairest, the best-bred, and the noblest Horses, selling them againe for breede or seruice, with plainnesse and honesty,) is as the Cheator to the faire Gamester: he is indeed a meere Jadish Nonopolitane, and deales for none but tyred, tainted, dull and diseased horses. By which meanes, if his picture bee drawne to the life, you shall finde euery Horse courser for the most part to bee in quality a coozener, by proffession a Knaue, by his cunning a Varlet, in fayres a Hagling Chapman, in the Citty a Cogging dissembler, and in Smith-field a common foresworne Villaine. Hee will sweare anything; but the faster hee sweares, the more danger tis to beleeue him; In one forenoone, and in selling a Jade not worth fiue Nobles, will hee forsweare himselfe fifteene times, and that so swearing too shall be by Equiuocation. As for example, if an ignorant Chapman comming to beate the price, say to the Horse-courser, your Nagge is very old, or thus many yeares old, and reckon ten or twelue, he clappes his hand presently on the buttock of the beast, and prayes hee may bee damb'd if the Horse be not vnder fiue; meaning that the horse is not vnder fiue yeares of age, but that he stands vnder fiue of his fingers, when his hand is clapd vpon him. These Horse-coursers are calld Iynglers, and these Iynglers hauing layd out their money on a company of Jades at some drunken Fayre, vp to London they driue them, and vpon the Market day into Smithfield brauely come they prancing.

APPENDIX 8

——— ∞ ———

ABUSES IN HORSE DEALING: THE CASE OF EDWARD HALL OF SOUTH GOSFORTH, YEOMAN

(Northumberland R.O., QSB Vol. 38 Mids. 1713 Hexham, folio 36)

The Informacion of Thomas Swan of East Denton made before me this 26th day of May 1713

This Informant maketh Oath that On Friday the twenty second instant One Edward Hall of South Gosforth yeoman hearing that James Swan an Infant About fifteen years of Age wanted a horse to drive ye Ginns came to Margaret Mitfords house grandmother to the said James Swan with whom he lived & brought a horse with him to sell him for that purpose, the said James carried the said Hall & Horse to his Vncle Thomas Swan of East Denton (who was his Guardian) to be directed in the purchase of the said horse Thomas Swan upon the View of the said Horse told the said Hall that the said Horse was by no means fit for the Vse & ordered his Nephew not to meddle with him   Hall answered there was no Harm done & so departed with his horse. But took the boy James Swan behind him pretending to carry him home to his Grandmothers House which was in the said Halls way home   But instead of carrying him home carryd him to an Alehouse Drunk him up & then prevailes with the Boy to buy his horse of him at the rate of six pound odd moneys which Sum is farr above the Value of the Horse & then went home with the said Boy prevaild with the Boyes said Grandmother to pay him the moneys Left the Horse there. & the Boy fuddled as this informant was told & so went home with the moneys

26th May 1713
John Ogle

his
Thomas ⤝ Swan
mark

─────── ○○○ ───────

ACTIVITIES OF THE HARRISON GANG
IN THE 1670s

(P.R.O. Palatine of Chester Depositions, CHES 38/41 part 2)

Examinacions taken before me Randolph Dod of Edge Esquire one of his Majesties Justices of the Peace and Quorum for this County the 25th of January and in the 26th yeare of the Raigne of our Soueraigne Lord King Charles the Second over England &c Annoque Domini 1674

John Normon aged 19 yeares or theirabouts upon his Examinacion saith that hee was the Sonne of Richard Normon & Elizabeth his wife who whilst they lived were House Keepers in Bood in the Parish of Whiston Three miles behind Warrington that his Father died Five yeares agon his Mother about one yeare and halfe agon after which time hee went abroad to gett reliefe till about Michaelmas last hee came into Cheshire to gett releife hee came to the House of Richard Newalls an Ale house at Acton Bridge where hee beged lodging in the Barne & that same night about Tenn of the Clocke Thomas Harrison & Richard Harrison who stiled themselves brethren came with either of them a Horse as Guests to Lie at that house finding this Examinant by the Fire before hee went to his Lodging in the barne asked this Examinant what calling hee followed Whoe sayd hee beged for his liveing to which they both replied if hee would goe with them hee should never need to begge againe & in the morning before Day hee went along with them to one Richard Bakers an Inn in Waverham where the[y] left him promiseing to pay for his meate and drinke till they came againe which was from Thursday till Tuesday following that they brought Three other horses telling Richard Baker and his wife that they had beene Fourteen Miles behind Shrewsbury & then they tooke this Examinant aside & perswaded him to take notice as hee went about the Contrey where likly horses were that they would come and steale them & thence they removed him to Widdow Fletchers an Alehouse in Cuddington in Waverham Parish where hee was lodged Three weekes payd for & maintained by them who often came & went and one brought one John Smith a Portly black man & another Slender youth about Twenty yeares of age brownish hair whom the[y] called Richard [ ] but doth not Know his other name haveing Three Horses amongst them then which they brought from Shrewsbury John Smith & Richard went towards Trafford to looke for more and Thomas and Richard Harrison keeping those three Horses one whole night and one day Close lockt up in Widdow Fletchers Stable themselves keeping the Key brought this Examinant to Nathaniel Williamsons who keeps the Red Lion in Over their to bee lodged & entertained Where hee stayed nine dayes at which time of their being with him their they tooke him sworne under an engagment with the breaking of six pence the one peice whereof is now found in this Examinants purse & the other peice is sowed within the Wast of Thomas Harrisons breeches That hee should bee true to them never discover or betray them or if they past by take notice that hee Knew them though hee was goeing to bee hanged That his charge at Over was to view the Grounds & fields their abouts & in Swanlow Lane to give them notice where likly Horses were for their purpose and that the sayd Harrisons Smith and Richard   whilst this Examinant lay at the Red Lion in Over brought Two lusty black Coults with long Tayles led in Halters each of them Four rideing upon other Horses where they came in late all Four sate up and went away againe two hours before day and as this Examinant heares them say towards Warrington And this Examinant saith that hee came along with them to Richard Bakers in Waverham & their dranke before Day and left this Examinant there Three dayes till they returned which was onely the Two Harrisons (this Examinant never since seene the sayd John Smith & Richard   ) who then tooke this Examinent along with them to one Thomas Fluitts house a little above the Three Cupps neer Sankey Street end in Warrington who Keeps a private house but is a noted dealer in Horses and whom this Examinant perfectly understood was the receivour and disposer of all such Horses as the sayd Harrisons or his Marrowes did bring to him & did further then and their hear of and understood that young Thomas Fluitt Sonn of the sayd Thomas Fluitt who lives at the Black Draggon in Shrewsbury but whether Hous keeper Sojorner or in quality of a Horse Coaser this Examinant cannot certainly declare did use to receive all such horses as the sayd Harrisons or his Marrowes had stolen in the Contreys about Warrington and that all the Horses as they Stole about Shrewsbury they brought to Thomas Fluitt to Warrington and hee received them but this Examinant doth not Know that ever Thomas Fluitt of Warrington sent any Horses by the sayd Harrisons or their Marrows to his sonne at Shrewsbury or that hee received any sent by them from his sayd sonn   This Examinant saith that at such time as hee was left at Cuddington as in this Examination is aforementioned hee gave the sayd Harrisons information of Two Naggs of Mr Gills of Cuddington the one a Light Bay with a Raw Nose and all four white feet the other a sad Bay without any white both which about Three weekes before Christmas last the sayd Harrisons stole out of a Field of Mr Gills but being discovered in the Ketching of them were soe hotly pursued that they were forced to quitt them upon Bartington heath but that day seaven night after by notice from this Examinant they tooke a Large sad Coloured Bay Mare of the sayd Mr Gills out of another pasture having a Lock on her foote and carried that clear away towards Shrewsbury & further saith that when hee lay at Over as aforesayd hee gave the sayd Harrisons notice of a Midle Siz'd light Bay Nagg with a starr in the forehead & with white in one Flanck a Whisk Tayle of Alderman Boziers of that Towne which they alsoe stole and carried away towards Shrewsbury

This Examinant further remembreth at that time hee was at Warrington with the Harrisons at Thomas Fluitts That Thomas Fluitt Knew him and whose Child hee was charged him to bee true to them and never to discover them   This Examinant saith that hee hath been at severall houses brought by the sayd Harrisons left and removed from place to place as oft as they came before Christmas last amongst which he remembreth they brought him to Ralph Poughtens a private house in Norley who was familliarly acquainted with them where hee staid Two nights at the first and for some few dayes removed to Widdow Fletchers in Cuddington & thence came to Poughtens in Norley again where hee staid for a weeke And further saith that hee hath laine Three nights at Two severall times at Randolph Haukies at Coate Brooke brought by the sayd Harrisons who had noe Horses there and alsoe that hee lay Five nights at Widdow Walkers in Little Budworth where the sayd Harrisons brought Two Horses fromwards Warrington & lay their one night & took this Examinant to Bunbury where they left him at Randolph Hitchins for one night and gave Nine Shillings to buy him the Breeches Drawers & Hose hee hath on gott made their & ordered him to come to John Fishers an Alehouse in Bickerton on Christmas Eve from thence they ordered him to call at Hugh Wixtids at Bellow Hill from thence to come to John Rawbones an Alehouse in Whitchurch in the street on the Lift hand below the Bull ring where hee met with both the Harrisons who had each of them a Horse one a Bay & thother a Gray one where hee lay with them upon Christmas day at night went with those Horses to Shrewsbury where they gave him seaven shillings to buy him the Coate & Wascoate hee hath on who came the next night to Hugh Wixtids aforesayd where hee staid for the space of a Fortnight at severall times being some dayes absent at John Fishers in Bickerton aforesayd that hee spent near Twenty Shillings at Hugh Wixtids which moneyes Harrison gave him to pay & bid him call for what hee had a mind of saith that the day after Christmas day at Night both the [sic] returned from wards Shrewsbury both on foote without Horses lay all night with this Examinant at Wixtids & from thence went towards Warrington where hee past the time as aforesayd untill Tuesday last in the afternoone both the sayd Harrisons came on Horse backe from Warrington haveing a third man in their company on Horse backe whom they tould him was young Thomas Fluitt rid upon a lusty black Nagg never staid to drink that Thomas Harrison rid upon a daple Gray Maire with a Bob Taile which hee hang on the Pales whilst hee dranke two or three Quarts & then went after young Thomas Fluitt towards Whitchurch or Shrewsbury that the sayd Thomas Harrison staid Three or Four hours being about a bargaine & change for that Gray Maire with John Carnill of Masfen for a Bay Nagg but not agreeing the sayd Harrison went that night to Whitchurch where they with Fluitt lay all night together who tooke all those Three Horses & Mairs towards Shrewsbury & the sayd Harrisons then ordering this Examinant to goe on Wednensday to goe to Fishers in Bickerton aforesayd & their to stay till they came to him that on Wednensday night about Midnight both Harrisons came by the sayd Fishers door where this Examinant lying on a Bench by the Fire side heard them give a Fute with an Instrument made like a hollow Key which they had each of them one to Whistle or call where hee saw them Two in a Turfe Coate with two Mairs the one being a Gray Maire with a white Tayle which Thomas Harrison platted up they haveing struck fire made alight thother a black Bay without any white with a Bob Taile saith that John Fisher & his wife being in Bed they saw them not nor did Harrisons come into the house or drink their but without Sadles rid away towards Shrewsbury which was the last time this Examinant ever saw them whoe promised to come to him their on Saturday night or if they mist they would lie at Wixtids on Sunday night or else would come in their before munday morning & would bee with him that night

This Examinant denied that hee ever saw or Knoweth anything of a Gray Maire of Mr Ashbrookes of Tattenhall or of another Gray Maire of John Massies of Bickerton both which were stolne the last weeke but by the Carrecter given of John Massies Maire their is great liklyhood that the Mair which Thomas Harrison platted the Taile vp in Fishers Turfe Coate on Wednensday last was Massies Maire which it seemes was stolne that night   This Examinant denies that hee ever stole Horse or was helping them to Ketch or Steale any Horse or Mair but further declareth & saith that hee verrily beleeves that Hugh Wixtid & his wife & Children doe verry well Know & perfectly understand the sayd Thomas Harrison & Richard Harrison what & whence they are & have been long privy & had Knowledge of their wayes & courses in Horse Stealing Conveying & returning of the same from Warrington to Shrewsbury & from Shrewsbury to Warrington who have followed these courses as they have acknowledged to this Examinant for six yeares last past & the sayd Thomas Harrison haveing declared to this Examinant great confidence which hee put in Hugh Wixtid & that house which hee sayd hee durst trust as much as hee durst his owne heart for betraying them & then this Examinant by his order payd Fifty shillings all in halfe Crownes to Hugh Wixtid in presence of his wife to lay up and Keep for the sayd Thomas Harrison

This Examinant further saith that about the time of his first falling into company with the sayd Harrisons Smith and Richard   as aforementioned being all Four together at Richard Bakers in Waverham aforesayd Thomas Harrison in the hearing of them all with this Deponent wished that hee had such another bout as when they Killed the man at Longford brooke behind Warrington Two yeares agon wherby hee gott agood Maire and all his money

This Examinant lastly being deposed upon his Oath declareth that the evidence & information given in this Examination concerning the Courses & practices Thomas Harrison Richard Harrison John Smith & Richard   their stealing & conveying to & from Warrington to Shrewsbury & againe & of the receiveing of the same by Thomas Fluitt the elder & Thomas Fluitt the younger & of the houses Inns & Alehouses where the[y] have been received & entertained as aforesayd is nothing but the truth and further saith not.

Taken before mee   the marke of
  Ran Dod   John E*m* Normon

Examinations further taken at Edge the 25th day of January
John Carnill of Masefen aged Thirty seaven yeares or theirabouts sworne and Examined deposeth and saith that on Tuesday last being the nineteenth of this Instant January this Examinant saw a little short Depper man about Thirty six yeares of Age Sad brownish Haire haveing a White Hatt a brownish Close bodied Coate a Buffe Belt and Henger with Bootes & spurrs in very good Fashion rideing upon a verry large light gray Maire not dappled verry long Coated with her Tayle tide up which seemed to bee much tired by his beating her caused this Examinant to draw near and enter into speech with him who tould him hee was newly come out

of Ireland from of Shippboard had betwixt Three & Fourscore miles to goe forwards into Herefordshire & his Maire was soe tired that hee would bee glad to change her away though it were for a Worse if hee could have some money too boote and a fresher Horse to carry him on his Jorney who went straight on the road to the Inn at Bellow=hill where hee sayd would stay till this Examinant would fetch his nagge & come to him to see if the[y] could bargaine whom hee found at the Inn and the stranger about to give his Maire some Corne to refresh her who asked this Examinant Thirty Shillings to change the Maire for his Nagge who sayd hee was an Irish Mair cost him Four pounds Fifteen Shillings their lately before & Thirty shillings carriage over & had a burn'd Marke below her hipp next to the man was about Seaven years old & according to this Examinants best Judgment hee doth verryly beleeve was come of Shipp board according to the mans relation   This Examinant offered him Twenty Shillings & Twenty Five Shillings at last came to his price & would have given him Thirty Shillings in change but this Examinant haveing bought a Coate & a pair of Breeches for Four Shillings three pence of the sayd Stranger whereby furnishing him with some money for his jorney seemed then not to like this Examinants Nagge soe well soe went away after drinking one quart of Ale & paying for his Oates   This Examinant saith that at the same time their was at Hugh Wixtids house the Boy now present at the takeing of this Examination who calls himselfe John Normon whom this Examinant had seene to be a Guest at that house lieing their most of Christmas but Knew not Whence hee came nor whither hee went nor of any company that came to him or left him their nor of any men to bee with him or to resort to that house called by the names of Thomas Harrison Richard Harrison John Smith and Richard   which hee hath given information to bee horse stealers

This Examinant further saith that dureing the time that the sayd Strang Travellir out of Ireland staid at the Inne aforesayd the sayd John Normon had never any words or speech with him or doth beleeve that hee ever Knew or had seene him This Examinant further saith that hee saw noe such persons as are reported by the sayd Normon by the name of Thomas Fluitt of Shrewsbury upon a Black Gelding to bee in Company with Richard Harrison who road upon a Bay Maire with a Bob Tayle or that they rid before and left the sayd Stranger & this Examinant to bargaine about the Gray Maire And further this Examinant upon Oath deposeth that hee doth not Know or hath ever heard that Hugh Wixtid or his house hath ever beene accustomed to receive & entertaine comeing or goeing in the night at unseasonable houres any men who might bee suspected for Horse stealers   And this Examinant further saith that the sayd John Normon on Wednensday last when hee came from Hugh Wixtids passing on the Roade by this Examinants house tould him that hee the sayd Normon had lent Hugh Wixtid Fifty Shillings which when this Examinant tould Hugh Wixtid & his wife they both utterly denied it and further saith not

John Carnill

Taken January the Twenty sixth

Hugh Wixtid of Tushingham aged Sixty Five yeares or theirabouts sworne & Examined deposeth & saith that about a Weeke before Christmas one Saturday night a young man who called himselfe John Normon who it seems was lately apprehended by the Constable of Bickerton came to this Examinants house for lodging and entertainment where he staid till Munday sayd hee was goeing to Shrewsbury and that morning went towards Whitchurch & returned to this Examinants house upon Tuesday night where hee stayd saying hee was weary till Thursday morning then pretended to goe home towards Warrington then return'd to this Examinants house againe upon Sunday after Christmas day stayd their Five or Six dayes & made a match for suteing with Bartlemew Larton of Agdon for Five shillings apeice to bee shott on Tuesday the nineteenth of this Instant January & to that end came to this Examinants house upon Sunday before & stayd their Wednensday following

This Examinant saith that the second time the sayd Normon came to his house in his returne as hee sayd from Shrewsbury not makeing any shew of much money offered to Lend this Examinant Fifty shillings which hee had in a Purse distinct by it selfe which this Examinant accepted of And promised to repay him in the Easter Hollidayes when hee came that way but it was not all in halfe Crownes whether Twenty or Forty Shillings was in halfe Crownes This Examinant cannot tell but denieth that Thomas Harrison was present or Councell'd the sayd Normon to deliuer the money to this Examinant

And further this Examinant doth utterly deny that hee doth Know Thomas Fluitt the elder of Warrington or Thomas Fluitt his sonn liveing at the Black Dragon in Shrewsbury or Thomas Harrison Richard Harrison John Smith or any of them according to the Carrecter given by the sayd Normon or that they were ever in Company with him at this Examinants house or came or went away in the day or night with Horses or saw any Stranger that came to him whilst hee was their saith hee payd his reckoning in this Examinants house that his expences were moderate that hee minded to play at Cards rather with some Naighbour for a Quart of Ale then drinking & further saith not

the marke of
Hugh **//** Wixtid

Examination further taken at Edge the Thirteenth of February
Daniel Cliffe sonne of Daniel Cliffe of Ash within the County of Salop husbandman aged Twenty one yeares or theirabouts sworne & Examined deposeth & saith that about Twelftide in Christmas last This Examinant in Company with Robert Purcill his Cozen servant to Rowland Salmon of Ash aforesayd Blacksmith came to his Vncle Hugh Wixtids house in Tushingham upon the invitation of his daughters in Guestwise where they stayed Three dayes who then found their the young man who called himselfe John Normon who pretending some lamenesse of a foote this Examinant & his Cozen left their had his company most whilst they stayed their dureing which time the sayd John Normon discovered to this Examinant some affection which hee had for his Cozen Elizabeth his Vncle Hugh Wixtids daughter then at home at which time this Examinant pulling six pence out of his Pockett to pay his shott the sayd Norman Twitch'd the sayd six pence out of his hand & broke it desireing this Examinant to give his Cozen Elizabeth the one peice of it as a Love Tie betwixt them which this Examinant offered her shee denying sayd shee would have nothing to doe with him whereupon

the sayd Normon desired this Examinant to take it as an engagement to bee his Groomes man if ever hee happened to Marry her & is the same peice of six pence as was then broken being produced & compared at the takeing of this Examination but this Examinant being disatisfied at the breaking of his sayd six pence the sayd Normon then gave him a Groate for amends This Examinant utterly denyeth that hee ever saw the sayd Normon before or since or doth know any thing of his wayes or courses in Horse stealing or doth know any such men as Thomas Harrison Richard Harrison John Smith or any other or Thomas Fluitt the elder of Warrington or Thomas Fluitt of Shrewsbury his Sonne or anything of the waies or Courses of their Stealeing & Conveying Horses from Shrewsbury to Warrington or from Warrington to Shrewsbury or the parts their adjacent or of any such like practices by or amongst them or any others and further saith not

Taken before mee   Ran Dod   the marke of Daniell ♂ Cliffe

Ambling: a gait of a horse in which the animal alternatively moves the legs on one side, an action which gives an easy comfortable ride.

Bills, bonds and specialties: debts secured by the signing of a contract and enforceable at law.

Book debts: debts owing to a tradesman or a dealer and (theoretically) entered into a ledger or a book of accounts.

To boot: the balance paid when two horses of different values were exchanged. Although normally made in cash, other commodities such as grain and beer were also used.

Chapman: a middleman, a person dealing in any commodity.

Clipping: paring off the edges of coins with the intention of making more coins from the shavings.

Common informers: persons who informed the authority of breaches of certain statutory regulations, many of which were of an economic nature. They received a portion of the fine or the proceeds accompanying a successful prosecution but were also in a position to extort money by blackmailing offenders. Looked upon with distaste by contemporaries, their influence declined with the relaxation, though not abandonment, of economic control in the late seventeenth century.

Cozen: deceive, cheat.

Destrier: a medieval warhorse, suitable for a knight and, as a result, a costly animal.

Earnest: a deposit given on the sale of a commodity, the balance being paid at a future date (or dates) agreed upon by both parties.

Farrier: a person who shod horses or who looked after them when ill. In practice, the work of a blacksmith and that of a farrier often overlapped.

Hackney services: public transport facilities for hire, either saddle horses or coaches.

Horse coper: a horse dealer.

Horse courser: a horse dealer, specifically one who bought and sold stock already broken in.

Horse leech: a horse doctor.

Impress: forced requisitioning of men, animals or goods for the army (or navy).

Manège: system of exercises for horses, now known as dressage.

Muster: the meeting of the county militia for display and inspection.

Nag: a male horse, normally (but not inevitably) referring to a saddle animal.

Pacing: a gait similar to racking (*q.v.*).

Pad: a saddle horse that paced.

Pedlar: an itinerant trader normally working on foot, who sold cheap consumer goods and small luxuries such as ribbons, laces, needles, threads, tobacco and chapbooks, to the population at large.

Racking: an ambling gait (*q.v.*) performed at the speed of a trot and a particularly easy-going comfortable action for the rider.

Reiving: taking goods by force, especially applied to the rustling and plundering that was carried on by inhabitants on either side of the Scottish border in the period before the Union of the Crowns in 1603.

Serviceable: a word used to describe a horse which because of its size, strength and pace was deemed suitable for use in the cavalry.

Stag: a North Country term for a young horse.

Toll books: books kept by a market official in which details of horse sales were entered (though other animals, especially cattle, were often listed too). Introduced by legislation in 1555, they were extended in scope in 1589.

Trotting: a gait in which the horse's feet move in diagonal pairs.

—— OOO ——

HORSE TOLL BOOKS

Cheshire
Chester (fair) *c.* 1567–79   Chester City R.O. Sheriff's Toll Books SBT/1
Chester (mkt) 1658–1723   Chester City R.O. Sheriff's Toll Books SBT/2

Cumbria
Carlisle 1631–4, 1653–4   Cumbria (Carlisle) R.O., Ca/4/152–5
Rosley Hill 1649–50   Cockermouth Castle, Leconfield Estate, D/Lec/323

Derbys.
Derby 1638–61, 1677, late C17, 1697–1700   Derby Ref. Lib., Derby Horse Fair Books

Devon
Barnstaple 1628–65   N. Devon Athenaeum, Barnstaple, Refs. 3973, 4143
Hartland (mkt) 1615–72   E. Devon R.O., Hartland Borough Records, 1201 A/B1
Plymouth (mkt) 1590–1606   W. Devon R.O., Plymouth Corpn. Records, W89

Essex
Blackmore 1679   Essex R.O., D/DB M154
Hatfield Broadoak 1644–59   D/DHt M50

Gloucs.
Bristol (mkt) 1705–14, 1735–58   Bristol R.O., Xerox copy of docts. not in B.R.O., 52

Hants.
Portsmouth (mkt) 1623–63   Portsmouth R.O., Sessions Book 1598–1638, CE 1/4
Winchester 1620–1, 1623, 1625, 1647, 1648   Winch. Cath. Lib., Cals. of Cath. Papers (plus date)

Herefs.
Leominster 1556–7   Herefs. R.O., Leom. Borough Records, Bailiffs' Accounts 8

Leics.
Hallaton 1720–8   Leics. R.O., DE 339/350–3
Leicester 1598   Leic. Borough Records, BR III/8/41
Market Bosworth 1603–32   Folger Shakespeare Lib., Washington DC, MS.V.b.165

Northants.
Boughton Green 1627   Northants. R.O., ZA 2455
Rothwell 1684–1721   MTM 595

Notts.
Nottingham 1634–64   Notts. R.O., CA 1504–5

Oxfords.
Banbury 1753–67   Oxfords. R.O., B.B. VIII/vii/1
Oxford (mkt) 1673–1745   Oxford Ref. Lib., Oxford City Records, F.4.4

Shrops.
Bridgnorth 1631, 1644–1720, 1767–78   Shrops. R.O., Bridgnorth Corpn. Records 4001/Mar/1/268–7
Ludlow 1646–9, 1687–95   Ludlow Corpn. Records 356/Box 297
   356/32/Box 466

Much Wenlock 1632–8   Guildhall, Much Wenlock, Transcript of Toll Bks 1632–8
Shrewsbury 1524/5–1674   Shrops. R.O., Shrews. Corpn. Records, 2645–68

Somerset
Taunton 1621–39, 1667, 1671, 1674, 1686–97   Somerset R.O., DD/SP 341
White Down Fair 1637–49   DD/HI By 53

Staffs.
Brewood 1661–2, 1683   Staffs. R.O., Giffard Colln., D590/435/1–3
Eccleshall 1691–2   Lichfield J.R.O., B/A/2/123307
Penkridge 1558, 1579, 1640   British Library, MSS Dept., Egerton MS 3008, fos 2v–22v
Stafford 1614–15   Staffs. R.O., Mat. Craddock's Commonplace Bk, D1287/10/2
Walsall 1628–c.1636   Walsall Town Hall, WTC II/40/1–15

Suffolk
Beccles (mkt) 1571–3, 1674–1710 — Beccles Town Hall, Rix Div. IV Proprietary IV, Markets and Fairs

Warwicks.
Stratford-upon-Avon 1602, 1646 — Shakespeare Lib., Stratford, Misc. Docts. V, VII, XIV
Sutton Coldfield 1750–9 — Birmingham Ref. Lib., Ref. 80–2
Warwick 1651–6, 1684–93 — Warwics. R.O., Warwick Borough Records, W 13/1

Worcs.
Dudley 1702–10 — Dudley Ref. Lib., Dudley Estate Colln., Misc. Box
Kidderminster 1694–1711 — Kidderminster Ref. Lib., KID 352/No. 1455
Worcester (fair) 1552–64 — Guildhall, Worc. Corpn. Archives, View of Frankpledge, vol. I
Worcester (mkt) 1635–56 — Liber Recordum

Yorks.
Adwalton 1631 — *Bradford Antiquary*, N.S. V, 1927, ed. W. Robertshaw, Notes on Adwalton Fair
Ripley 1708, 1721–30, 1773–7 — Leeds City R.O., Ingilby Papers 3117–18

MANUSCRIPT SOURCES

I. NATIONAL REPOSITORIES

Bodleian Library
MS Gough Shropshire 12

British Library
Add. MSS 33144–7, 9 Account Books of the Pelhams of Haland, Sussex 1626–1702
Harleian MS 29443 MS History of the Reresby family of Thrybergh written by Sir John Reresby

National Library of Wales
Oakley Park Estate (Shrops.) Accounts: deed no. 21924 account 1653–4; deed no. 14854 account 1678; deed no. 21206 accounts 1682–7
Powis deeds: no. 16751, Account and Memo. Book of Sir Charles Foxe of Bromfield 1569–1607; no. 21922 Account Book of Sir Charles Foxe of Bromfield 1593–1630
Court of Great Sessions in Wales, Gaol Files, Class WALES 4, 141–4 (Montgs.); 334–5 (Brecons.); 478 (Radnors.); 974–5 (Flints.)

Public Record Office
Assize records;
The following records were searched for references to horse stealing. Particular attention was given to the Northern Assize records because they had already been indexed.
Oxford Circuit ASSI 2/1–5; ASSI 5/1–4
Northern Circuit ASSI 45/1–33
Palatine of Chester CHES 24/95–104
Palatine of Lancaster PL 27/1–2
Chancery Records:
C1/1009/58; C2/Charles I/C12/28; C3/141/98; C3/185/47; C3/405/29
Exchequer Records:
Equitium Regis (E101)
E101/107/17, 27–9, 33–5; E101/533/11–5
Taxation (E179)
Hearth Tax: E179/160/320; E179/254/30
Port Books (E190)
E190/737/3, 18–9; E190/738/10
Prerogative Court of Canterbury, Probate:
PROB 11/71 PCC 42 Spencer
Requests Records:
REQ 2/3/293; REQ 2/4/60; REQ 2/12/115; REQ 2/19/35; REQ 2/157/163; REQ 2/162/16; REQ 2/176/11; REQ 2/245/5; REQ 2/396/80; REQ 2/397/77; REQ 2/411/113; REQ 2/420/57

Star Chamber Records:
STAC 5/C54/17; STAC 8/225/21 Misc. James I
State Papers (Commonwealth Papers, Class SP 28)
SP 28/128(8); SP 28/130 Part 3
State Papers Domestic
SP 46/83/fo.91

2. LOCAL REPOSITORIES

Beccles Town Hall, Suffolk
Beccles Corporation Records: Rix Division IV, Proprietary IV, Markets and Fairs

Bedfordshire R.O.
Judicial: Transcripts of Depositions
HSA 1671 W75; HSA 1676 W26; HSA 1677 S50; HSA 1678 S75; HSA 1678 W51; HSA 1678 W58; HSA 1689 W77; HSA 1684 W82–6
Family and Estate Papers:
Becher Family Account Book 1663–89, PO 3
Boteler Family Accounts, TW 800, 802/1–34, 805/1, 809

Birmingham Reference Library
Family and Estate Papers:
Gough Family of Perry Barr: 330, Account Book of Walter Gough 1707–21

Bradford City Library
Family and Estate Papers:
Cunliffe-Lister Colln. Box 1, Accounts by Thomas Johnson for Mashamshire beginning in 1688

Bristol R.O.
Judicial:
04438–9 Deposition Books 1643–7, 1657–61
Family and Estate Papers:
Correspondence of the Smyth Family of Ashton Court, AC/C46/9

Buckinghamshire R.O.
Family and Estate Papers:
Chester of Chicheley Accounts, D/C/32/36(iii); D/C/4/8, 10–11

Cheshire R.O.
Probate:
Richard Stockton of Malpas WS 31/27

Cornwall R.O.
Family and Estate Papers:
Rashleigh Papers, DDR 4337

Cumbria R.O. (Carlisle)
Judicial:
  Calendar of Cumberland Q.S. Petitions Mich.1686–Easter 1762
Family and Estate Papers:
  Lowther Family Accounts, D/LONS/W/unlisted; List of Pit Horses 1733;
  Millom Castle Papers, D/SEN/8; Cash Book of Mrs Bridget Hudleston 1700–3;
  Day Book of Accounts of Mrs Bridget Hudleston's Estate at Millom 1707–20, Day
  Book of Accounts of Mrs Bridget Hudleston 1710–15
Probate:
  Michael Lightfoot of Kirkland, Wigton, 1670
  Adam Pearson of Stoneraise, Westward, 1670
Taxation:
  Photo-copy of Hearth Tax Returns N.D. (*c.* 1664)

Cumbria R.O. (Kendal)
Family and Estate Papers:
  Lonsdale Family Correspondence, D/LONS/W/Tickell Correspondence Box 5

Derbys. R.O.
Family and Estate Papers:
  Gell Family Correspondence D258/31/9a
  Vernon of Sudbury Papers, 410M/2A 17th Century Disbursements

East Devon R.O.
Judicial:
  Quarter Sessions Rolls, Q/SB Boxes 30–64

West Devon R.O.
Judicial:
  Plymouth Borough Records W326, Examination and Information Book 1674–8

Durham R.O.
Family and Estate Papers:
  Bowes Family Accounts V606, V609

Durham University Dept. of Palaeography and Diplomatic
Family and Estate Papers:
  Baker-Baker of Elemore Hall, Notebook of George Baker BB72/251
  Howard of Naworth Castle Accounts C708–10; List of Tenants' Duties N.D.
  201/9

Essex R.O.
Family and Estate Papers:
  Clopton Diary 1648–52, D/DQs 18
  Langley's (Great Waltham) Estate: D/DTu 276 Samuel Tufnell's Accounts
  1701–21
  Petre Family Correspondence D/DP/2 37/16; Accounts D/DP/A16, 55

Gloucestershire R.O.
Family and Estate Papers:
  D149/F13, Commonplace Book of Nathaniel Clutterbuck 1603–1721
  D23 5/E2, Farming Accounts and Memo. Book of Henry Sturmy of Swindon

Hampshire R.O.
Probate:
  Inventory of John Whit of Eling 1573 B Wills 143/2

Herefordshire R.O.
Family and Estate Papers:
  Foley Family of Stoke Edith, FH/111 Steward's Accounts 1672–93

Hertfordshire R.O.
Family and Estate Papers:
  Grimston of Gorhambury Accounts, Box 54/XI.15, 22–3, 26
  Henry of Nassau's Papers, D/ENa/03, 05–06, 011, 019–020; D/ENa/A27, A44
  Wittewronge Family Accounts, D/ELW F18, D/ELW F20–2

Kent A.O.
Family and Estate Papers:
  Sackville of Knole Papers, Lists of Horses, U269/E201/1/Bundles 34– 5, U269/
  E201/3/Bundles 24, 27, 33, 36, 85

Lambeth Palace Library
Probate:
  Probate Inventories of the Parishes of Burstow, Charlwood, Cheam, East
  Horsley, Merstham (all in Surrey)

Lancashire R.O.
Family and Estate Papers:
  Clifton of Lytham Accounts. DDCl/399–400

Leicestershire R.O.
Family and Estate Papers:
  Finch of Burley-on-the-Hill Accounts, DG 7/1/16, 19a, 22

Lichfield Joint R.O.
Probate:
  Charles Frizwell of Bedworth (Warwicks.) 23 Apr. 1696; John Frizwell of
  Bedworth 25 Oct. 1728; Humphrey Hanbury of Bedworth 24 Apr. 1722; Thomas
  Jones of Kemberton (Shrops.) 1695; Luke Satchwell of Bedworth 11 May 1733

Lincolnshire A.O.
Family and Estate Papers:
  Ancaster Papers, Accounts, ANC/10/356/2; ANC X/A/3, 7–8

Massingberd Family of Gunby, Accounts, MG 5/2/1–13; Diary of George
  Langton, 1690, MASS 28/1
Massingberd Family of Mumby, Accounts, MM 6/1/2–5
Monson Papers, Accounts, MON 10/1/A/14, 16, 18–9; MON 10/3/1–3
Diocesan:
Lincoln Diocesan Records Box 58/2/66
Probate:
Horbling Parish Inventories
Parochial:
Horbling Parish Rates, Horbling Parish Records 7/1, 7/3, 12/2

Corporation of London R.O.
Journals 9–11
Family and Estate Papers:
  114 C Survey of the Manor of Lympsham 1622

Middlesex R.O.
Family and Estate Papers:
  Wood Papers ACC 262/43/29

Norfolk R.O.
Family and Estate Papers:
  Hare of Stow Bardolph, Disbursements 1683–93, Hare 5284
  Ketton-Cremer of Felbrigge Hall, Accounts of Windham Family, WKC 5/150–210
  Knyvett-Wilson Colln. Accounts, KNY 575–6, 939
  Pratt of Ryston Hall, Account and Memo. Book of Sir Roger Pratt, NRO m/f reel
218/7
  Walsingham (Merton) Colln. Accounts, WLS LXIX/26–7
  Wych of Hockwold Hall, no ref. Accounts 1680–9, 1690–9, 1700–9, 1710–19

Northamptonshire R.O.
Family and Estate Papers:
  Cartwright of Aynho Colln. Account Book C(A)3489
Account Book of Thomas Thornton Esq.Thornton family Papers, Microfilm 40
  Westmorland (Apethorpe) Colln. Accounts, Misc. Vols. 4, 7–9, 15

Northumberland R.O.
Judicial:
  Q.S. Papers and Order Books, beginning in 1663 (Class QSB). Searched for
references to horse dealing and stealing.
Family and Estate Papers:
  NRO 1973, Survey of the Manor of Haltwhistle 1653
  Blackett (Matfen) MSS, Accounts 1690–1717, ZBL 273/2–4, 6–9

Norton Conyers Hall
Family and Estate Papers:
  Accounts of Sir Richard Graham, Gentleman of the Horse to the Duke of
Buckingham, 1620s.

Nottinghamshire R.O.
Probate:
  Inventory of Thomas Brown of Farnsfield, PR SW 85/6

Nottingham University Library, MSS Dept.
Family and Estate Papers:
  Middleton Family Accounts, Mi A/1–87
  Portland Colln. Pw V4, accounts *c.* 1592–1662; Pw 2/325–44, Papers relating
to the studs of the Duke and Duchess of Newcastle

Shropshire R.O.
Judicial:
  Shrewsbury Borough Records, Q.S. 1564–1713, Bundles 2204–2304
Family and Estate Papers:
  Charlton Family Papers, Rentals 625/, Boxes 10, 15; Survey *c.* 1676, 2340
  Forester Family Papers, Accounts, 1224/Boxes 296–7
  Marrington Colln., Account Book 1717–70, 631/2/1
  Sandford of Sandford Colln., Accounts, 2/135, 138
  Sutherland Colln., Leases 1592, 38/143–4
Parochial:
  Newport Parish Register, Microfilm 412
Borough:
  Ludlow Corporation Records, 356/2/Box 2, 356/297

Somerset R.O.
Judicial:
  Quarter Sessions Records(Q/SR) 1607–1702 searched for references to horse
dealing and stealing

Staffordshire R.O.
Judicial:
  Quarter Sessions Depositions and Examinations: Q/SR 26, 29, 40, 42, 50, 55,
57, Epiphany 1612/3–Mich. 1617
Family and Estate Papers:
  Bagot Family Papers, Accounts, D(W)1721/3/195, 202
  Bradford Colln. D1287/3/6B, Disbursements 1716–47
  D1287/10/2, Matthew Craddock's Commonplace Book 1614–15
  HM 27/2, Account Book of Edward James of Kinvaston
  Paget Family Accounts, D(W)1734/3/3/276, 279
  Sutherland Colln. Accounts, D593/F/2/5–14, 37–40; Rentals D593/G/1/1/1–2,
4, 13; D593/4/1/6; Lease D593/I/1/4; Correspondence D593/P/8/2/4

East Suffolk R.O.
Family and Estate Papers:
  Blomfield Family of Stonham, HD 330/7, Accounts 1661–96

West Suffolk R.O.
Judicial:
P516 Transcript made by Peter Christie of P.R.O. ASSI 16/59/6
Borough:
Bury St Edmund's Borough Records D8/1/1

Surrey R.O.
Family and Estate Papers:
Slyfield Estate Papers 65/4/22–4

Warwickshire R.O.
Family and Estate Papers:
Newdigate of Arbury Colln. CR 136/A/3 Diary of Sir John Newdigate 1608;
Accounts CR 136/B/593–5, 615–23, CR 136/V/142
Earl of Northampton's Estate, Accounts CR 556/274–5
Warwick Castle Colln. Accounts, CR 1886/Boxes 411–13

Wiltshire R.O.
Judicial:
Quarter Sessions Depositions searched for references to horse dealing and
stealing cases, Trinity 1604–Michaelmas 1699
Family and Estate Papers:
Cole Park Colln. 161:57, Account Book 1664–85

Woodstock Town Hall
Judicial:
Portsmouth Book 1618–35

Worcestershire R.O.
Family and Estate Papers:
John Gibson's Farm Book 1683–95 B.A.4221, Ref. 705:66/51(vi)
Bishop of Worcester's Colln. Rental 1682, R.A. 2636/4(ii) Ref. 009.1

Yorkshire Archaeological Society (Leeds)
Family and Estate Papers:
Clifford of Skipton Castle Accounts, DD121 Bundle 36A/2–4
Slingsby of Scriven Accounts DD56/J3/2–8

North Riding of Yorkshire R.O.
Judicial:
Calendar of Q.S. Papers QSB 1691/303, QSB 1693/223, QSB 1699/219;
Quarter Sessions Roll DC/RMB 3/3–4
Borough:
Scarborough Borough Records DC/SCB no further reference; Scarborough
Corporation Minute and Sessions book MIC 833

Family and Estate Papers:
  Cholmley/Strickland of Whitby Archive, Accounts ZCG/IV/5/2/6–7
  Commonplace Book of Richard Cholmeley of Brandsby, no ref.
Manorial:
  Beresford-Peirse Colln. ZBA 17/1/19, Court Book of the Manor of Bedale
1594–1604

PRIMARY PRINTED WORKS

Blome, Richard, *The Gentleman's Recreation* (1686)
Blundeville, Thomas, *The Foure Chiefest Offices Belongyng to Horsemanship* (1580 edn.)
Camden, William, *Britannia*, trans. Philemon Holland (1610)
Carew, Richard, *The Survey of Cornwall*, ed. F. E. Halliday (New York, 1969)
Cavendish, William, *A New Method and Extraordinary Invention to Dress Horses* (1667)
Defoe, Daniel, *A Tour through the Whole Island of Great Britain*, ed. P. Rogers (Harmondsworth, 1971)
Dekker, Thomas, *Lanthorne and Candle-light* (1608)
Ellis, William, *Modern Husbandman* (1744–5)
Fienes, Celia, *The Journies of Celie Fennes*, ed. C. Morris (1947)
Fitzherbert, John(?), *The Boke of Husbandrie* (1523?)
Fuller, Thomas, *The History of the Worthies of England*, ed. P. A. Nuttall (1840)
Furnivall, F. J., ed., *Harrison's Description of England* (1881)
Gough, Richard, *The Antiquityes and Memoyres of the Parish of Myddle* (Shrewsbury, 1875)
Harman, Thomas, *A Caveat for Common Cursitors* (1567)
Johnson, Benjamin, *Bartholomew Fair* (1614)
London Gazette (1685)
Markham, Gervase, *How to chuse, ride, traine and diet, both Hunting-horses and running Horses* (1599)
Marshall, William, *Rural Economy of the West of England* (1796; repr. Newton Abbot, 1970)
Morgan, Nicholas, *The Perfection of Horsemanship* (1609)
Noble, T., ed., *History and Gazeteer of the County of Derby* (Derby, 1831)
Owen, William, *An Authentic Account published by the King's Authority of all the Fairs in England and Wales* (1756 edn.)
Peacham, Henry, *Coach and Sedan* (1636)
Pilkington, James, *A View of the present State of Derbyshire* (1803)
Reyce, Robert, *The Breviary of Suffolk*, ed. Lord F. Hervey (1902)
Robinson, C. B., ed., 'Rural Economy in Yorkshire in 1641, being the Farming and Account Books of Henry Best of Elmeswell in the East Riding', *Surtees Soc.*, 33 (1857)
Spreull, John, *The Accompt current between England and Scotland Balanced* (1706)
Worlidge, John, *Systema Agriculturae* (1675)

PRINTED CALENDARS OF RECORDS

Acts of the Privy Council, N.S. 7 (1558–70); N.S. 11, 1578–80; N.S. 26, 1596–7; 1616–17; 1621–3

Brewer, J. S. and Bullen, W. eds., *Calendar of the Carew Manuscripts (at Lambeth) 1515–1574* (1867)

Cockburn, J. S. ed., *Calendar of Assize Records: Hertfordshire Indictments Elizabeth I* (1975)

Cockburn, J. S. ed., *Calendar of Assize Records: Hertfordshire Indictments James I* (1975)

Cockburn, J. S. ed., *Calendar of Assize Records: Sussex Indictments Elizabeth I* (1975)

Cockburn, J. S. ed., *Calendar of Assize Records: Essex Indictments Elizabeth I* (1978)

Cockburn, J. S. ed., *Calendar of Assize Records: Kent Indictments Elizabeth I* (1979)

Cockburn, J. S. ed., *Calendar of Assize Records: Surrey Indictments Elizabeth I* (1980)

Calendar of State Papers Domestic, Addenda 1566–79; Addenda, 1580–1625; 1649–50; 1651–2

Calendar of State Papers Venetian, II, 1509–19; III, 1520–6; VI, iii, 1557–8

Historical Monuments Commission, 12th. Report, Duke of Rutland's MSS, I–II; Duke of Rutland's MSS, IV; 12th. Report, Appendix, vii, Lord Muncaster's MSS; 13th. report, ii; De L'Isle and Dudley MSS, VI; Duke of Portland's MSS, V; Marquis of Salisbury's MSS, V, XIX, XX

Letters and Papers of Henry VIII, VIII, i, 1509–14; XII; XIV; XIX, i; 1542; Addenda, I, i

STATUTES

11 Henry VII c.13
1 Edward VI c.5
1 Edward VI c.12
5 & 6 Edward VI c.7
5 & 6 Edward VI c.14
2 & 3 Philip and Mary c.7
22 Henry VIII c.7
23 Henry VIII c.16
27 Henry VIII c.6
32 Henry VIII c.13
33 Henry VIII c.5
5 Elizabeth I c.8
5 Elizabeth I c.12
8 Elizabeth I c.8

RECORDS SOURCES IN PRINT

Atkinson, C. ed., 'Quarter Sessions Records', *North Riding Rec. Soc.*, 6 (1888)

Bagley, J. S. ed., 'The Great Diurnall of Nicholas Blundell of Little Crosby', *Lancs. & Cheshire Rec. Soc.* (3 vols. Manchester, 1968–72)

Batho, G. R. ed., 'The Household Papers of Henry Percy Ninth Earl of Northumberland', *Camden Society*, 3rd. ser. 93 (1962)

Bestall, J. M. and Fowkes, D. V. eds., 'Chesterfield Wills and Inventories, 1521–1603', *Derbys. Rec. Soc.*, 1 (1977)

Brears, P. C. D. ed., 'Yorkshire Probate Inventories 1542–1689', *Yorks. Arch. Soc.*, 124 (1972)

Bruce, J. ed. 'The Letters and Papers of the Verney Family', *Camden Society*, O.S., 56 (1853)

Burne, S. A. H. ed., 'Staffordshire Quarter Sessions Rolls IV, 1598–1602', *Staffs. Hist. Collns.* (1935)

Dell, R. F. ed., 'Rye Shipping Records 1566–1590', *Sussex Rec. Soc.*, 64 (1965–6)

East Anglian Miscellany, Jan.–March 1909

Emmison, F. G. ed., 'Jacobean Household Inventories', *Beds. Hist. Rec. Soc.* 20 (1938)

Everitt, A. M. ed., 'Suffolk and the Great Rebellion', *Suffolk Rec. Soc.* 3 (1960)

Ferguson, R. S. and Nanson, W. eds., 'Some Municipal Records of the City of Carlisle', *Trans. Cumb. & Westmor. Antiq. & Arch. Soc.*, extra ser. 4 (1887)

Forster, A. M. C. ed., 'Selections from the Disbursement Book (1691–1709) of Sir Thomas Haggerston, Bart.', *Surtees Soc.*, 180 (1965)

Fussell, G. E. ed., 'Robert Loder's Farm Accounts 1610–1620', *Camden Soc.* 3rd. ser. 53 (1936)

Gibson, J. S. W. and Brinkworth, E. R. C. eds., 'Banbury Corporation Records: Tudor and Stuart', *The Banbury History Society*, 15 (1977)

Harland, J. ed., 'The House and Farm Accounts of the Shuttleworths of Gawthorpe Hall in the County of Lancaster at Smithils and Gawthorpe from September 1582 to October 1621', *Chetham Soc.*, 35 (1856)

Harrison, J. V. ed., 'Five Bewcastle Wills 1587–1617', *Trans. Cumb. & Westmor. Antiq. & Arch. Soc. N.S.*, 67 (1967)

Havinden, M. A. ed., 'Household and Farm Inventories in Oxfordshire 1550–90', *Oxford Rec. Society*, 44; and *H.M.C.* Joint Publication, 10 (1965)

Hearnshaw, F. J. C. and D. M. eds., 'Court Leet Records, I, ii, 1578–1602', *Southampton Rec. Soc.* (1906)

Hey, D. ed., *The Letters of James V* (Edinburgh, 1954)

Hill, J. W. F. ed., 'The Letters and Papers of the Banks Family of Revesley Abbey 1704–1760', *Lincs. Rec. Soc.*, 45 (1952)

Hodgson, J. ed., 'Calendars of ... Prisoners ... in the High Castle and in Newcastle-upon-Tyne and the Assizes for Northumberland in the Years 1628 and 1629', *Archaeologia Aeliana*, 1 (1822)

Hudleston, C. R. ed., 'Naworth Estate and Household Accounts 1648–60', *Surtees Soc.*, 168 (1953)

Jackson, C. ed., 'Yorkshire Diaries and Autobiographies in the Seventeenth and Eighteenth Centuries', II, *Surtees Soc.*, 77 (1883)

Jeaffreson, J. C. ed., 'Middlesex County Records', *Middlesex County Rec. Soc.* (4 vols. 1886–92)

Kennedy, P. A. ed., 'Nottinghamshire Household Inventories', *Thoroton Society Rec. Ser.* 22 (1963)

le Hardy, W. ed., 'Middlesex Sessions Records', *Middlesex County Records* N.S. (4 vols. 1935–41)

Leighton, W. A. ed., 'Early Chronicles of Shrewsbury', *Trans. Shrops. Arch. Soc.*, 3 (1880)

Lewis, R. A. ed., Local History Source Book L19 (Stafford, n.d.)

Lodge, E. C. ed., *The Account Book of a Kentish Estate 1616–1704* (1927)

Marlow, N., trans., *The Diary of Thomas Isham of Lamport (1658–81)* (Farnborough, Hants., 1971)

Meads, D. M. ed., *Diary of Lady Margaret Hoby 1599–1605* (1930)

Moore, J. S. ed., *Clifton and Westbury Probate Inventories, 1609–1761* (1981)

Myddleton, W. M. ed., *Chirk Castle Accounts A.D. 1605–1666* (St Alban's, 1908)

Myddleton, W. M. ed., *Chirk Castle Accounts A.D. 1666–1753* (Manchester, 1931)

Ornsby, G. ed., 'Household Books of Lord William Howard of Naworth Castle', *Surtees Society*, 68 (1878)

Parsons, D., *The Diary of Sir Henry Slingsby of Scriven bart.* (1836)

'Penney, N., ed., *The Household Account Book of Sarah Fell of Swarthmoor Hall 1673–8* (Cambridge, 1920)

Pollard, A. F. and Blatcher, M. eds., 'Henry Townshend's Journal', *Bull. Inst. Hist. Research*, 12 (1934–5)

Raine, J. ed., 'Wills and Inventories . . . of the Northern Counties of England', *Surtees Society*, 2 (1835)

Ramsay, G. R. ed., 'John Isham, Mercer and Merchant Adventurer', *Northants. Rec. Soc.*, 21 (1962)

Robertson, S. ed., 'The Expense Book of James Master Esquire A.D. 1646 to 1676', *Archaeologia Cantiana*, 15–18 (1883–9)

S.H.A.H. ed., *The Diary of John Hervey First Earl of Bristol with Extracts from his Book of Expenses 1688 to 1742* (Wells, 1894)

S.H.A.H. ed., *Letter books of John Hervey First Earl of Bristol 1651 to 1750: I, 1651 to 1715* (Wells, 1894)

Salt, D. H. G. eds., 'Staffordshire Quarter Sessions Rolls, Easter 1608 to Trinity 1609', *Staffs. Hist. Collns.* (1948–9)

Squires, H. L. and Rowley, E. eds., 'Early Montgomeryshire Wills at Somerset House', *Montg. Hist. Collns.* 22 (1888)

Thwaite, H. ed., 'Abstracts of Abbotside Wills 1552–1688', *Yorks. Arch. Soc.* 130 (1980)

Tibbutt, H. G. ed., *The Letter Books 1644–45 of Sir Samuel Luke: Parliamentary Governor of Newport Pagnell* (1963)

Turner, J. H. ed., *The Reverend Oliver Heywood B.A.* (Bingley, 1885)
Verney, M. M. ed., *Memoirs of the Verney Family during the Commonwealth 1650 to 1660* (1894)
Verney, M. M. ed., *Memoirs of the Verney Family from the Restoration to the Revolution 1660 to 1696* (1899)
Warner, Sir G. F. ed., 'The Nicholas Papers IV, 1657–60', *Camden Soc.* 3rd. ser. 30 (1921)
Watkins-Pitchford, W. ed., *The Shropshire Tax Roll of 1672* (Shrewsbury, 1949)
Wheatley, H. B. ed., *The Diary of Samuel Pepys* (1905)
Whitaker, T. D. ed., *The Life and Correspondence of Sir George Radcliffe knight Ll.D.* (1810)
Witty, J. R. ed., 'Documents relating to Beverley and District', *Yorks. Arch. Soc.* 36 (1944)

SECONDARY WORKS

(Place of publication is London unless otherwise stated.)
Albert, W., *The Turnpike Road System in England 1663–1840* (Cambridge, 1972)
Awan, S., 'An Analysis of Agriculture and Society in Seventeenth Century Oadby, Leicestershire', Roehampton Institute of Higher Education BA thesis (1980)
Aydelotte, F., *Elizabethan Rogues and Vagabonds* (Oxford, 1913)
Beattie, J. M., *Crime and the Courts in England 1660–1800* (Oxford, 1986)
Beresford, M. W., 'The Common Informer, the Penal Statutes and Economic Regulation', *Econ. Hist. Review*, 2nd. ser., 10 (1957–8)
Bettey, J. H., *Rural Life in Wessex 1500–1900* (Bradford-upon-Avon, 1977)
Bowden, P. J., *The Wool Trade in Tudor and Stuart England* (1971)
Boynton, L., *The Elizabethan Militia 1558–1638* (Newton Abbot, 1971)
Brereton, J. M., *The Horse in War* (Newton Abbot, 1976)
Burley, K. H., 'The Economic Development of Essex in the Later Seventeenth and Early Eighteenth Centuries', London University PhD thesis (1957)
Chalklin, C. W., *Seventeenth Century Kent* (1965)
Chartres, J. A., 'Markets, Fairs and the Community in Seventeenth and Eighteenth Century England', *University of Leeds School of Economic Studies, Discussion Paper Series*, no. 6 (Leeds, 1974)
Chartres, J. A., *Internal Trade in England 1500–1700* (1977)
Chartres, J. A., 'Road Carrying in England in the Seventeenth Century: Myth and Reality', *Econ. Hist. Review*, 2nd. ser., 30 (1977)
Chartres, J. A., 'The Marketing of Agricultural Produce', *The Agrarian History of England and Wales V ii, 1640–1750*, ed. J. Thirsk (Cambridge, 1985)
Chell, R. W., 'Agriculture and Rural Society in Hampshire *circa* 1600', Leicester University MPhil thesis (1975)
Chivers, K., *The Shire Horse* (1978)
Clark, P., 'The Alehouse and the Alternative Society', *Puritans and Revolutionaries*, eds. D. Pennington and K. Thomas (Oxford, 1978)
Clarkson, L. A., *The Pre-Industrial Economy in England 1500–1700* (1971)

Cliffe, J. T., *The Yorkshire Gentry from the Reformation to the Civil War* (1969)
Cockburn, J. S., 'The Northern Assize Circuit', *Northern History*, 3 (1968)
Cockburn, J. S., *A History of English Assizes, 1558–1714* (Cambridge, 1972)
Cockburn, J. S., 'Early-Modern Assize Records as Historical Evidence', *Journal of the Society of Archivists*, 5 (1974–5)
Cockburn, J. S. ed., *Crime in England 1550–1800* (1977)
Coleman, D. C., *The Economy of England 1450–1750* (Oxford, 1977)
Cornwall, J. C. K., 'The Agrarian History of Sussex 1560–1640, London University MA thesis (1953)
Crofts, J., *Packhorse, Waggon and Post* (1967)
Davis, R. H. C., 'The Medieval Warhorse', *Horses in European Economic History: A Preliminary Canter*, ed. F. M. L. Thompson (Reading, 1983)
Dyer, A. D., 'The Market Towns of Southern England 1500–1700', *Southern History*, 1 (1979)
Edwards, P. R., 'The Farming Economy of North-East Shropshire in the Seventeenth Century', Oxford University DPhil thesis (1976)
Edwards, P. R., 'The Development of Dairy Farming on the North Shropshire Plain in the Seventeenth Century', *Midland History*, 4 (1978)
Edwards, P. R., 'The Horse Trade of the Midlands in the Seventeenth Century', *Agric. Hist. Review*, 27 (1979)
Edwards, P. R., 'The Horse Trade of Chester in the Sixteenth and Seventeenth Centuries', *Journal of the Chester Arch. Soc.*, 62 (1979)
Edwards, P. R., 'The Cattle Trade of Shropshire in the late Sixteenth and Seventeenth Centuries', *Midland History*, 6 (1981)
Edwards, P. R., 'The Horse Trade in Tudor and Stuart England', *Horses in European Economic History*, ed. F. M. L. Thompson (Reading, 1983)
Edwards, P. R. 'Shropshire Agriculture 1540–1750', *Victoria County History of Shropshire*, ed. G. Baugh (forthcoming)
Emmison, F. G., *Elizabethan Life and Disorder* (Chelmsford, 1970)
Everitt, A. M., 'Farm Labourers', *The Agrarian History of England and Wales IV, 1500–1640*, ed. J. Thirsk (Cambridge, 1967)
Everitt, A. M., 'The Marketing of Agricultural Produce', *The Agrarian History of England and Wales IV, 1500–1640*, ed. J. Thirsk (Cambridge, 1967)
Everitt, A. M., 'Change in the Provinces: The Seventeenth Century', *Leicester University, Dept. of English Local History, Occasional Papers*, 2nd. ser., no. 1 (Leicester, 1969)
Everitt, A. M., *Perspectives in English Urban History* (1973)
Fleming, D., 'A Local Market System: Melton Mowbray and the Wreake Valley 1549–1720', Leicester University PhD thesis (1980)
Fletcher, A., *A County Community in Peace and War: Sussex 1600–1660* (1975)
Gibson, T. E., *Blundell's Diary* (Liverpool, 1895)
Gillett, E. and MacMahon, K. A., eds., *A History of Hull* (Oxford, 1980)
Goodacre, J., 'Lutterworth in the Sixteenth and Seventeenth Centuries: A Market Town and its Area', Leicester University PhD thesis (1977)
Goodall, D. M., *The Foals of Epona* (1962)
Goodall, D. M., *A History of Horse Breeding* (1977)

Havinden, M. A. and Wilkinson, F., 'Farming', in *Dartmoor: A New Study*, ed. C. Gill (Newton Abbot, 1970)

Hey, D. G., *An English Rural Community: Myddle under the Tudors and Stuarts* (Leicester, 1974)

Hey, D. G., *Carriers and Packhorse Roads* (Leicester, 1980)

Hill, C., *The World turned upside down* (Harmondsworth, 1975)

Hodgen, M. T., 'Fairs in Elizabethan England', *Economic Geography*, 18 (1942)

Holderness, B. A., 'Aspects of Inter-Regional Land Use and Agriculture in Lincolnshire 1600–1850', *Lincs. Hist. & Arch.*, 9 (1974)

Hoskins, W. G., 'The Leicestershire Farmer in the Sixteenth Century', *Essays in Leicestershire History*, ed. W. G. Hoskins (Leicester, 1950)

Hoskins, W. G., *The Midland Peasant* (1965)

Houston, R. A., 'The Development of Literacy: Northern England, 1640–1750', *Econ. Hist. Review*, 2nd ser., 35 (1982)

Howard, M., *War in European History* (Oxford, 1976)

Hull, F., 'Agriculture and Rural Society in Essex 1560–1640', London University PhD thesis (1950)

Ingram, M. J., 'Communities and Courts: Law and Disorder in Early-Seventeenth Century Wiltshire', *Crime in England 1550–1800*, ed. J. S. Cockburn (1977)

Jones, W. R. D., *The Tudor Commonwealth 1529–1559* (1970)

Kerridge, E., 'The Agrarian Development of Wiltshire 1540–1640', London University PhD thesis (1951)

Kerridge, E., *The Agricultural Revolution* (New York, 1967)

Kirby, J. L., 'Border Service 1662–1757', *Trans. Cumb. & Westmor. Antiq. & Arch. Soc. N.S.*, 48 (1949)

Langdon, J., *Horses, Oxen and Technological Innovation* (Cambridge, 1986)

Large, P. F. W., 'Economic and Social Change in North Worcestershire', Oxford University DPhil thesis (1980)

Long, H. W., 'Regional Farming in Seventeenth Century Yorkshire', *Agric. Hist. Review*, 8 (1960)

MacDermot, E. T., *The History of the Forest of Exmoor* (Newton Abbot, 1973)

Macfarlane, A., *The Justice and the Mare's Ale* (Oxford, 1981)

McCutcheon, K. L., 'Yorkshire Fairs and Markets to the End of the Eighteenth Century', *Thoresby Society*, 39 (1940)

Milward, R., 'The Cumbrian Town between 1600 and 1800', *Rural Change and Urban Growth 1500–1800*, eds. C. W. Chalklin and M. A. Havinden (1974)

Moir, E., *The Justice of the Peace* (Harmondsworth, 1969)

'Montgomeryshire Horses, Cobs and Ponies', *Montg. Hist. Collns.* 22 (1888)

Morehouse, H. J., 'A Dyurnall or Catalogue of all my Accions and Expence from the 1st. January, 1646', *Surtees Society*, 65 (1875)

Nares, G., *Arbury Hall Guidebook* (1969)

Newton, R., 'The Decay of the Borders: Tudor Northumberland in Transition', *Rural Change and Urban Growth*, eds. Chalklin and Havinden (1974)

Palliser, D. M., *The Age of Elizabeth: England under the Later Tudors 1547–1603* (1983)

Pam, D. O., 'Tudor Enfield, the Maltmen and the Lea Navigation', *Edmonton Hundred History Society, Occasional Paper*, N.S., no. 18 (n.d.)

Pennington, D. H., 'The War and the People', *Reactions to the English Civil War 1642–1649*, ed. J. Morrill (1982)

Pickles, M. F., 'Agrarian Society and Wealth in Mid-Wharfdale 1664–1743', *Yorks. Arch. Soc.*, 53 (1981)

Plumb, J. H., *The Commercialisation of Leisure in Eighteenth Century England* (Reading, 1973)

Prior, C. M., *The Royal Studs of the Sixteenth and Seventeenth Centuries* (1935)

Prior, M., *Fisher Row: Fishermen, Bargemen and Canal Boatmen in Oxford 1500–1900* (Oxford, 1982)

Robertshaw, W., 'Notes on Adwalton Fair', *Bradford Antiquary*, N.S., 5 (1927)

Robinson, H., *The British Post Office: A History* (Princeton, N.J., 1948)

Rowlands, M., *Masters and Men* (Manchester, 1975)

Salgado, G., *The Elizabethan Underworld* (New Jersey, 1977)

Sharpe, J. A., 'Crime and Delinquency in an Essex Parish 1600–1640', *Crime in England 1550–1800*, ed. J. S. Cockburn (1977)

Sharpe, J. A., *Crime in Seventeenth-Century England: A County Study* (Cambridge, 1983)

Sharpe, J. A., *Crime in Early Modern England 1550–1750* (1984)

Sherwood, R., *The Court of Oliver Cromwell* (1977)

Skipp, V. H. T., *Crisis and Development* (Cambridge, 1978)

Spence, R. T., 'The Pacification of the Cumberland Borders, 1593–1628', *Northern History*, 13 (1977)

Spence, R. T., 'The Graham lands on the Eve of the Jacobean Pacification', *Trans. Cumb. & Westmor. Antiq. & Arch. Soc.*, N.S., 80 (1980)

Spufford, M., *Petty Chapmen and their Wares in the Seventeenth-Century: The Great Reclothing of Rural England* (1984)

Stone, L., 'The Residential Development of the West End of London in the Seventeenth Century', *After the Reformation: Essays in Honour of J. H. Hexter*, ed. B. C. Malament (University of Pennsylvania, 1980)

Surtees, R., *The History and Antiquities of the County Palatine of Durham* (1816; repr. 1972)

Tennant, A. J., 'Brailes: A Felden Community 1500–1800', Leicester University MPhil thesis (1977)

Thirsk, J., *English Peasant Farming* (1957)

Thirsk, J., *The Agrarian History of England and Wales IV, 1500–1640* (Cambridge, 1967)

Thirsk J., *Horses in Early Modern England; for Service, for Pleasure, for Power* (Reading, 1978)

Thirsk, J., *The Agrarian History of England and Wales V, 1640–1750* (2 vols. Cambridge, 1985)

Thwaites, W. 'The Marketing of Agricultural Produce in Eighteenth Century Oxfordshire', Birmingham University PhD thesis (1980)

Veasey, E. A., 'The Frizwell Family of Bedworth' (unpubd. MS, 1982)

Watts, S. W., *From Border to Middle Shire: Northumberland 1586–1625* (Leicester, 1975)

Wedgwood, C. V., *The King's War 1641–1647* (1958)

West, F., 'The Social and Economic History of the East Fen Village of Wrangle 1603–1837', Leicester University PhD thesis (1966)

Westerfield, R. B., *Middlemen in English Business* (New Haven, 1915)

Wheeler, W. H., *A History of the Fens of South Lincolnshire* (Boston, 1868)

Willan, T. S., *The Inland Trade* (Manchester, 1976)

Williams, M. I., 'Agriculture and Society in Glamorgan 1660–1760', Leicester University PhD thesis (1967)

Williams, P., *Life in Tudor England* (New York, 1964)

Wilson, C., *England's Apprenticeship 1603–1763* (1983)

Winchester, A., 'Rural Economy in Sixteenth Century Copeland', Durham University PhD thesis (1978)

Wrightson, K. and Levine, D., *Poverty and Piety in an English Village: Terling 1525–1700* (New York, 1979)

Yelling, J. A., 'Probate Inventories and the Geography of Livestock Farming: A Study of East Worcestershire 1540–1750', *Pre-Industrial England: Geographical Essays*, ed. J. A. Patton (Folkestone, 1979)

Yelling, J. A., 'Livestock Numbers and Agricultural Development 1540–1750', *Field and Forest: An Historical Geography of Warwickshire and Worcestershire*, eds. T. R. Slater and P. J. Jarvis (Norwich, 1982)

Young, P. and Holmes, R., *The English Civil War* (1974)

INDEX